Y0-AGG-957

A17000 212981

Reproduced under license from United Feature Syndicate

REED ORGANS ON PARADE

. . . a pictorial review of the many parlour, cabinet, boudoir, philharmonic, and other types of reed organs made over a 100-year period by the famous Estey Organ Company, together with a brief corporate history . . .

ROBERT B.
WHITING

THE • VESTAL • PRESS • LTD

P. O. BOX 97 • VESTAL • NY • 13850 • USA

FORBES LIBRARY
Northampton, Mass.

PREFACE

I dedicate this book to the memory of my parents, James and Ethel Whiting, who always encouraged my musical studies and interest in organs, and also to the memory of the Estey family and their thousands of skilled craftspersons who for over a century created organs of superior quality.

I appreciate the kindness of those listed in the Foreword who loaned material for this book, and I want to give special thanks to Harvey N. Roehl of the Vestal Press Ltd., for all of his guidance, helpful suggestions, and personal efforts in preparing this book for publication.

Robert Bruce Whiting
Schwenksville PA 19473
May 1981

VXOR+
Ep85

Library of Congress Cataloging in Publication Data
Main entry under title:

Estey reed organs on parade.

Includes music and index.
1. Reed organs—Catalogs, Manufactures'.
2. Estey Organ Company—History and criticism.
I. Whiting, Robert B., 1917- II. Estey Organ Company.
ML155.E88 786.9'4 81-7545
ISBN 0-911572-21-X AACR2

© By The Vestal Press Ltd

First Printing — August 1981

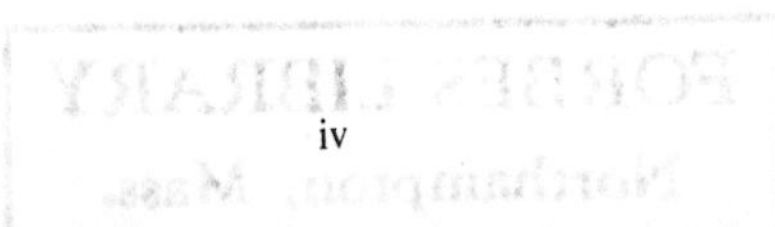

FOREWORD

In the eighteen-eighties there were something on the order of 250 companies in the United States engaged in the manufacture of reed organs. It took no vast amount of capital to be in this business, so many of these firms were small and obscure and have long since been generally forgotten.

From among this number there were nevertheless several which made a big mark on the industry, and Estey tops the list not only for the quantity of instruments they produced, but for longevity what with having endured for well over a century.

This book makes no pretense of being a comprehensive history of the company, and such a book remains to be written. The tragic death of Stephen Greene of Brattleboro, who founded the publishing company of the same name, in the Chicago DC-10 disaster put an end to the project that he was about to initiate which would have accomplished this — and one can hope that someone will be sufficiently interested, as he was, to pick up the pieces and go forward with the total story of this fascinating company.

Rather, the purpose of this book is to give the student of the reed organ scene an overall view of the products of the company, and most particularly to be able to study the styles as they changed from year to year.

It would be quite impossible without having a volume of encyclopaedic proportions to include everything and all the variations that Estey did in the way of reed organ production, but this assortment of material renders a pretty good over-all view of their accomplishments.

In its later years Estey was into pipe organs in a big way, and they produced several famous instruments not only for residential use but for churches and theatres as well. Henry Ford was the proud possessor of an Estey pipe organ built especially for his new home "Fairlane" constructed near the great River Rouge factories at Dearborn, Michigan, and many other wealthy individuals were also fortunate enough to own such an instrument. But you didn't have to be rich to share the Estey heritage; they made instruments in all prices ranges for all tastes, all evidently sharing the same standards of quality established by Jacob Estey right from the beginning.

Professor Whiting is both a mathematician and an organist by profession. He is Professor of Mathematics at Drexel University Evening College and also Minister of Music at the historic Old First Reformed Church (founded 1727) in Philadelphia. He has for years collected and restored reed organs, and in his research has assembled one of the largest collections of reed organ catalogs and literature in existence.

We are indeed fortunate that he has seen fit to share this material with his readers at a time when antiques in general are very much a subject of wide interest.

He is joined by Jim Andrews of Troy, New York, who generously made available much material from his private collection (including the exceedingly-rare 1867 catalog), Reed and Mary VanGorder of Flemington, New Jersey who were fortunate enough to get into the Estey offices within hours of the trash-man who was about to haul hundreds of pounds of documentary material to the town dump, thus saving many important historical papers and photographs, and Ed Jameson of Berlin, Massachusetts who now owns many rare glass negatives made by a professional photographer at the Estey plant in the late 1800's.

Harvey N. Roehl
Vestal, New York
May 1981

TABLE OF CONTENTS

ESTEY'S ORGANS.

AMONG the exhibitors at the Centennial Exhibition may be mentioned the well-known organ manufacturers of Brattleboro,' Vt., MESSRS J. ESTEY & Co. "The prominent absence" of such a firm from the "list of awards" has, doubtless, occasioned many questions as to the reason. The explanation is simple, indeed. *They did not compete.* They simply exhibited their instruments on their intrinsic merits, with no efforts to obtain recognition except from the public.

We cannot too highly commend such a course, as compared with some exhibitors, whose sole aim seemed to be *not* to give the public pleasure in examining their wares, but to obtain the bronze medal.

Inquiry elicits the fact that ESTEY & Co. are the largest manufacturers and the heaviest exporters of their class, one-half of the entire amount of Organs shipped to European markets being from this house.

RICHARD WAGNER, of whose ability to judge there can be no doubt, writes: "The tone of the ESTEY ORGAN is very beautiful and noble and gives me the greatest pleasure. My great friend, Franz Liszt, is also charmed and delighted with them."

MME. ESSIPOFF says: "I can play with exquisite enjoyment for hours on these beautiful instruments."

OLE BULL: "Excel in fine, powerful tone."

MME. LUCCA: "I am surprised at their full, noble, and organ-like tone."

RUBENSTEIN: "Tone full, noble, and exceedingly animating."

There is no doubt about the meaning of such expressions as these, from the leading musicians of the age, and ESTEY & Co. may well claim to lead the world.

ESTEY & GREEN, Manufacturers of the

PERFECT MELODEON,

Which has invariably drawn the highest prize for purity, sweetness, and evenness of tone; to which is added their new Patent "**Base Damper,**" without which no Melodeon is complete. Also, dealers in **PIANO FORTES.**

BRATTLEBORO, VERMONT.

13 Vt. Register 1857

JACOB ESTEY & CO.'S
Cottage Organ Triumphant!
Cottage Organ Triumphant—Growing Improvement!

The Vox Humana Tremolo—Growing Improvement!

in addition to the

Patent Harmonic Attachment and Patent Manual Sub-Base!

ESTEY & CO. have now further than ever eclipsed all rival makers of Reed Instruments, by the introduction of their

PATENT VOX HUMANA TREMOLO.

This most wonderful addition to the Cottage Organ is acknowledged by leading musical characters in the country to be the *ne plus ultra* of all improvements on reed instruments.

It is *very important* that the purchasers bear in mind that the ORIGINAL AND GENUINE COTTAGE ORGAN is made by the house of J. ESTEY & CO., *only*.

The chief points of superiority are *patented by them*, and of course are found in the instruments of *no other maker*. They have taken over 100 FIRST PREMIUMS at the principal fairs in the country.

☞ Send for a Circular.

J. ESTEY & CO.,

BRATTLEBORO, ... VERMONT

Walton's Vt. Register 1868

ADVERTISEMENTS. 85

JACOB ESTEY & CO.,

MANUFACTURERS OF

The Cottage Organ,

1866

Admitted by all to be the best instrument of the kind made in the world. Also the

HARMONIC ORGAN, &C.,

With Patent Bass Dampers, Harmonic Attachment and Manual Sub-Bass Improvements,

found in instruments of no other makers.

The Vocal Tremulo,

Will be found *only* in our instruments. It is considered by all leading Artists the most beautiful, and far surpassing all other improvements ever added to a reed instrument.

Send for Circular.

Brattleboro,* - - - - *Vermont.

8

Have you seen CLARK'S INDELIBLE PENCIL? Every Housekeeper should have one.

The Estey Organ Company in its advertisements always stated that the firm was established in 1846. Actually, a company in Brattleboro, Vermont, began to manufacture melodeons in 1846, and after a number of changes in ownership Jacob Estey bought the company in 1853. The 1876 Estey Cottage Organ Catalog (1) gives the story as follows: "The manufacture of reed musical instruments was begun in Brattleboro, Vermont, in the year 1846. The original organ factory occupied a room belonging to Mr. Jacob Estey, and, after considerable urging, that gentleman reluctantly consented to accept an interest in the business as payment of rent due him. The little concern struggled along until 1852, when its originators lost heart in the enterprise and it fell bodily into Mr. Estey's hands. Six workmen were then employed in the establishment, and its estimated total value was $2,700."

A detailed account of the early years of the Estey Organ Company is given in "The Perfect Melodeon: The Origins of the Estey Organ Company, 1846-1866" by Milton J. Nadworny (2). The original melodeon business had various changes in ownership and reorganizations as listed chronologically below:

1. Samuel H.Jones, along with John Woodbury and Riley Burditt (later Burdett) in 1846 formed the firm of S. H. Jones & Company. The first melodeon was finished late in 1846.
2. In May, 1847, Burdett acquired Woodbury's interest in S. H. Jones & Company. The new firm was called Jones & Burditt. By 1850 the firm employed 10 men and produced 75 instruments per year.
3. In August, 1850, Jones & Burditt dissolved their partnership. Edwin B. Carpenter joined Burdett and the firm became Burditt & Carpenter.
4. In January, 1852, E. B. Carpenter & Company succeeded Burditt & Carpenter. It is probable that Jacob Estey bought Burdett's share of the business.
5. In May, 1853, Isaac Hines, Jacob Estey and H. P. Green purchased the firm and formed I. Hines & Company.
6. In February, 1855, the firm of Estey & Green succeeded I. Hines & Company. This firm made "The Perfect Melodeon". In September, 1857, a fire destroyed the shop. Estey & Green's new shop was completed in February, 1858. In April, 1858, Estey & Green employed 20 men and made 10 instruments per week.
7. Jacob Estey bought out H. P. Green in January, 1863, and assumed full control. Early in 1864 another fire burned down part of the factory, but new buildings were soon erected.
8. In 1865 the firm was reorganized as J. Estey & Company, with ownership shared among Jacob Estey, Riley Burdett, Silas Waite and Joel Bullard.
9. In April, 1866, the former partnership was dissolved and Jacob Estey reorganized J. Estey & Company with two new partners: Julius J. Estey, his son, and Levi K. Fuller, his son-in-law. This was the last reorganization of ownership in the nineteenth century.

In 1869 a flood seriously damaged the factory. New factory buildings were built on higher ground overlooking Brattleboro. A charter for the Estey Organ Company was obtained in 1872, with the following officers: President, Jacob Estey; Vice President, Levi K. Fuller; Secretary and Treasurer Julius J. Estey (3). During the following years, under the leadership of Jacob Estey, Levi Fuller and Julius Estey, the Estey Organ Company had a period of great expansion, achieved much financial success, and made many improvements in reed organ design.

For over ten years from the early 1870's, the Estey Organ Company was engaged in litigation over a patent infringement case with Riley Burdett. The case was sensational because of accusations of fraud against Jacob Estey, Levi Fuller, and Julius J. Estey; attempted destruction of evidence, and claims of bribery and perjury.

On October 12, 1867, Riley Burdett, then of Chicago, Illinois, filed an application for a patent for "an improvement in reed organs". The principal claims were for a reed board with two and one-half sets of reeds, the half set commencing at tenor F and running through the treble in reed cells placed obliquely in the space between the diapason and the octave sets, and tuning the half set slightly above or below the diapason set to form a celeste. On November 4, 1867, the application was rejected by the Patent Office on the grounds that reed boards as described had been fully anticipated by previous patents, and the method of tuning had been in use for many years in pipe organs.

On November 26, 1867, Burdett amended his application and added additional claims, and on December 11, 1867, the application was again rejected by the Patent Office. Burdett appealed to the Examiners-in-Chief, and on August 29, 1868 they reversed some of the decisions of the Examiner. A patent was granted to Burdett on February 23, 1869.

In January, 1872, Silas M. Waite filed suit under that patent against Jacob Estey, Levi Fuller and Julius Estey, and swore the bill of complaint, which actually Burdett never signed or swore to, charging that Estey organs in their construction infringed on some of the claims of the patent. The money for carrying on the litigation was furnished by Silas M. Waite, who was a prominent banker and power in Vermont at the time.

The Estey defense was based on the fact that a small reed organ builder, Arvid Dayton, of Wolcottville, Connecticut, had made organs with two and one-half sets of reeds with the half set tuned as a celeste, well before the date of the Burdett patent. Jacob Estey bought several of these older

Arvid Dayton organs. At the request of Waite's counsel, one of these organs had been sent to New York City for an examination. While there, the organ was made incapable of producing music, and hence valueless in the patent suit. It also had dust removed, brass parts polished, and some wood made to look new, in an effort to make the organ look like a more recent fabrication. In retaliation, on March 23, 1874, J. Estey & Company filed a $5,000 damage suit in the Windham County Court, State of Vermont, against Riley Burdett, Charles B. Stoughton and Silas M. Waite for mutilation of exhibits in the patent case (7).

When the exhibit organ was brought to New York, it had the signature of Arvid Dayton. Later this signature was missing. Counsel for Waite attempted to prove that Jacob Estey had been alone with the organ a few minutes and had removed it (8).

Waite produced witnesses to prove the organ was a false exhibit. One witness, Nichols, had previously attempted to blackmail Mr. Estey and extort one thousand dollars from him, under a threat that he would go over to Waite and damage the Estey cause (8).

The Arvid Dayton organ had been purchased by a Dr. Newbury for his daughter, Eva Newbury, a teacher. Both testified that it had been bought in 1866. The desperate Waite, through an intermediary, tried to bribe Dr. Newbury to retract his testimony; and also put pressure on a School Commissioner, under whom Eva Newbury worked, to influence Eva to retract her testimony (8).

Waite's counsel then asserted that the Newbury organ was originally a single reed instrument when sold, and that Dayton, Estey and Fuller had fraudulently conspired to convert it to two and one-half sets. Their character before the community and the Grand Jury was at stake; and it was assailed virulently, both outside of the court and in it (8).

In a related issue, an 1867 Estey catalog which had been introduced as an exhibit in the case was found to have extra pages inserted in it. This implied that Jacob Estey had introduced false evidence. Fortunately for the Estey case, Levi Fuller recalled that the 1867 catalogs had extra pages inserted in them and were used in 1868. Fuller produced letters to the printers and paid printing bills for this work, thus demolishing the accusation of fraud.

The case, because of the large interests involved in it and for reasons growing out of the character of some of the evidence, was heard before the Circuit Judge and District Judge sitting together. The court decided in favor of Burdett, granting him an account of the profits and damages on some of the claims. A Master was appointed to ascertain these profits and damages and on the report of the Master a final decree was made for the plaintiff, Riley Burdett, for over $161,000., without costs to either party (6).

Jacob Estey, Levi K. Fuller and Julius J. Estey appealed to the Supreme Court of the United States in October 1883. The damages by this time amounted to about $205,000. The brief for the appellants (8) goes over the entire case in great detail. It pointed out that Arvid Dayton since 1855 had made organs with two and one-half sets of reeds with the half set tuned to form a celeste; that Henry K. White, an Estey employee, discovered for himself celeste tuning of reed organs in 1865; that Burdett's patent application, after being rejected twice, was issued after a third examination because of political letters of recommendation, presumably obtained by Waite; that Silas M. Waite schemed to damage the Arvid Dayton organ; that many efforts were made to damage the character and credibility of Jacob Estey and Levi Fuller; and that several of Burdett's patent claims were false.

The case was finally settled by the Supreme Court of the United States, thus ending one of the most bitterly fought patent cases of the nineteenth century. The decision was that the decree of the Circuit Court must be reversed, and the case remanded to that court, with direction to dismiss the bill (9).

The history of Jacob Estey's life is an interesting "rags-to-riches" story (3). He was born in Hinsdale, New Hampshire, on September 30, 1814. His parents were poor, and at the age of four he went to work on a neighboring farm. At thirteen, having been mistreated, he ran away to Worcester, Mass., where he became apprenticed in a plumbing business and where he also graduated from the Worcester Manual Labor Academy. In 1834 he returned to Hinsdale to attend the funeral of his father, and immediately afterward invested his hard-earned capital of $200 in the purchase of a plumbing business at Brattleboro, Vermont. He was successfully engaged in the plumbing business from 1835 to 1855. In 1848 he erected a large building on Main St., Brattleboro. Sometime later, he rented part of this building to Mr. Carpenter for use as a small factory for making melodeons. Subsequently he formed a partnership with Mr. Carpenter, as described above, and began to take an interest in manufacturing melodeons and reed organs. To the day of his death, April 15, 1890, he took an active interest in directing the Estey Organ Company, for whose growth he was mainly responsible.

Levi Knight Fuller was born February 24, 1841, at East Westmoreland, Cheshire County, New Hampshire (3). At the age of thirteen he went to Brattleboro and learned the printer's trade, also attending the Brattleboro High School. He then went to Boston, Mass., where he served an apprenticeship in the machinist's trade and also studied science and electricity at the evening schools. He became a skillful electrician, the inventor of an improvement in steam engines, and an excellent amateur astronomer. In 1860 he became engineer of the Estey organ works, and in 1866 was admitted into the firm of J. Estey & Company. He married Abby, the only daughter of Jacob Estey. He made numerous improvements in reed organ design. He visited Europe in 1873, 1878, and 1884 and laid the foundation of the firm's great system of foreign agencies. The adoption of a uniform pitch in piano manufacture in this country was largely due to his efforts (4). He rose to great eminence and became Lieutenant Governor and later Governor of Vermont.

Julius J. Estey (1845-1902) was a native of Brattleboro, Vt. He spent a year in Chicago, Illinois, in 1865, for Estey & Burdett and then in 1866 entered the firm of J. Estey & Company. As treasurer of the Estey Organ Company he built up the credit of the firm and placed it on a sound financial basis. He served in the Civil War as a Captain of the Vermont militia. He was also Colonel of the First Regiment of the Vermont National Guard, later becoming Brigadier General. He served in both houses of the Vermont legislature (3). Upon the death of Jacob Estey, he became president of the Estey Organ Company (5). A musical composition, the "Estey March", by Robert O. Eaton, has his portrait on the cover and the inscription "Dedicated to General Julius J. Estey" (10).

In 1891 the Estey plant covered 3½ acres of floor space. Around the factories the beautiful town of Esteyville grew up, peopled mainly by employees of the company. There were 500 workers on the payroll, and the capacity of the factories was 1500 to 1800 organs per month (3). The firm also had an interest in the Estey Piano Company in New York City.

By the start of the twentieth century, the two sons of General Julius Estey, Jacob Gray Estey and Julius Harry Estey, were in the company (4). The firm had a paid-up capital of $1,000,000. Estey organs were known all over the world, in the English colonies, as well as in South America. The company had special catalogs for Canada (11), for England, with prices in guineas, as early as the 1880's (12), and for South America, written in Spanish (13).

From 1846 to 1900, the Estey Organ Company made reed organs only. In 1900 the firm began building pipe organs and since then built both pipe and reed organs (14). At the start of pipe organ manufacture, Estey specialized in building small tubular pneumatic pipe organs in standard stock models. Estey also made self-playing pipe organs, operated automatically from perforated paper rolls (15). The history of Estey pipe organs lies outside of the scope of this book.

From 1900 on, reed organs began to lose favor with the general public. The piano, player piano, and phonograph became the popular home musical instruments. Reed organ manufacturers even built "Piano-Organs", which were reed organs fitted into upright piano cases with full 88 note keyboard (17), (18). Thus a person would appear to have in the home a modern piano rather than an old-fashioned reed organ. The first two decades of the twentieth century were a period of price cutting and intense competition among reed organ manufacturers. For example, Sears, Roebuck & Company in 1902 sold their "Happy Home" reed organ for only $22.00 and a portable folding organ for $21.50 (19). Companies discontinued making reed organs and went out of business or made pianos only. Of the several hundred American reed organ manufacturers before 1900, by the third decade of the twentieth century only three of any importance survived: the Estey Organ Company; The Hinners Organ Company of Pekin, Illinois, manufacturers of pipe and reed organs, and legally dissolved in 1942 (16); and the A. L. White Company of Chicago, manufacturers of small portable reed organs, and liquidated in December, 1956.

By the 1920's, the fourth generation of the Estey family were in the business: Jacob Poor Estey and Joseph Gray Estey, sons of Jacob Gray Estey; and Paul Chase Estey, son of Julius Harry Estey (20). In the early 1930's, the Estey Organ Company was reorganized as the Estey Organ Corporation. From this time on, Estey adopted new ideas in reed organ construction and developed innovative styles of organs. Electric suction units were used in some one manual organs, as well as in the two manual organs. A small Children's Organ and a somewhat larger Junior Organ were made with modern styling. Both could be had either pedal or motor operated. In addition to the bulky older style two manual and pedal organs, Estey brought out a "Student Organ" with self-contained suction unit. It had two sets of reeds on each manual and on the pedal; a 30 note pedal board which folded up underneath the keyboards when not in use; stop tablets; and separate expression pedals for each manual. The action was mechanical (21). About ten years later, a compact two manual and pedal "Practice Organ" was developed (22). The console dimensions and the full 32 note concave radiating pedal board were to American Guild of Organists standards. It had one 8' set of reeds on each manual; 16' and 8' sets on the pedal; expression pedals for each manual; and a self-contained electric suction unit.

New styles were also added to the Estey line of one manual organs: the "Modernistic Organ" and the "Gothic Organ", both either pedal operated or motor operated (23). In 1934 Estey put out a melodeon in a modernized four-legged melodeon case but with stop tablets and an electric suction unit (24). During World War II, Estey made many folding portable organs for the armed forces. In the late 1940's, Estey introduced the "Estey Cathedral Organ", a one manual organ designed for chapels and small churches, with 5 sets of reeds and a Sub Bass, internal suction unit, and trim styling (25). Other one manual organs of the late 1940's and the 1950's were the "Estey Chorus Organ", a compact organ of four octaves and two sets of reeds (26); and the "Estey Symphonic Organ", an organ for homes, chapels and schools, with five octaves, 3½ sets of reeds and Sub Bass, and graceful styling (27).

In the middle 1930's, the Estey Organ Corporation developed an entirely new two manual and pedal reed organ with electropneumatic action, ten sets of reeds, American Guild of Organists dimensions and pedal board, self-contained suction unit, and a full set of 16', 8', and 4' couplers (23), (28). During the early 1950's, the case and specifications were slightly modified, and the instrument was called the "Estey Virtuoso" (29). This was the crowning achievement of the Estey family in reed organ manufacture. The "Estey Virtuoso" was the finest reed organ ever made by an American company. Because of increased competition from electronic organs, it was only in production for a few years.

By 1950, the fifth generation of the Estey family was in the business. The company had made almost 500,000 reed organs and about 3,500 pipe organs. The factory consisted of some twelve buildings, and one hundred and thirty persons were employed. The company made nearly everything that went into both the pipe and reed organs, including the pipes and reeds (14). In 1950 Estey made the Miniature (Children's) Organ, Folding Organs, the Junior Organ, Symphonic Organ, Cathedral Organ, and the Two Manual Practice Organ.

In the 1950's, the Estey Organ Corporation began to manufacture electronic organs. One was the "Estey Spinet Electronic Organ". It had two 49 note manuals, 18 pedals, 54 harmonic control tablets, 3 vibrato control tablets, 8 pre-set keys, and two built-in 12-inch speakers (30). By the middle 1950's, the only organs made were the Child's Organ, Folding Organ, Chorus Organ, Symphonic Organ, and the Spinet Electronic Organ. The company continued to develop electronic organs and in 1959 established a plant at Torrance, California, for their manufacture (31).

There were several changes in management in the late 1950's, and eventually reed organ manufacturing at Brattleboro, Vermont, was discontinued. The firm became Estey Electronics, Inc., of Torrance, California. In 1961, the 115-year-old firm merged with the Organ Corporation of America, of West Hempstead, New York. The management of the Organ Corporation took over the direction of the surviving corporation, which was called Estey Electronics Inc. (31). Thus ended the reed organ industry in the United States.

In its long history, the Estey firm made over a half million reed organs, under the direction of five generations of the Estey family. Estey organs were noted for their fine craftsmanship and pure tone.

Many of them are still in existence today, and after a bellows restoration these old organs continue to produce beautiful music at the hands of a sympathetic player. Estey organs are part of the heritage of the United States and are an everlasting credit to the Estey family. May they always be lovingly preserved.

REFERENCES

1. Illustrated Catalogue of Cottage Organs Manufactured By J. Estey & Company, Brattleboro, Vermont, New York, 1876.
2. Nadworny, Milton J. "The Perfect Melodeon: The Origins of the Estey Organ Company, 1846 - 1866". The Business History Review, Vol. XXXIII, No. 1, Spring 1959.
3. General History of the Music Trades of America. Bill & Bill Publishers, New York, 1891.
4. The Piano and Organ Purchasers Guide for 1903, prepared by John C. Freund. The Music Trades Co., New York, 1903.
5. Gellerman, Robert F. "The American Reed Organ". Vestal Press, Vestal, New York, 1974.
6. Circuit Court of the United States for the District of Vermont. Riley Burdett vs. Jacob Estey, Julius Estey and Levi K. Fuller. Decision on final hearing before Judges Blatchford and Wheeler, at New York.
7. State of Vermont, Windham County Court. J. Estey & Co. vs. Riley Burdett, Chas. B. Stoughton, Silas Waite. Charge of His Honor, Judge Rowell.
8. Supreme Court of the United States. Jacob Estey, Levi K. Fuller and Julius J. Estey, Appellants, vs. Riley Burdett, Appellee. October term, 1883, No. 85. Brief for the Appellants.
9. Supreme Court of the United States, No. 85, October Term, 1883. Jacob Estey, Levi K. Fuller and Julius Estey, Appellants, vs. Riley Burdett. Appeal from the Circuit Court of the United States for the District of Vermont.
10. Eaton, Robert O. "The Estey March". Published by Estey & Bruce, Philadelphia, Pa. 1898.
11. Catalogue of Estey Organs. Canadian Representatives Gourlay, Winter & Leeming, Toronto, Hamilton, Winnipeg. Estey Organ Company, Brattleboro, Vermont. 1906.
12. Estey American Organs. Illustrated Price List. J. Estey & Company. (No date; circa 1880).
13. El Organo Estey. Unicos Representantes Para Sud America: The Dé Rees-Bush Co., New York. Estey Organ Company, Brattleboro, Vermont, U.S.A. (No date; early 1900's).
14. Estey Organ Corporation. Letter of October 31, 1950, from J. P. Estey.
15. Estey Pipe Organs. Estey Organ Co., Manufacturers of Church Organs of the Highest Grade. Brattleboro, Vermont. Catalogue, no date (early 1900's).
16. Hinners, John R. "Chronicle of the Hinners Organ Company". The Tracker, Official Publication of The Organ Historical Society, Vol. VII, No. 2, December, 1962.
17. Sears, Roebuck & Co., catalogue No. 111, 1902, page 178.
18. Descriptive Catalogue of Estey Organs, 1905, pp 11-12. Estey Organ Company, Brattleboro, Vermont.
19. Sears, Roebuck & Co., catalogue No. 111, 1902, page 180.
20. The Estey Organ - A Booklet on the Construction of the Estey Organ. Estey Organ Company, Brattleboro, Vermont. (No date; early 1920's).
21. The Estey Student Organ. Estey Organ Company, Brattleboro, Vermont. (No date; circa 1930).
22. Practice Made Perfect. The Estey Practice Organ. Estey Organ Corporation, Brattleboro, Vermont. (No date; 1940's).
23. Here's Music For Your Home. Estey Organ Corporation, Brattleboro, Vermont, 1939.
24. The Estey Melodeon. Estey Organ Corporation, Brattleboro, Vermont. 1934.
25. The Estey Cathedral Organ. Estey Organ Corporation, Brattleboro, Vermont. (No date; late 1940's).
26. The Gem of Small Organs - The Estey Chorus Organ. Estey Organ Corporation, Brattleboro, Vermont. (No date; late 1940's).
27. The New 38-Action Estey Symphonic Reed Organ. One page Broadside. Estey Organ Corporation, Brattleboro, Vermont. (No date; 1950's).
28. Estey Organ - A New Two Manual and Pedal organ. Estey Organ Corporation, Brattleboro,

Vermont. (No date; 4 page brochure circa 1937).

29. The Estey Virtuoso Two Manual and Pedal Organ. Estey Organ Corporation, Brattleboro, Vermont. (Pamphlet, 1953).
30. The Estey Spinet. Big Organ Features, Prismatic Tone, In A Spinet Console. Estey Organ Corporation, Brattleboro, Vermont. (No date; six page brochure of the middle 1950's).
31. The Music Trades, July 1961, page 95.

Where the work began in 1846

Part of this building only was used, the rest of it being occupied as a grist mill.

ESTEY ORGAN WORKS,

BRATTLEBORO, VT.

The Largest of the Kind on the Globe.

ESTEY ORGAN CO. BRATTLEBORO VT. U.S.A.
ORGAN MANUFACTORY
BRATTLEBORO, VT., U.S.A.
ESTEY
ORGANS AND PIANOS
BRATTLEBORO & NEW YORK
PIANO MANUFACTORY
NEW YORK U.S.A.
ESTEY
PIANOS & ORGANS
NEW YORK. BRATTLEBORO.
ESTEY ORGAN CO.
BRATTLEBORO, VT. U.S.A.
BRATTLEBORO VT. U.S.A.
ESTEY ORGAN COMPANY
THE ESTEY PHONORIUM.
ESTEY ORGAN CO.
BRATTLEBORO, VT.
U.S.A.
Compliments
ESTEY ORGAN CO.
BRATTLEBORO, VT. U.S.A.
ESTABLISHED 1846.
J. ESTEY & CO.,
MANUFACTURERS OF THE CELEBRATED
Estey Cottage Organs,
The Beautiful VOX HUMANA TREMOLO, and the Wonderful
VOX JUBILANTE, are new stops peculiar to the Estey Organs.
CATALOGUES SENT FREE.
J. ESTEY & CO.,
Sole Manufacturers,
BRATTLEBORO', VT.
Vermont Directory 1870
FOLD THIS BACK
Listen!
THE ESTEY ORGAN
FOLD THIS BACK
Listen!
THE ESTEY ORGAN

COMPLIMENTS OF
CLUETT & SONS,
TROY N. Y.
ESTEY ORGANS
The
ESTEY
ORGAN
MANUFACTORIES:
BRATTLEBORO, VT.
THE SONG JOURNAL.
ESTEY
Cottage Organs
THE CELEBRATED
ESTEY ORGANS
Combine more Perfections than any other Reed Instruments in the market, resulting from
The Patent Harmonic Attachment.
The Patent Manual Sub-Bass.
The Patent Knee Swell.
The Patent Organ Bellows.
The Patent Vox Jubilante, and
The Patent Vox Humana Tremolo.
These Improvements belong exclusively to the ESTEY Organs, which, for sweet, full, round sympathetic and powerful tone surpass all others.
C. J. WHITNEY & CO.,
General Agents.
831 BROADWAY, New York
188-190 STATE STREET, Chicago, Ill.
203 NORTH FIFTH STREET, St Louis, Mo.
18 Nº SEVENTH STREET, Philadelphia.
601 WASHINGTON STREET, Boston.
BROAD & ALABAMA STREETS, Atlanta, Ga.
42 HOLBORNE VIADUCT, London E.C. England.
Estey Organ Co.
Brattleboro, Vt.
Jacob Estey, PRESIDENT.
Levi K. Fuller, V. PRESIDENT.
Julius J. Estey, TREASURER.
THE PERFECT MELODEON.
With Bass Damper and Harmonic Attachment,
Both recently patented, and two of the most valuable improvements ever made on the Melodeon.
Also the New Harmonic Organs for Churches, Concert or Lecture Rooms, the best Instrument for the price yet invented, Manufactured by
ESTY & GREEN,
BRATTLEBORO, ... VERMONT,
Who have exclusive control of the Patents.
PIANOS FOR SALE OR TO RENT.
Vt Directory 1863
THE ESTEY OVERTURE
1866
ESTEY'S COTTAGE ORGANS!
ESTEY'S HARMONIC ORGANS!
ESTEY'S BOUDOIR ORGANS!
ESTEY'S PERFECT MELODEONS!
40
Different Styles and Prices!
40
MADE AND SOLD EVERY WEEK!
PRICES FROM $100 TO $400.
The Best and the Cheapest!
12,000 NOW IN USE!!
FOR THE PARLOR! THE LODGE ROOM! THE CHURCH!
Send for a Circular to
442 Broadway, Albany, N. Y.
A. C. ROSE, Agent.
The Bootblack Boy
"What are you doing, Bootblack boy?"
"I'm trying to shine," said he,
Like the Estey Organ, great and grand,
That shines as first in this big, broad land,
And sounds so sweet to me!
It began at the foot, like me," he said,
"But now it has climbed right up to the head."
S. S. S.
The Match Girl
"What are you doing, matchgirl, blonde?"
"I'm trying to think," said she,
"If in this box that I have here,
There's a match for the Estey Organ clear
That's famed from sea to sea!
Its match, I fear, will never be found
For wondrous worth and beautiful sound!"
S. S. S.
ESTEY
Every buyer should Select an Organ That guarantees good Every day work and Years of service.
Every Estey Organ Sold is made Throughout with Equal fidelity, and Yields unrivaled tones.
ORGAN
Send for Illustrated Catalogue.
leboro, Vt.
Estey's Cottage Organs,
$100 TO $500.
These popular instruments excel all others in QUICKNESS OF ACTION, ROUNDNESS, PURITY, AND VOLUME OF TONE, accomplished by PATENT IMPROVEMENTS. The crowning perfection is the
VOX HUMANA TREMOLO,
a wonderful imitation of the sympathetic sweetness of the human voice.
They are strongly endorsed by Geo. W. Morgan, Wm. A. King, Chas. Fradel, and many others, the highest musical authority in the United States.
Good Agents wanted everywhere.
Send for illustrated catalogue or call at the New Warerooms.
GEO. G. SAXE & CO.,
417 Broome Street, N. Y.

J. ESTEY & COMPANY,

MANUFACTURERS OF

Cottage Organs, Harmonic Organs,

BOUDOIR ORGANS, AND MELODEONS,

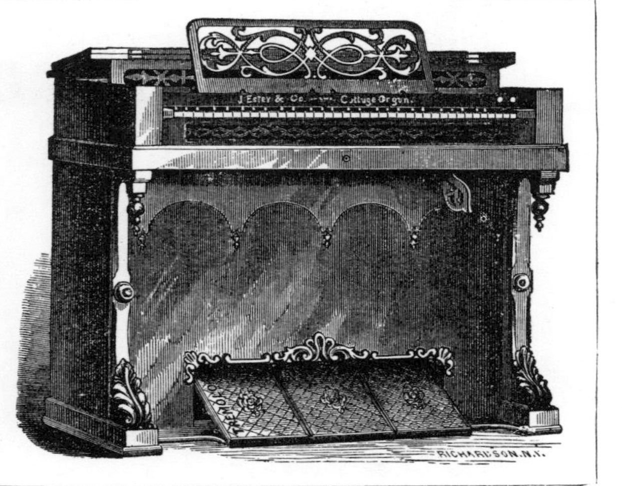

Brattleboro, Vt.

NEW YORK:

L. H. BIGLOW & CO., PRINTERS AND STATIONERS, No. 13 WILLIAM STREET.

1867.

A CARD.

The undersigned respectfully invite attention to the peculiar merits of their instruments, as partially set forth in this circular. They have been before the public for more than twenty years, and from a small beginning have steadily increased and improved their manufacturing facilities, notwithstanding the entire destruction of the establishment by fire in 1857, *and again in* 1864, *until they have now one of the most complete and extensive manufactories in the world.*

This vast amount of patronage has been secured more by the actual merits of the instrument than by extensive advertising and the pretentious parade of their wares before the public. They have employed and retained, from the first, some of the finest mechanics and inventors of the age, and have adopted and patented more valuable improvements than any other establishment in the land. As the result, their instruments stand unrivaled by anything found in this country or in Europe, as is admitted by all impartial judges. The most eminent Pipe-Organ builders and performers—the last to discover excellence in reed tones—pronounce them vastly superior to all others.

Thanking their friends for their continued favors, they invite the severe scrutiny and candid criticism of all.

Respectfully,

JACOB ESTEY,
L. K. FULLER,
J. J. ESTEY.

J. ESTEY & CO.

The 1867 catalog reproduced on pages 10 through 19 is one of the earliest known to exist, and comes from the Jim Andrews collection. The factory pictures on 18 and 19 presumably show the ones that were damaged by flood in 1869. Note particularly the third pedal on several models, used to operate the "Vox Humana Tremolo", an idea that evidently was found wanting as it does not appear in subsequent catalogs.

Four Octave Cottage Organ.

Nos. 14, 15, - - - - - - Length, 3 ft.; Height, 2 ft. 10 in.

Five Octave Cottage Organ.

Nos. 16, 19, 20, 21, 22, - - - Length, 3 ft. 6 in.; Height, 2 ft. 10 in.

Six Octave Cottage Organ.

Nos. 28, 29, 30, 31, 32, - - - - Length, 4 ft.; Height, 2 ft. 10 in.

Rosewood Cottage Organ.

Nos. 23, 24, 25, 26, 27, - - - Length, 3 ft. 6 in,; Height, 2 ft. 10 in.

The Boudoir Organ,

With all our Patent Improvements.

No. 33, - - - - - Length, 3 ft. 8 in. Height, 3 ft. 11 in.

The Most Complete and Elegant Instrument in Use.

BEAUTIFULLY FINISHED IN BLACK WALNUT

DESIGNED FOR THE PARLOR OR DRAWING ROOM.

Harmonic Organ,

FOR

Parlors, Lecture Rooms, Sunday Schools & Churches,

BEAUTIFULLY FINISHED IN BLACK WALNUT.

Nos. 34 and 35. - - Length, 4 ft. 3 in.; Height, 3 ft. 10 in.

Has a Powerful Sub Bass, with Independent Reeds,

Harmonic Attachment and Vox Humana Tremolo,

And has GREAT POWER, being nearly equal to a PIPE ORGAN of THREE TIMES ITS COST.

THE

DOUBLE BANK HARMONIC ORGAN,

FOR

CHURCHES, LECTURE AND SOCIETY ROOMS, &C.

In massive Black Walnut Cases.

No. 36, - - - - - - Length, 4 ft. 3 in.; Height, 3 ft. 2 in.

Five Sets of Reeds Eight Stops, viz: BOURDON, DIAPASON, PRINCIPAL BASS, PRINCIPAL TREBLE, DULCIANA, SUB-BASS, COUPLER, VOX HUMANA.

The MANUAL SUB-BASS, an octave of the same size as the pedal reeds, has more power than was ever obtained on the manuals by any reed instrument maker in the world.

THE DOUBLE BANK HARMONIC ORGAN,

WITH AN OCTAVE AND A HALF OF PEDALS.

No. 37, - - - - - - Length, 4 ft. 3 in.; Height, 3 ft. 2 in.

This instrument differs from No. 36, only in having PEDALS instead of the MANUAL SUB-BASS.

It will be observed that we avoid the custom of many manufacturers of multiplying stops by dividing; every reed stop, with one exception, drawing a full set.

The Estey Organs,

WITH PIPE ORGAN TOP.

The great power and pipe-like tone of the Estey Organs have created a demand for an instrument which shall imitate the appearance, as well as the tone, of the pipe organ; and we are happy to announce to our friends and patrons, that we have now perfected new and beautiful gilt pipe tops for three different styles of our Organs, which, for elegance of proportion, chasteness of style and beauty of finish, are unexcelled by anything in the market.

Churches which are unable to bear the expense of a pipe organ have here a beautiful substitute. The tone and touch are, without doubt, unapproached by any other reed organ in existence, while the style of case will prove an appropriate addition to the architectural beauty of any church or the furnishing of the most elegant parlor.

THE VOX JUBILANTE

Is a new and beautiful stop, peculiar to the Estey Organs. The character of the tone is marked and wonderfully effective, giving a style of music hitherto unattained in instruments of this class. This is accomplished by an extra set of reeds, ingeniously arranged, after long and careful experiment, to meet this special and hitherto unsupplied want. It is considered by competent judges a great success.

The Boudoir Organ,

WITH PIPE ORGAN TOP.

No. 40. Height, 7 ft., 6 in. - - - - Price, $350.

(Similar to No. 33.)

We have no hesitation in saying that our Boudoir Organ, with the addition of the Pipe Organ Top, has no equal for a parlor instrument.

The Double Bank Harmonic Organ,

With Pipe Organ Top.

No. 45. Height, 8 ft., 2 in. - - - - Price, $650.

This Organ corresponds with our No. 36 in every particular, with the addition of PIPE ORGAN TOP with richly gilt pipes and elegantly carved ornaments of solid walnut.

The Double Bank Harmonic Organ,

With Pipe Organ Top.

No. 46. Height, 8 ft., 2 in. - - - - Price, $700.

This Organ corresponds with our No. 37 in every particular, with the addition of the PIPE ORGAN TOP, and we feel warranted in saying, that for elegant appearance, combined with the quality and power of its tone, it has NO EQUAL. The pipes are richly gilt, and the ornaments are elegantly carved out of solid walnut.

The Perfect Melodeon.

Portable Melodeon.

Nos. 1, 2, 3, 4, 5,

Piano Style.

Nos. 6, 7, 8, 10, 11, 12, 13.

Rosewood, Round Corners, Serpentine Mouldings.

THE ESTEY PERFECT MELODEONS

Are so well known, and their reputation so firmly established, that a minute description is unnecessary; they are finished in Walnut and Rosewood, and we spare no pains in making them PERFECT, as heretofore.

Patented Improvements.

That we have invented and adopted more valuable improvements in reed instruments than any other house in the world, is evidenced by the fact that other prominent establishments, after vainly endeavoring to depreciate, have been driven to the scarcely more honorable course of imitating them. But let it be well understood that the credit for originality and superior excellence belongs to THE ESTEY ORGAN; and purchasers should beware of dealers who offer a spurious article posessing only some of the general features of the genuine, orginal invention.

THE PATENT HARMONIC ATTACHMENT

Is an octave coupler used on a single manual, and doubles the power of the instrument without increasing its size or number of reeds. Thus, by the use of this improvement an Organ containing two sets of reeds is instantly made equivalent to one of four; and a tri-reed equals an instrument of six sets of reeds, making the MOST POWERFUL instrument of its size yet known in this country.

THE PATENT MANUAL SUB-BASS

Brings into use an independent set of large and powerful SUB-BASS REEDS, which are played with the ordinary keys and controlled by a stop. The manner in which this set of reeds is placed upon the air-chamber increases the volume of tone at least one-third. This new and valuable invention requires no extra room, and has all the effect of pedal bass, and can be used by any ordinary performer.

The Vox Humana Tremolo.

PATENTED JUNE 27, 1865.

This late and really wonderful invention, (so acknowledged by all leading artis's), is to be found only in our instruments.

In attempting to describe the effect of this stop, we are at a loss for language; its beauties cannot be written, but must be heard to be appreciated. By this stop an ordinary performer can produce an effect which requires a lifetime of practice for an artist upon the violin.

It entirely changes the reed-tone, giving the sympathetic sweetness of the HUMAN VOICE, making it so melodious and pure that it never fails to enchant the appreciative listener.

CONSTRUCTION

OF THE

VOX HUMANA TREMOLO ATTACHMENT.

Various attempts have been made in years past by organ makers to imitate the Tremolo of the human voice, resulting in nothing better than the common valve tremolo, which acts upon the wind before the tone is formed ; thus producing a rigid, mechanical effect really distressing to cultivated ears. It occurred to the inventor of the new "Vox Humana" in using a fan, while listening to the music of an organ and choir, that the vibrations thus produced might be applied to an organ. Acting on this hint, months of careful experimen resulted in the FIRST AND ONLY MECHANICAL REPRODUCTION OF THE TREMOLO OF THE HUMAN VOICE ever given to the world.

The Tremolo is produced by means of a REVOLVING FAN placed just back of the swell, which imparts to the tone a charming wave-like effect hitherto unknown in instrumental music.

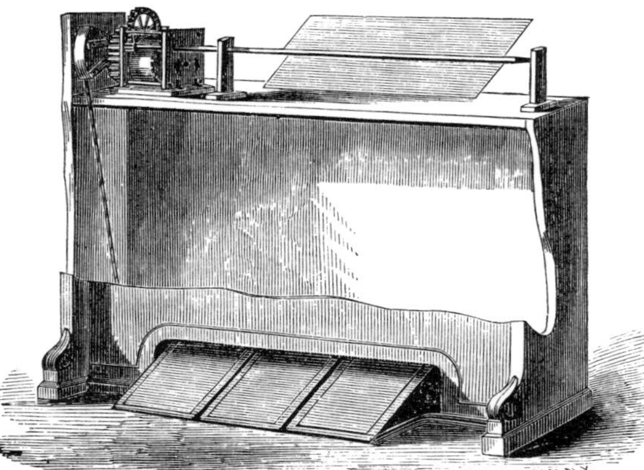

The control of this great discovery was at once secured by LETTERS PATENT, and two years' trial and the largely increasing demand for it attest the value of the invention and its appreciation by the public.

MANNER OF USING.—This Tremolo, unlike all others, is managed by the foot with an ordinary Pedal—the left one of the three—the other two being used as in all instruments of this kind. Whenever the player desires to use the Tremolo, draw the stop and change the left foot to the left or Tremolo Pedal, leaving the right foot to blow. With a few moments' practice, any person at all acquainted with the instument can readily learn to use this most beautiful of all stops. It should be played mostly as a solo stop, with a light, short accompaniment with the left hand.

CAUTION TO PURCHASERS.—One of the results of the great success of the Vox Humana Tremolo is the introduction of various inventions, aiming to accomplish the same results by different means; they are, however, little better than failures, and purchasers are cautioned against receiving the statements of interested parties, who represent their so called Tremolos as the same or nearly the same in effect as ours. The genuine VOX HUMANA TREMOLO is found only in the ESTEY Organ, with three Pedals.

DESCRIPTIVE PRICE LIST.

FOUR OCTAVE COTTAGE ORGAN, Black Walnut, Oil Finish.

No. 14.	Single Reed,	$100
No. 15.	Double Reed, one Stop,	125

FIVE OCTAVE COTTAGE ORGAN, Black Walnut, Paneled Cases,

No. 16.	Single Reed,	130
No. 19.	Double Reed, one Stop,	160
No. 20.	" " Harmonic Attachment, two Stops,	180
No. 22.	" " Sub Bass, two Stops,	180
No. 21.	" " Harmonic Attachment and Manual Sub Bass, three Stops,	200

FIVE OCTAVE ROSEWOOD COTTAGE ORGAN, Finely Polished.

No. 24.	Single Reed,	150
No. 25.	Double Reed, one Stop,	180
No. 26.	" " Harmonic Attachment, two Stops,	200
No. 23.	" " Sub Bass, two Stops,	200
No. 27.	" " Harmonic Attachment and Manual Sub Bass, three Stops,	220

SIX OCTAVE COTTAGE ORGAN, Black Walnut, Paneled Cases.

No. 28.	Single Reed,	150
No. 29.	Double Reed, one Stop,	200
No. 30.	" " Harmonic Attachment, two Stops,	225
No. 32.	" " Sub Bass, two Stops,	225
No. 31.	" " Harmonic Attachment and Manual Sub Bass, three Stops,	250

Any Six Octave Organ in Rosewood $25 extra.

The ***Vox Humana Tremolo $25*** on each number after No. 15.

BOUDOIR ORGAN, Five Octave, Black Walnut, Fancy Paneled, Oil Finish.

No. 33.	Double Reed, with all improvements,	275
"	" " " " finely polished,	290

HARMONIC ORGAN, Five Octave, Black Walnut.

No. 34.	Double Reed, Har. Attach., Sub Bass, Vox Humana Tremolo, six Stops,	325
No. 35.	Tri-Reed, " " " " "	375

Nos. 34 and 35, with Pedal Bass, ***$50*** extra.

No. 36.	Two Banks Keys Man. Sub Bass, four sets Reed, eight Stops,	500
No. 37.	" " Pedal Bass, " "	550

Any of the above styles with Pipe Organ Top, furnished to order.

PORTABLE MELODEONS.

No. 1.	Five Octaves, Black Walnut,	95
No. 2.	" Rosewood,	110
No. 3.	" Rosewood, Harmonic Attachment, one Stop,	135
No. 4.	" Rosewood, Double Reed, two Stops,	160
No. 5.	Six Octaves, Rosewood Single Reed,	135

PIANO STYLE MELODEONS, Rosewood.

No. 6.	Five Octaves,	150
No. 7.	" Harmonic Attachment, one Stop,	175
No. 8.	" Double Reed, three Stops.	200
No. 10.	Six Octaves,	180
No. 11.	" Harmonic Attachment, one Stop,	210
No. 12.	" Double Reed, four Stops	235
No. 13.	" Double Reed, Harmonic Attachment, five Stops,	260

Carved Legs, $10 Extra. No charge for boxing and shipping.

DIRECTIONS.—When the Reeds are disturbed by dust or other foreign substance, take out the Sounding-Board, which is just back of the Keys, fastened by small brass thumbscrews; then by opening the Swell, the Reeds may be reached, and, if necessary, drawn out with the Reed Hook, which accompanies each instrument. Oftener, however, a slight thump or pressure with the Hook is all that is required. In double Reed instruments, the front set may be reached by removing the small fret-work board in front, below the Keys. In the Cottage Organ, if necessary, the upper part of the Case may be taken off after unfastening a small hook at each end, on the inside.

EVERY INSTRUMENT WARRANTED TO GIVE SATISFACTION.

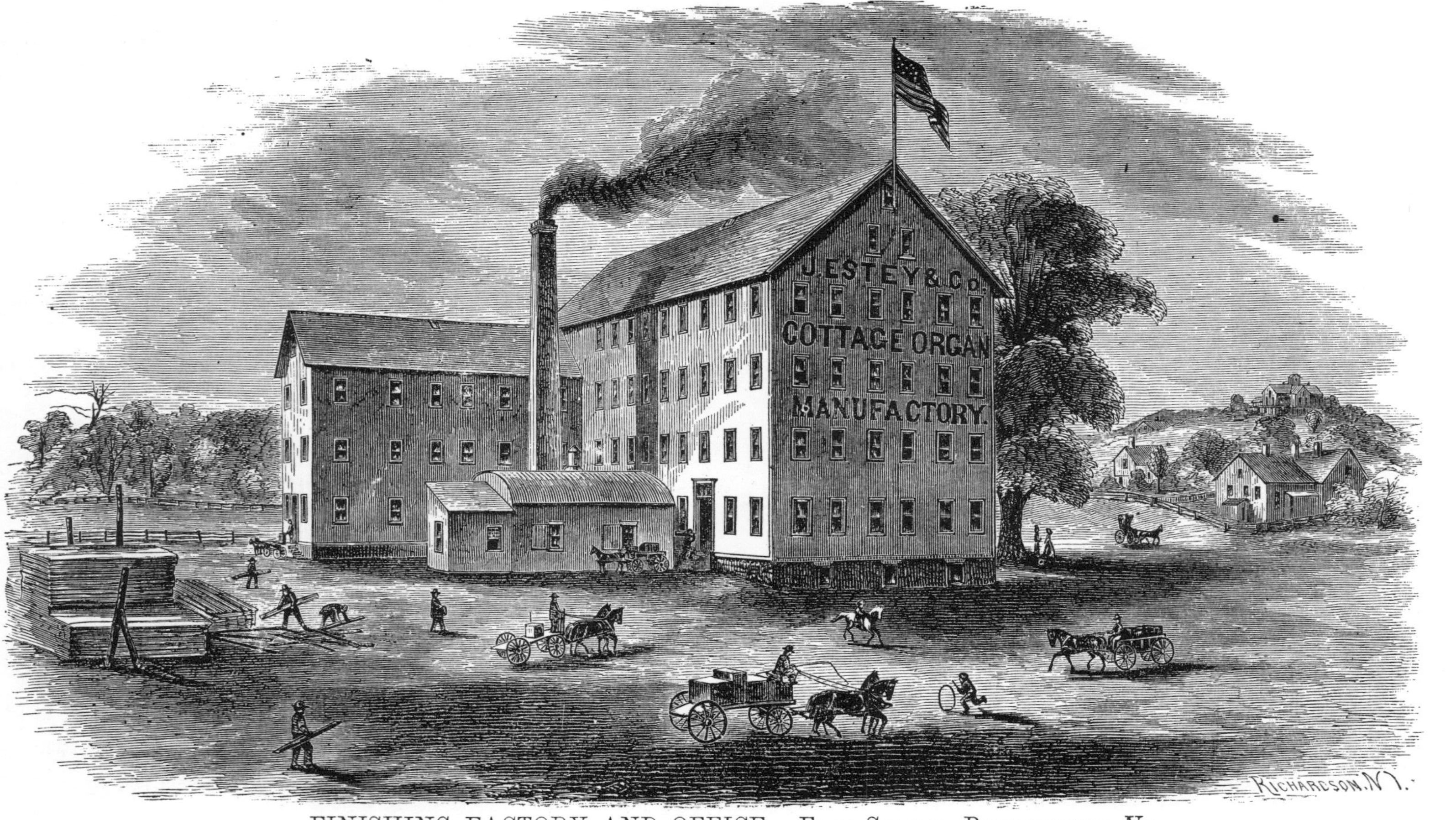

FINISHING FACTORY AND OFFICE.—FLAT STREET, BRATTLEBORO, VT.

From C. B. SEYMOUR, Musical Critic of the N. Y. Times:

"An invention so simple and perfect as the Vox Humana Tremolo invented by R. W. CARPENTER, must commend itself to every one's appreciation. That it adds to the quality, humanity and sensibility of the tone, no one can for a moment deny. More than this, it gives character to what, in inferior instruments, is seldom more than a level, dry monotony of scale. It is vocal, which is the highest praise that can be bestowed on any instrument."

From WILLIAM A. JOHNSON, Organ Builder, Westfield, Mass.:

"I am happy to express my conviction that no Tremolo has yet been invented that will in any degree compare with this for beauty of effect. In fact, it seems to me to be absolutely perfect, leaving nothing to be desired."

From Professor L. O. EMERSON, of Boston:

"It redeems reed instruments from harshness, and makes them more sympathetic and beautiful. Hereafter, with the addition of your valuable patent, I shall enjoy the music of the Reed Organ."

From the Rev. Bishop SIMPSON:

"I am much pleased with the musical instruments which I purchased of you. The COTTAGE ORGAN combines sweetness and power in an unusual degree, and is quite a favorite in our family circle. The Piano is also an excellent instrument, and fully sustains your recommendations."

REED AND CASE FACTORIES.—SOUTH MAIN STREET.

The following from the NEW YORK INDEPENDENT, October 11th, 1866:

"NOTES AT THE FAIR OF THE NEW YORK STATE AGRICULTURAL SOCIETY.—Floral Hall and Domestic Hall never before appeared so much like an Eden of delight as when every standing was occupied by enraptured listeners, drinking in the Heaven-born music of ESTEY'S COTTAGE ORGANS, which received the Gold Medal. I never want to hear another piano, if I can hear such an ORGAN with the Vox Humana Tremolo Attachment, which consists of a revolving fan placed just back of the swell of the organ, and which is put in motion by a pedal. There is no use in attempting to describe this prize instrument. Language fails in adequacy to convey a fair idea of its perfectly enchanting power. It must be heard to be appreciated. I saw old iron-sided Ajaxes, at Saratoga, wiping the unbidden tears, because the entrancing music not only charmed the ear, but sank into the very fountains of life."

From the SPRINGFIELD REPUBLICAN:

"The Masons of this city have purchased, for the use of the different bodies that meet in Masonic Hall, a fine reed organ, from the manufactory of J. ESTEY & Co. A peculiar and admirable feature of this instrument is the Vox Humana Tremolo, recently invented and patented. Tremulants are usually in Pipe as well as Reed Organs, a clattering, superfluous, unmanageable nuisance; offensive to a correct taste and undesirable in every way. This one, however, is as beautiful as the others are worthless; being under perfect control as to rapidity, its delicate pulsations appeal to the listener, with a power and pathos impossible to resist."

ILLUSTRATED CATALOGUE

OF

Cottage Organs,

MANUFACTURED BY

J. ESTEY & COMPANY,

Brattleboro, Vermont.

Giving a Brief Account of the most extensive Cottage Organ Establishment in the World; together with a Description of the different Styles of Organs manufactured, their Peculiarities and Patented Improvements.

ALSO,

THE WRITTEN STATEMENTS OF CELEBRATED MUSICIANS, ORGANISTS, AND CRITICS, WHO HAVE EXAMINED OUR ORGANS, AND A FEW FROM THE THOUSANDS OF OTHER TESTIMONIALS RECEIVED FROM PURCHASERS AND USERS.

ESTABLISHED 1846.

HOLMES & SOUTHWORTH,

Agents, Lansing, Mich.

New York:
L. H. Biglow & Co., Printers and Stationers, No. 13 William Street.
1871.

J. Estey & Company.

The year 1846 witnessed in BRATTLEBORO, VERMONT, *the establishment of the manufacture of Reed Musical Instruments. Although humble in the beginning, the work has grown from year to year, until the house of* **J. ESTEY & CO.** *has become the most extensive manufacturers of Cottage Organs in the world.*

Mr. JACOB ESTEY, *the senior member of the firm, has been connected with the business for a quarter of a century, and under his watchful care it has assumed gigantic proportions.* Mr. LEVI K. FULLER *has been with this establishment for twelve years, and has planned and developed the most complete system of Reed Organ manufacture extant. Scientific men, and manufacturers from all parts of the world, have visited the* ESTEY ORGAN WORKS, *and declare them unsurpassed for perfectness of system and detail of arrangements.* Mr. JULIUS J. ESTEY, *son of the senior member, and brought up in the business, inherits the genius of his father, and has had a large share in the responsibility and labor of bringing the business up to its present standard.*

The manufacturers invite a careful examination of the following pages, which contain a description of their works, the improvements they have made and now use in their Instruments, and a full description and engravings of the prominent styles of Organs manufactured by them.

Their Organs have been sold not by extensive advertising and puffing, but by the real merits of the Instruments themselves. Wherever they have been introduced they have won their way into the admiration and confidence of the people; and this is not mere chance, but comes as the inevitable consequence of skill, high attainment, and unremitting application and labor. From the first the manufacturers have employed the finest mechanicians and inventors of the age. The leading improvements now in vogue in Reed Organs were perfected and brought out in this establishment. Their Instruments now stand unrivalled by anything found in this country or Europe.

Thanking their friends for their continued favors, they invite the severe scrutiny and candid criticism of all, feeling confident that the more searching the test, the greater will be the triumph for

The Estey Organ.

J. ESTEY & COMPANY'S

Cottage Organ Manufactory.

These Works are situated on BIRGE STREET, in the beautiful Village of BRATTLEBORO, VERMONT. In 1869, finding that we must enlarge our already extensive works, in order to keep pace with the great demand or Instruments of our make, we purchased a large tract of land suitable for Factories, Dry-Houses and Lumber Yards, and proceeded at once to erect the most complete and extensive Reed Organ Factories in the world.

The Works consist of six main factories, placed in a row, fronting Birge Street, forty feet apart, each one hundred feet long and three stories high, varying from thirty to thirty-eight feet in width, according to the work to be done in them. The Dry-Houses are placed in the rear of the main factories, and are two in number, one 36 × 52 feet, the other 21 × 135 feet, both two stories high, heated and ventilated in the most thorough manner. The buildings are all connected at the second story by a bridge, containing a track, on which is run a car conveying material from one shop to another.

The Lumber is taken in at the first story of building No. 2, where it is cut and planed ready for the more complicated machinery placed in other parts of the building. The other stories of this building, also the whole of No. 1, is devoted to case making. In the basement is placed a Patent Steam Exhaust Fan, which takes all of the shavings and dust from the machinery and shops, and deposits them in a building near the furnaces, making our room free from dust, giving pure and wholesome air to the workmen.

No. 3 is devoted to making Reeds and Actions. In the rear of No. 3 is a fire-proof Engine and Boiler House, containing four large boilers, furnishing steam for the engine and heat for the buildings. The Engine is of the celebrated Corliss patent, and of one hundred horse power.

After the different parts of the Organ have been made they are "assembled" together in No. 4, which is used exclusively for "SETTING UP" the Organs.

In No. 5 our Tuning rooms are situated. The offices of the establishment are here located, where is conducted the extensive correspondence, and all matters of business with the firm are transacted.

No. 6 contains a few Tuning rooms, the rest of the building being devoted to finishing the Organs.

From the office there goes out a net-work of speaking-tubes, bringing all parts of the establishment into instantaneous communication with it.

On each floor of every building is placed a row of water pails filled with water, also a Fire Extinguisher. For greater security against fire, an Amoskeag Steam Fire Engine is kept on the premises ready for use at a moment's warning.

In fact, everything that skill and capital can do to secure the comfort, convenience and health of the workmen, and the safety, perfection and economical working of the establishment has been done.

Thus, in brief, we have given an outline of this extensive establishment. Other improvements are being made, buildings erected to carry out the grand scheme projected by the MESSRS. ESTEY & Co., in order to furnish instruments in sufficient numbers to meet the great demands of the public.

In this circular, we give the facts as they are, and have not detailed prospective things as already existing.

We have not been accustomed to secure the designs of our Cases by Patent, but in order to preserve to ourselves the benefit of our labors we have Patented all the designs here represented.

The write-up in this 1871 catalog describes what takes place in the factory buildings. Note that it refers to six main factories in a row, yet the various pictures of the establishment show eight. Possibly the last two were owned by other concerns. The danger of fire putting the firm out of business was obviously lessened by having several individual structures instead of one large one.

IMPROVEMENTS.

THAT we have invented and adopted more valuable improvements in REED INSTRUMENTS than any other house in the world, is evidenced by the fact, that other prominent establishments after vainly endeavoring to depreciate, *have been driven to the scarcely more honorable course of imitating them*, and we have been obliged on several occasions to call to our aid the LAW to protect our rights. But let it be well understood, that the credit for originality and superior excellence belongs to **THE ESTEY ORGAN,** and purchasers should beware of dealers who offer inferior instruments, possessing only some of the general features of the ORIGINAL and GENUINE ESTEY INSTRUMENT.

Among the many improvements, we would call attention to

The Patent Vox Humana.

This wonderful invention was perfected and brought out in the ESTEY ORGANS in 1865. It consists of a revolving fan placed just back of the Reeds, which, when set in motion, imparts to the tone a charming, wave-like effect hitherto unknown in instrumental music. The control of this great discovery was at once secured by Letters Patent, and after years of trial, the largely increasing demand for it attests the value of the invention and its appreciation by the public. Since its introduction by us, and its great success, other manufacturers have introduced various inventions, aiming to accomplish the same result by different means, calling theirs by the same or similar names; they are, however, that old and dilapidated idea—the "Valve," "Clapper," or "Cut-off" Tremulant, and are little better than failures; and purchasers are cautioned against receiving the statements of interested parties who represent their so-called Tremolos, as the same or *nearly* the same in effect as ours.

After vainly endeavoring to decry this great improvement, a certain firm has been compelled to adopt it, paying a liberal royalty for the same, and are now advertising it as *their* new improved *Vox Humana*, patented by them. It is the old story of the cautious (?) man, waiting for bolder men to venture and achieve success, and then come in to share the fruits; in this case the fruit has to be well paid for.

Several firms, regardless of the rights of others, who have seen fit to infringe this patent, have been prosecuted in the *Courts of the United States*, and compelled to pay heavy damages for pirating away this invention, and enjoined from further infringement. Purchasers of other Organs will do well to ascertain whether they are licensed under the original Patent of June 27th, 1865, re-issued October 5, 1869, before they invest their money in what hereafter may be a source of financial trouble to them.

Our **Vox Humana** entirely changes the reed-tone, giving it the sympathetic sweetness of the HUMAN VOICE; its gentle, wave-like tones vibrate so melodious and pure that it never fails to enchant the appreciative listener; in fact it is the FIRST AND ONLY MECHANICAL REPRODUCTION OF THE HUMAN VOICE EVER GIVEN TO THE WORLD.

THE USE OF THE VOX HUMANA.—The finest effects of the *Tremolo* are produced in using it as a Solo Stop. On all SINGLE BANK ORGANS it should be used with the *Diapason* Stop; though in Organs that have the *Harmonic Attachment* or *Vox Jubilante* Stop, a fine effect is produced by using that in connection with the *Diapason*. On DOUBLE BANK ORGANS it is used ON THE UPPER BANK, and with the *Dulciana* Stop, though the taste and skill of the performer will lead him to produce beautiful effects by coupling other sets with it.

The Patent Vox Jubilante

Is a new and beautiful stop, peculiar to the ESTEY ORGANS. The character of the tone is marked and wonderfully effective, giving a style of music hitherto unattained in instruments of this class. This is accomplished by an extra set of reeds, ingeniously arranged and peculiarly tuned, the patent for which Messrs. ESTEY & Co. have owned for a long time, and not until after long and careful experiment were they adjusted to meet this special and hitherto unsupplied want. It is considered by competent judges a great success, and is destined to create a great revolution in the manufacture of Reed Organs.

With this attachment on an ESTEY ORGAN, the most thrilling effects can be produced, the listener can hear the sweet *Dulciana* in the distance, increasing in beauty and grandeur, until mingling with the royal tones of the ***Jubilante***, like a full band, it breaks upon the ear, charming and delighting beyond our ability to express.

The Patent Harmonic Attachment

Is an octave coupler used on a single manual, and doubles the power of the instrument without increasing its size or number of reeds. Thus, by the use of this improvement, an Organ containing two sets of reeds is instantly made equivalent to one of four; and a tri-reed equals an instrument of six sets of reeds, making the MOST POWERFUL instrument of its size yet known in this country.

The Patent Manual Sub-bass

Brings into use an independent set of large and powerful SUB-BASS REEDS, which are played with the ordinary keys and controlled by a stop. The manner in which this set of reeds is placed upon the air chamber increases the volume of tone at least one-third. This new and valuable invention requires no extra room, and has all the effect of pedal bass, and can be used by any ordinary performer. The invention is covered by ***three*** patents.

The Patent Knee-Swell,

Whereby the player has a complete control over the instrument, obtaining a perfect ***crescendo*** or ***diminuendo***, more beautiful than the Automatic Swell, or any other ever before used.

The Patent Organ Bellows

Greatly enhances the power and quality of the tone without increasing the size of the case.

The Patent Reed Board,

Whereby the tone is greatly improved, and rendered more like a Pipe Organ than by any other instrument in the market. This important improvement is covered by two patents.

Improved Tone.

The days of the old fashioned Melodeon have passed. The great improvements in modern Reed Organs have brought them to the front rank of musical instruments. No matter how good a case it may have, how costly or stylish its apparel, unless the tone of the instrument be pure, sweet and musical, beyond the *twang* usually found in reeds, it is little else than a failure. As regards quality of tone, the Estey Organ stands pre-eminently above every other. Its sweetness, purity and pipe-like quality is the wonder of all who hear it. Round and full, without sacrifice of power, and capable of the most delicate articulations—breathing forth the soft tones of the Dulciana, it can also produce the deep and thrilling tones of the Pipe Organ. The question is often asked, "How do you produce such tones, why! I never heard anything to equal it?" Our answer is, a great many things go to make up this quality of tone. In the first place we have two patents covering the method in which our reed boards are constructed, and these improvements are not found elsewhere. The Reeds have no small part to play in giving us these beautiful tones. It would be perfectly ridiculous for a person with a husky, cracked and ugly voice to attempt to imitate a *Prima Donna*, or for an untutored and harsh voice to appear as Parepa or Nillson. There is as wide a difference in reeds as in voices. Our reeds are the fruit of long and patient study. The stock is of a fine and peculiar texture, melted and rolled especially for our use. The most costly and exact machinery known to modern times is used by us. After the reeds are fashioned by machinery as far as it is possible so to do, skillful hands manipulate them in the most delicate and exquisite manner. Some of our workmen have been with us from the start. Our leading tuners have spent their whole lives in this particular branch, and although we do not claim for them, or for ourselves, the discovery of Reeds, the Electric Telegraph or the Steam Engine, we do claim that our method of manufacture, our skill and experience enables us to fashion our reeds and produce a tone which others have in vain attempted to imitate. In relation to our machinery for doing the above work, we have one word more to say. It is well known that we have the finest in the world, and others have often applied to us for copies or drawings of it. As we have spent many thousands of dollars in perfecting it, we have declined all such invitations. And yet, one of the leading city manufacturers during the past year has kept an agent in town for weeks at a time, vainly attempting to bribe our workmen, and get a knowledge of it.

Cases.

The American public demand in all those things which are manufactured for their convenience and comfort, that there should be a proper display of useful and beautiful ornamentation. In fact, no more annoying problem is presented to artizans and manufacturers than how to gratify this demand.

The days of plain and severe style of cabinet work have passed. Modern skill and machinery have enabled us to thoroughly satisfy the refined taste of the people, and at a moderate cost. We have the gratification of presenting to the public new styles of Organ Cases, which for chasteness of design, elaborate embellishment and beauty of finish, have never been excelled or equalled—styles which will prove an appropriate addition to the architecture of any church, or the furnishing of the most elegant parlor.

Material.

The material used in the construction of the Estey Organs is tested in the most thorough manner known to modern science. The most scrupulous care is taken in every stage of the work. The lumber is first exposed to the open air for a given period, that nature may do her own seasoning, after which it runs the gauntlet of kilns built especially for this purpose. When thus prepared, it is proof against climatic changes, and assists materially in giving tone and excellence to the instrument. In fact, nothing but the most carefully selected material, and that which has been proven to be the very best, is allowed to enter into the construction of any of the parts of the Estey Organs.

Prices.

Many firms are advertising a reduction of prices, and it behooves the public to examine carefully what they buy. There has been no real reduction of prices, and cannot be so long as labor and material are so high. To be sure, some articles are cheaper, but others have increased in value. Nevertheless, a cheaper class of instruments has been introduced, made of what would be refuse material in the manufacture of first-class Organs, and these are sold cheap, the better class of goods remaining the same. We have seen the reputation of too many firms shaken or ruined by putting upon the market goods of an inferior grade, and we will not risk ours by palming off upon the public goods which are *cheap, trashy* or *second class.* Our success has been achieved by giving the public nothing but a first-class article, and for such we believe they are still willing to pay.

What to Buy.

In looking over the list of Organs now before the public, purchasers are sometimes bewildered to know whose make to select, and still more, the particular style of instrument it is best to procure. For this reason we have attempted to set forth in as full and clear a manner as possible, the peculiarities and distinctive qualities of the Estey Organs.

Tastes differ so much, circumstances are so varied, places for and the surroundings of instruments so dissimilar, that it is impossible to give any general rule for buying an Organ. But there are some HINTS which will be found useful to all intending to purchase. In the first place, the purchaser must be assured that he is getting a good article, thoroughly made, that will stand the test of climate for years, and will not easily get out of order.

In fact, the public now demand that there shall be a *good reputation* back of their purchase—the mere getting of an instrument through the terms of warranty will not do.

The case must be well made, of good proportion, and with a degree of elegance commensurate with the price. The bellows, being of vital importance, must be of sufficient capacity to sustain a *strong* and *steady* tone. The reeds must be of an excellence that will produce *round, full* and *pipe-like* tones, entirely musical, of which the ear does not tire. They must not be *twangy* nor *reedy*, but pure and sweet, and of sufficient power to meet their requirements.

All of these qualities are obtained in the Estey Organs. To enable those who may not be able to examine Organs before ordering, we make a few explanations in regard to the different styles.

Those who do not care so much for *power*, but want a beautiful, soft tone, with some variety, Nos. 16, 17 and 18 are very desirable and popular.

No. 19 is the "Gem of the Parlor," being moderate in price, and of sufficient power for the parlor, and of great variety and sweetness of tone.

No. 21 is the sample instrument. It has *all* the improvements. Its variety is almost endless. It has the power of about six sets of reeds, and combines every quality produced in the styles described; and we challenge the world to produce any Reed Organ of its size and price that will bear a favorable comparison with it.

In our Boudoir Organ, No. 33, will be found more elegance than in any other instrument in the market. It is beautifully finished, and designed for the most elegant parlor or drawing room.

Churches must be governed by the size of their audience room, position of the Organ, and their circumstances; but to those who can afford them, we recommend strongly the larger instruments. They have greater depth of tone, power sufficient for most of our Church edifices, and are more desirable than Pipe Organs costing less than $2,000.

For further particulars in regard to Organs with Gilt Pipe Tops, and full description of other styles, we refer the enquirer to the following pages.

The styles of Organs described on this page have CASES alike; they are the finest in appearance of any Instruments in the market of their size and cost, the difference in them being in the *number* and *kind* of *Stops*, or the action controlled by them. When we put a Stop into an Organ, it adds to its value; in no case do we put them in to fill up or to make a show.

No. 16.

This style contains One and three-fifths Sets of Reeds, *Vox Jubilante* and *Vox Humana*. 4 Stops. The Key-board is of five octaves compass. Case—Solid Black Walnut, Oil Finish.

No. 17

Contains Two full Sets of Reeds and *Vox Humana*. 5 Stops. The Key-board has a compass of five octaves.

No. 18

Contains Two and three-fifths Sets of Reeds, including *Vox Jubilante*. 5 Stops. The Key-board is of five octaves compass.

No. 19

Contains Two and three-fifths Sets of Reeds, including *Vox Jubilante* and *Vox Humana*. 6 Stops. This Instrument is a combination of Nos. 17 and 18, and is the "GEM OF THE PARLOR." The price is moderate; tone sweet, with power and volume sufficient for the parlor, and of great variety.

No. 20

Contains Two full Sets of Reeds, *Vox Humana*, *Harmonic Attachment* and *Manual Sub-Bass*. The power and variety is doubled in this Instrument, while there is great depth of tone.

No. 21

Contains Two and three-fifths Sets of Reeds, including *Vox Jubilante* and *Vox Humana*. It has also the *Harmonic Attachment* and *Manual Sub-Bass*. 8 Stops. Key-board is of five octaves compass; Case of solid Black Walnut, Oil Finish. This is the sample Instrument. It has all the Improvements mentioned in the others; its variety is almost endless; it has the power of about six sets of reeds, and combines every quality produced in the styles described; and we challenge the world to produce any Reed Organ of its size and price that will bear a favorable comparison to it.

All Organs described on this page contain our improved Knee-Swell, Reed-Board and Bellows, with Double Blow-Pedals.

Five Octave Cottage Organ.

Length, 3 ft., 10 in.; Depth, 2 ft.; Height, 3 ft., 2 in.

No. 16,	Price, $180	No. 19,	Price, $210
" 17,	" 185	" 20,	" 235
" 18,	" 200	" 21,	" 260

From A. M. SHERWOOD, Trumansburgh, N. Y.

Eighteen months ago I purchased one of your Double Bank Reed Organs, with sub-base and *Tremolo* attachment, and I am happy to say we are greatly pleased with it. It is very prompt and brilliant in secular music, and in sacred music it has a richness of tone and depth of harmony that I have never heard in any other Organ. The *Tremolo* produces one of the most beautiful musical effects.

From WILLIAM ROBJOHN, late of London, now with C. & J. H. Odell, Organ Builders, New York.

I accidentally saw one of your Organs in the St. Paul's M. E. Church, Peekskill, and its appearance induced me to try it. I was so much pleased with its touch and quality of tone that my former prejudices against such instruments completely gave way, and I have great pleasure in saying that they are the best reed instruments I have met with; the *Tremolo* is certainly very ingenious and beautiful, and well adapted to instruments of its class.

From H. M. WELCH, Potsdam, N. Y.

After carefully examining the Organs of various manufacturers, I have come to the conclusion that none that I have ever seen are equal to the ESTEY in construction and in in the quality of tone as well as power. The one I have is remarkably free from the coarse, open, reedy sound that characterizes reed Organs generally, and more nearly approaches the full, round tone of the pipe Organ. All who have this express the same opinion.

From ISAIAH SMITH, Farmer Village, N. Y.

I purchased one of your Cottage Organs, and my daughter has used it nearly eighteen months, and it has given myself and family perfect satisfaction. The reeds are voiced so evenly that it is perfectly natural and easy to sing with, and we think the *Tremolo* the finest arrangement we have ever seen in an Organ.

Six Octave Cottage Organ.

Length, 4 ft., 4 in.; Depth, 2 ft.; Height, 3 ft., 2 in.

No. 29, - - - - - **Price, $250** | **No. 31,** - - - - - **Price, $300**

No. 29

Contains Two and three-fifths Sets of Reeds, including *Vox Jubilante* and *Vox Humana.* 6 Stops. It differs from No. 19 in the Key-board having a compass of six octaves.

No. 31

Contains Two and three-fifths Sets of Reeds, including *Vox Jubilante and Vox Humana.* It has also the *Harmonic Attachment* and *Manual Sub-Bass.* 8 Stops. This Instrument differs from No. 21 in having a Key-board of six octaves compass. All the Improvements mentioned as attached to the five octave Organs are contained in these. Although the greater part of music is now written for five octave Instruments, there are a few who want a six octave Organ. From our great experience in Organ making, we have selected the combinations contained in these two styles as the best suited to their wants.

Extra Styles will be made to order.

Boudoir Organ.

Length, 3 ft. 11 in.; Depth, 2 ft.; Height, 3 ft. 7 in

No. 33, - - - **Price, $325**

No. 33.

Our Boudoir Organ contains Two and three-fifths Sets of Reeds, including *Vox Jubilante* and *Vox Humana.* It has also the *Harmonic Attachment* and *Manual Sub-Bass.* 8 Stops. Key-board of five octaves compass. Improved Knee-Swell, Reed-board and Bellows. We believe this to be the most complete and elegant Instrument in use, beautifully finished in Black Walnut, designed for the parlor or drawing-room.

Although the outward style of this case is now for the first time presented to the public, the internal features of it were perfected in 1866. We then introduced sounding chambers in the upper part of an Organ, and have used them in our Boudoir Organ since.

There are very many minor things that might be spoken of in relation to our Organs, such as Ivory fronts to the Keys, the best quality of Ivory being used by us; Keys bushed to prevent rattling, and always preserving an even and delicate touch. In fact everything connected with our Organs is of the very best quality and workmanship.

Harmonic Organ.

Length, 4 ft., 4 in.; Depth, 2 ft., 5 in.; Height, 3 ft., 7 in.

No. 35, . . . Price, $400.

No. 35.

This is especially designed for large Parlors, Lecture Rooms, Sunday Schools and Churches, beautifully finished in Black Walnut. It has a powerful Sub-Bass, with independent Reeds, and is the most powerful single bank Organ made; and is so simple in its arrangements that the most ordinary player can manage it.

Contains Two and three-fifths Sets of Reeds, including *Vox Jubilante* and *Vox Humana, Harmonic Attachment* and *Manual Sub-Bass.* 8 Stops. Key-board of five octaves compass, and improved Knee-Swell. The case is large enough to admit of great size in the air chambers and bellows, thus giving greater power and a depth of tone unattainable in smaller Instruments.

Double Bank Organ.

Length, 4 ft., 4 in.; Depth, 2 ft., 5 in.; Height, 3 ft. 7 in.

No. 36, . . . Price, $500.

No. 36.

This Organ is designed for Churches, Lecture and Society Rooms. This case is similar in size and appearance to No. 35.

It contains two Manuals and 10 Stops, three full and and two and three-fifths sets of Reeds. including *Vox Jubilante, Vox Humana* and *Manual Sub-Bass,* with independent set of reeds. Manual Coupler. It also contains our improved Knee-Swell, Reed-boards and Bellows, with double Blow Pedals.

The *Manual Sub-Bass,* of the same size as pedal reeds, has more power than was ever before obtained on the manuals by any reed instrument maker in the world.

Pedal Organ.

Length, 4 ft., 6 in.; Depth, 2 ft., 8 in.; Height, 3 ft., 9 in. Including the Pedals in, ready for use, the Depth is 4 ft.

No. 39, - - - Price, $650.

No. 39.

This Instrument is of great variety as well as power, and is suitable for LECTURE ROOMS, HALLS and CHURCHES.

This style contains Four full and Two three-fifths Sets of Reeds, including the *Vox Jubilante* and *Vox Humana.* Has Two Manuals of five octaves compass. The Pedal-Bass is of two octaves and very heavy. The Stops are fourteen in number—*Vox Humana, Trumpet, Viola, Dulciana, Principal Bass, Principal Treble, Diapason, Forte, Bourdon, Delecante, Pedals, Vox Jubilante, Coupler, Manual Coupler.*

Boudoir Organ.—Pipe Organ Top.

Length, 3 ft., 7 in.; Depth, 1 ft., 10 in.; Height, 7 ft., 3 in.

No. 40, - - - Price, $400.

No. 40.

This Organ corresponds with our No. 33 as regards the stops and attachments, but the Case has a different appearance, also the addition of PIPE ORGAN TOP.

From the VERGENNES VERMONTER.

ESTEY'S ORGANS.—There are some musical instruments in all good society which it is quite as unnecessary to commend to public favor as it would be to advise a thoughtful housekeeper to always have a barrel of good flour on hand; and among these we class the ESTEY ORGAN. Why occupy the space in our columns to say that the Messrs. J. ESTEY & Co., of Brattleboro, have exhausted musical skill, ingenuity and taste in getting up the most perfect instrument of the kind made—when all know that they have!

From the OGDENSBURGH JOURNAL.

Twenty years ago reed music met with comparatively little favor; but under the watchful care of JACOB ESTEY it has attained a wonderful state of perfection. Of the many improvements made, none is more admired than the *Vox Humana Tremolo*, introduced four years ago. It is probably the nearest approach to an imitation of the human voice ever invented, and gives to music a mellow cadence and pathos hitherto unknown

Double Bank Organ.—Pipe Organ Top.

Length, 4 ft., 1 in.; Depth, 2 ft., 8 in.; Height, 9 ft., 8 in.

No. 45, - - - Price, $600.

No. 45.

This Organ corresponds with our No. 36 in every particular, with the addition of Pipe Organ Top, with richly Gilt Pipes and elegantly Carved Ornaments, and Case of solid Black Walnut.

Pedal Organ.—Pipe Organ Top.

Length, 4 ft., 6 in.; Depth, 2 ft., 8 in.; Height, 9 ft., 4 in. Including the Pedals in, ready for use, the Depth is 4 ft.

No. 46, - - - Price, $750.

No. 46.

This Organ corresponds in every particular with our No. 39, with the addition of the Pipe Organ Top, and we feel warranted in saying, that for elegant appearance, combined with the quality and power of its tone, it has NO EQUAL. The Pipes are richly gilt, the ornaments elegantly carved, and the Case of solid Black Walnut.

Two Manual Organ.

Length, 4 ft. 7 in.; Depth, 2 ft. 8 in.; Height, 5 ft. 4 in.

Style 87; Price, $750.

This Organ is designed for CHURCHES, LECTURE and SOCIETY ROOMS, and is a great favorite with Organists. It contains Two Manuals and Sixteen Stops, one Five Octave Set of PRINCIPAL REEDS, one Five Octave Set of DIAPASON REEDS, one Two and one-half Octave Set of FLUTE REEDS, one Two and one-half Octave Set of DULCIANA REEDS, one Two and one-half Octave Set of CLARIONET REEDS, one Two and one-half Octave Set of VIOLETTA REEDS, one Two and one-half Octave Set of CREMONA REEDS, one Two and one-half Octave Set of GAMBA REEDS, one Two and one-half Octave Set of BOURDON REEDS, one Two and one-half Set of DELICANTE REEDS, one One and one-half Octave Set of MANUAL SUB-BASS REEDS, the VOX HUMANA, and the MANUAL COUPLER. It also has the patent improved KNEE-SWELL, REED-BOARDS and BELLOWS, with Double BLOW-PEDALS.

The MANUAL SUB-BASS, of the same size as Pedal-Reeds, possesses more power than has ever before been obtained on Manuals by any Reed Instrument maker in the world. The new improved Independent Bellows, with Blow-Lever, has been introduced into this style of Organ.

The Case is of Solid Black Walnut, of new and elegant design, finished in Shellac and Oil SIXTEEN STOPS:

Viola, Flute, Melodia, Diapason, Principal, Dulciana, Delicante, Clarionet, Violetta, Cremona, Gamba, Bourdon, Vox Humana, Sub-Bass, Manual Coupler, Forte.

Grand Organ. Knee-Swell.

Two Manual Pedal Organ.

Length, 4 ft. 9 in.; Depth, 2 ft. 8 in.; Height, 5 ft. 10 in. With the Pedals in, ready for use, the Depth is 4 ft. 2 in.

Style 89; Price, $900.

This instrument is of great variety as well as power, and is suitable for LECTURE ROOMS, HALLS, CHURCHES, and CONSERVATORIES OF MUSIC. It contains Two Manuals and Sixteen Stops, one Five Octave Set of PRINCIPAL REEDS, one Five Octave Set of DIAPASON REEDS, one Two and one-half Octave Set of FLUTE REEDS, one Two and one-half Octave Set of DULCIANA REEDS, one Two and one-half Octave Set of CLARIONET REEDS, one Two and one-half Octave Set of VIOLETTA REEDS, one Two and one-half Octave Set of CREMONA REEDS, one Two and one-half Octave Set of GAMBA REEDS, one Two and one-half Octave Set of BOURDON REEDS, one Two and one-half Set of DELICANTE REEDS, the VOX HUMANA, and the MANUAL COUPLER.

It has, in addition, a full PEDAL-BASS of twenty-seven notes, which is very powerful. There is a Stop operated by the foot to couple the Pedals with the Manuals. Also, FOOT-SWELL, KNEE-SWELL, and DOUBLE BELLOWS. There are two Blow-Pedals which can be used, if desired, as in an ordinary Cottage Organ, and a Blow-Lever which can be worked by an assistant, if necessary, and also operated independently of the Pedals, which ensures a steady and constant supply of air. A seat for the Organist accompanies the instrument. The Case is of Solid Black Walnut, elegantly carved and richly finished, SIXTEEN STOPS:

Viola, Flute, Melodia, Diapason, Principal, Dulciana, Delicante, Clarionet, Violetta, Cremona, Gamba, Bourdon, Vox Humana, Pedal-Bass Manual Coupler, Forte.

Grand Organ, Knee-Swell, Pedal Coupler. Foot-Swell.

Boudoir Organ, Pipe Organ Top.

Length, 4 ft. 6 in.; Depth, 2 ft. 1 in.; Height, 7 ft. 7 in.

Style 91; Price, $470.

THIS Organ corresponds with Style 84 in Stops and Attachments, while the Case has a handsome

PIPE ORGAN TOP,

which gives a grandeur and elegance not otherwise attainable, and will be found very desirable for those who can afford it.

From I. GEORGE HEPWORTH, Dome-Organist, in Schwerin, Mecklenburg.

I have had often the opportunity to try the American Harmoniums or Cottage Organs of J. ESTEY & CO., in Brattleboro, and find that in consequence of their original construction, by which the tone comes near the character of labial voices, they are qualified to take the place of a Pipe Organ.

From ANTON RUBENSTEIN, Director of the Imperial Conservatory, and the Musical Society at Moscow.

It gives me great pleasure to give due praise to Messieurs J. ESTEY & CO. for their really splendid Organs. The tone of these instruments is full, noble and charming, and has the advantage of pleasing and captivating the ear. To these ARTISTIC qualities must be added that they are of SOLID WORKMANSHIP and of the most elegant finish, and I doubt not their having an extraordinary success in Russia.

Two Manual Organ, Pipe Organ Top.

Style 94; Price, $900.

Length, 4 ft. 7 in.; Depth, 2 ft. 8 in.; Height, 8 ft. 11 in.

Style 96; Price, $1050.

Length, 4 ft. 9 in.; Depth, 2 ft. 8 in.; Height, 9 ft. 3 in. With the Pedals in ready for use, Depth, 4 ft. 2 in.

THESE noble Organs correspond in every particular with Styles 87 and 89, and have, in addition, the PIPE ORGAN TOP. For elegant appearance and quality and power of tone, they have NO EQUAL. The Pipes are richly gilt, the ornaments are deftly carved, and the Case is of Solid Black Walnut.

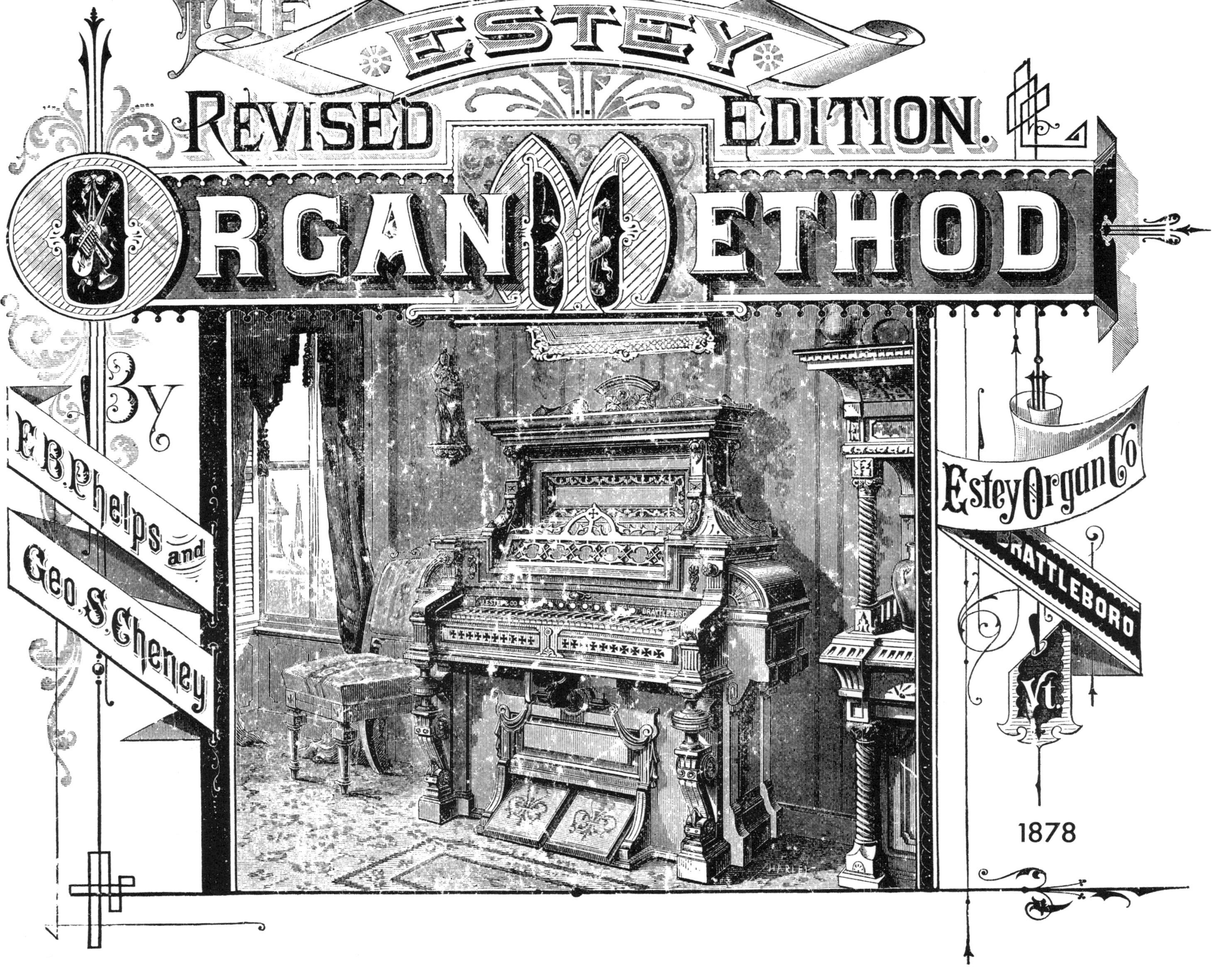
The Estey
Revised Edition.
Organ Method
By
F. B. Phelps and
Geo. S. Cheney
Estey Organ Co
Brattleboro
Vt.
1878

DESCRIPTION OF STOPS USED IN THE ESTEY ORGAN.

By referring to the following description of Stops, it will be noticed that they are designated as being eight feet pitch, four feet pitch, &c. For the information of those persons who are not familiar with the technical phrases used by Organists and Organ builders, a slight explanation is necessary.

A given tone requires a pipe of a certain length to produce it; hence it is customary to say that a certain tone is of four feet pitch or eight feet pitch, as the case may be, by which is meant that a pipe must be four or eight feet long to produce this tone. The same terms are used when referring to the Stops of an Organ. When a key is depressed with an eight feet Stop drawn, and a corresponding key depressed on the Piano forte, the two sounds will be in unison, provided the two instruments are tuned to the same standard pitch.

A four feet Stop produces sounds which are really an octave ***higher*** than the keys depressed.

A two feet Stop produces sounds *two* octaves higher than the keys depressed.

A sixteen feet Stop produces sounds which are an octave ***lower*** than the keys depressed.

A thirty-two feet Stop produces sounds which are ***two*** octaves lower than the keys depressed.

For instance: if the Middle C be the key depressed, the sounds produced by the different Stops, drawn separately, will be the following:

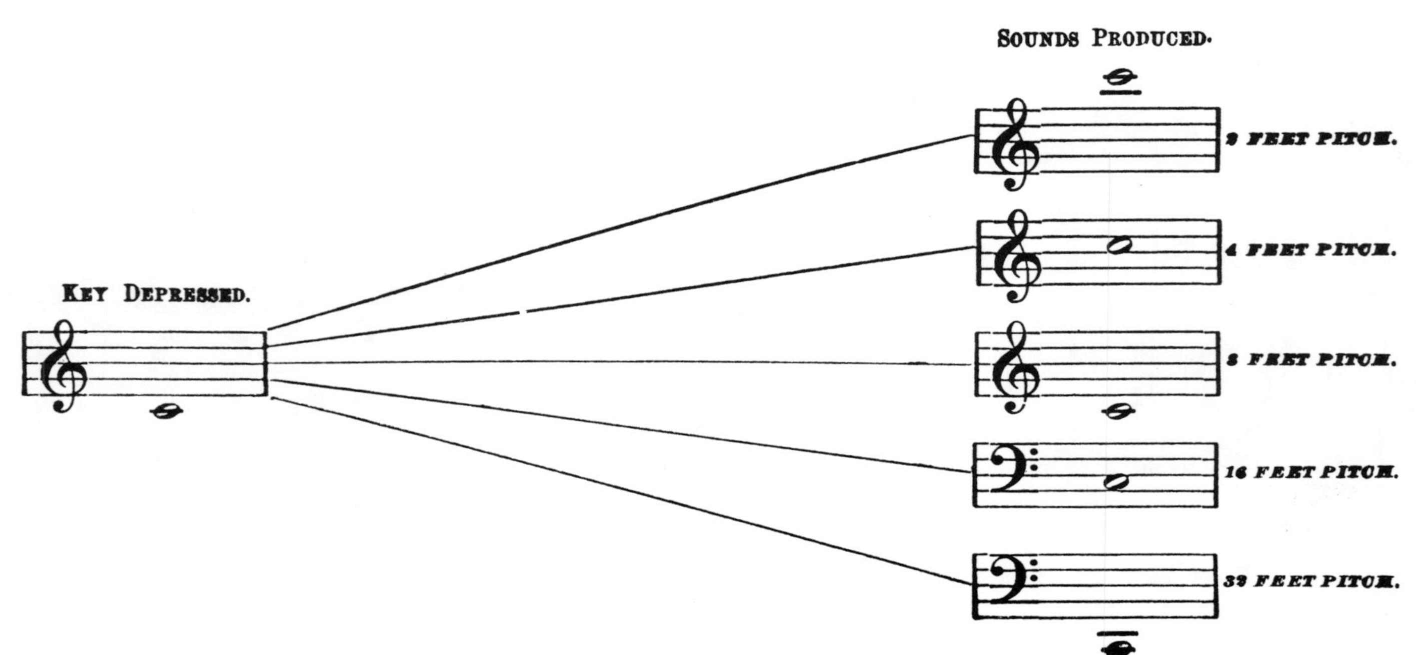

In speaking of a stop as a Treble Stop or a Bass Stop, we mean a set of reeds situated in the *upper*, or *treble* part of the organ, or in the *lower* or *bass* part. With this explanation, the following enumeration of stops will be readily understood.

Name.	Pitch.	Characteristics.
BARYTONE.	32 ft.	*Treble.* Full in tone, but slightly reedy; generally used in combination with other stops, but can be made very effective as a solo stop.
BASSET.	16 ft.	*Bass.* Rich, pervading tone.
BASSOON.	16 ft.	*Bass.* Very powerful.
BOURDON.	16 ft.	*Bass.* Full and round.
CLARIONET.	16 ft.	*Treble.* Resembles the Clarionet in quality.
CREMONA.	8 ft.	*Bass.* Soft and rich. Very fine for accompaniment.
CORNET ECHO.	2 ft.	*Bass.* Very soft echo effect.
CORNETTINO.	2 ft.	*Bass.* String tone, beautiful for solo or accompaniment.
DELICANTE.	8 ft.	*Treble* Brilliant, piquant. Chiefly for solo, but valuable in combination.
DIAPASON.	8 ft.	*Treble.* Foundation set of reeds by which all others are tuned. Round, full tone. Used more generally than any other stop, except Melodia.
DULCIANA.	8 ft.	*Treble.* Very similar in quality to Diapason, but softer
DOLCE.	8 ft.	*Bass.* Similar to Melodia, but softer in tone.
FLUTE.	4 ft.	*Treble.* Brilliant, but not reedy. Generally used in combination.
GAMBA.	8 ft.	*Bass.* Smooth and pipe-like in tone.
HARP AEOLIENNE.	2 ft.	*Bass.* Closely resembles the tones produced by the vibrations of the strings of an Æolian Harp. Very fine for accompaniment.
HAUTBOY.	8 ft.	*Treble.* Reedy in character, and very effective as a solo stop.
MELODIA.	8 ft.	*Bass.* Same quality as the Diapason, of which it is the continuation.
PEDAL BASS.	16 ft.	A pedal stop, deep, round and full.
PRINCIPAL.	4 ft.	*Treble.* Very bright and clear.
ROYAL JUBILANTE.	16 ft.	*Treble.* Very fine solo stop. Large, round tone.
SUB-BASS.	16 ft.	*Bass.* Very deep and powerful.
SUB-BOURDON.	32 ft.	*Treble.* Beautiful solo stop, Full, rich tone.
VIOLA.	4 ft.	*Bass.* Same character as Flute set, of which it is the continuation. Used much for accompaniment.
VIOLETTA.	4 ft.	*Bass.* Very soft, smooth tone; for accompaniment and echo effects.
VOX JUBILANTE.	8 ft.	*Treble.* Its name well indicates its character; very effective as a solo, and when used in combination with other stops, imparts a peculiar brilliancy to all.
WALD FLUTE.	2 ft.	*Treble.* Very clear and penetrating Used almost entirely with full organ.

MECHANICAL STOPS.

Name.	Characteristics.
FORTE.	Opens, swells, and augments the tone.
GRAND ORGAN (Knee)	Brings into use all the reeds in the organ without the necessity of drawing a stop.
HARMONIQUE.	So constructed that when any key is depressed, its octave above is also depressed, thereby causing both to sound simultaneously.
KNEE SWELL.	Gives same effect as Forte, only more gradual if desired.
MANUAL COUPLER.	Used in organs with two manuals, and so connecting them that, when a key on the lower manual is depressed, it also depresses the corresponding key of the upper manual.
PEDAL COUPLER.	Used in organs having Pedal Keys, and so connecting the manual, that when the Pedal is depressed its corresponding key in the manual is depressed and responds also.
VOX HUMANA.	A revolving fan, placed just back of the reeds, which, when set in motion imparts to the tone a thrilling wave-like effect. It changes the reed tone completely, giving it the sympathetic sweetness of the human voice.

A few Suggestions as to the Use of Stops.

There are no rigid rules for the combination and use of the various Stops. Every experienced organist will produce such effects as his taste, judgment, and familiarity with the instrument may teach him. The following hints are offered merely as suggestions to those unaccustomed to the use of the organ. These hints are limited to Estey Organs having two or three sets of reeds, as the larger instruments will naturally find their way into the hands of those whom it would be superfluous to instruct.

In general, then, for legato playing, the stops DIAPASON and MELODIA are the first to be drawn. These are the foundation stops to which the others are added as more power is wanted. The next in importance are the stops FLUTE and VIOLA. These add brilliancy as well as power. With these four stops drawn, the touch may be either staccato or legato, according to the character of the music to be played. Then comes the VOX JUBILANTE, whose bright, cheerful tones are heard above all the others. This stop is of great service where it is desired to make the treble prominent. The VIOLETTA adds little to the power of instrument, but is mainly used for an accompaniment to a Solo stop, or to produce an Echo, as hereafter explained.

If a still softer effect is desired, as is very often the case, draw the DOLCE and DULCIANA stops alone. The DULCIANA is very fine as a solo stop with the VIOLETTA for accompaniment. In general, however, the DIAPASON is more desirable. In either case, the organ is prepared for a soft, smooth solo with corresponding accompaniment. Play solo in smooth legato style above Middle C, and accompaniment in full chords in the lower octaves of the instrument. Now add the FLUTE, and more lively music can be played with good effect. For bright and joyful effects, use VOX JUBILANTE with VIOLETTA accompaniment, as before. In using VOX JUBILANTE and FLUTE together, it will be found that the VIOLA will give a better accompaniment than the VIOLETTA. As an example of the foregoing, take some simple galop, play the first part with all stops drawn except the VOX HUMANA and FORTES; for the trio, use the VOX JUBILANTE alone, with VIOLETTA for accompaniment, returning to the Full Organ for the close. The VOX HUMANA adds much to the variety of the instrument when judiciously used. It should be employed solely with the DIAPASON, used as a solo stop, but never with the Full Organ.

A fine Echo effect can be produced by drawing the DIAPASON and VIOLETTA, and play in full chords, with both hands above Middle C, with the swell open; then repeat the last four or more chords, with both hands below Middle C, and having the swell closed.

In instruments having the Grand Organ attachment, this effect can be better produced by drawing the VIOLETTA stop alone, and, after throwing open the GRAND ORGAN, play in the same manner as indicated above, closing the Grand Organ and transferring the hands to the lower octaves of the instrument for the Echo.

In accompanying a solo voice, the DIAPASON and MELODIA are generally of sufficient power to give the proper sustaining effect, unless the room is very large, and the voice more than usually powerful; in that case, the FLUTE and VIOLA should be added. For a quartette or chorus, the DIAPASON, MELODIA, FLUTE, and VIOLA will usually be needed. The accompanist, however, should always bear in mind that the tone of the instrument is but the *background* of the voices and not the leader. In accompanying a solo voice, the constant effort should be to move with the voice in all its variations of expression and time, and not attempt to direct by a rigid adherence to the time of the written music. For quartette and chorus singing a more strict regard for exact time is necessary; but the instrument should be entirely secondary in power to the voices, the accompanist remembering always that it is the voices that are to be heard, and that an accompaniment is not the work by which he ought to display either the power of his instrument, or his own proficiency as an organist. With these simple suggestions as a guide, learners will rapidly acquire such familiarity with the organ as will enable them to devise for themselves many other very desirable effects.

The Care of the Estey Organ.

The Estey Organ is not easily affected by heat or cold, dampness, or extremely dry weather; but it is obvious that no instrument should be needlessly exposed thereto. Frequently instruments are reported as "out of order" and, in some cases, returned to the factory when a day's open exposure in a warm, dry room would have made them all right.

One of the worst things is to place an organ away in the "front parlor," which is only opened when "company" comes, and then gives a damp, chilly feeling to every one entering it.

Especially, should care be taken when sweeping, that the organ is closed and, if convenient, covered with a cloth, as any small atom of dust when drawn into a reed may prevent it from speaking.

Should a reed remain silent when its key is depressed, it can be very easily removed and the dust blown out of it when it will be found to work all right.

Purchasers are particularly cautioned against allowing travelling workmen or "quacks" to *tune* their organs. Reed organs very rarely need tuning. In some instances, an individual reed, through some little defect in the material, or otherwise, may sound falsely, or become flattened in pitch, on account of corrosion, caused by dampness. In all such cases, the offending reed should be mailed to the factory with the reed an octave above or below it (to insure the accurate pitch), when a new one will be promptly supplied without charge, if the number of the organ is given. If, from any cause a reed gets lost, or cannot be sent, state the *set* from which it is taken (i. e., give the name of the stop-knob), and state the octave and letter, counting from the left hand. For instance, "Letter G (or G sharp) in second octave of Melodia."

Directions for Blowing.

Have a seat high enough to give a sufficient command of the instrument and pedals. Sit close enough to bring the KNEE-SWELL into full command.

Each foot should be set firmly on its Blow Pedal, the heel being even with the lower part of the Pedal. In blowing, the feet move alternately, one Pedal being made to descend while the other is ascending. The motion should be regular and uniform, and not by JERKS. Each Pedal should move its full extent up and down at each movement; it being much easier to supply the instrument with wind by so doing. In Single and Double Reed Organs, a slow, even motion will give the desired effect; in those having a Sub-Bass, Harmonic Attachment and Vox Jubilante, a strong, vigorous action of the pedals will be necessary to produce the FULL POWER and tone of the Organ.

The Knee-Swell is controlled by the right knee, so that the slightest pressure of the knee, without the least inconvenience in position, will increase the tone, while a spring causes it to return, when it is desirable to diminish the tone; thus the most perfect Crescendo and Diminuendo can be obtained, more beautiful than the Automatic Swell, or any other ever before used. The ease with which it is managed, and the PERFECT CONTROL which the performer has over it, make it the best Swell now in use.

HAPPY FARMER.

Con spirito.
Diapason & Flute.

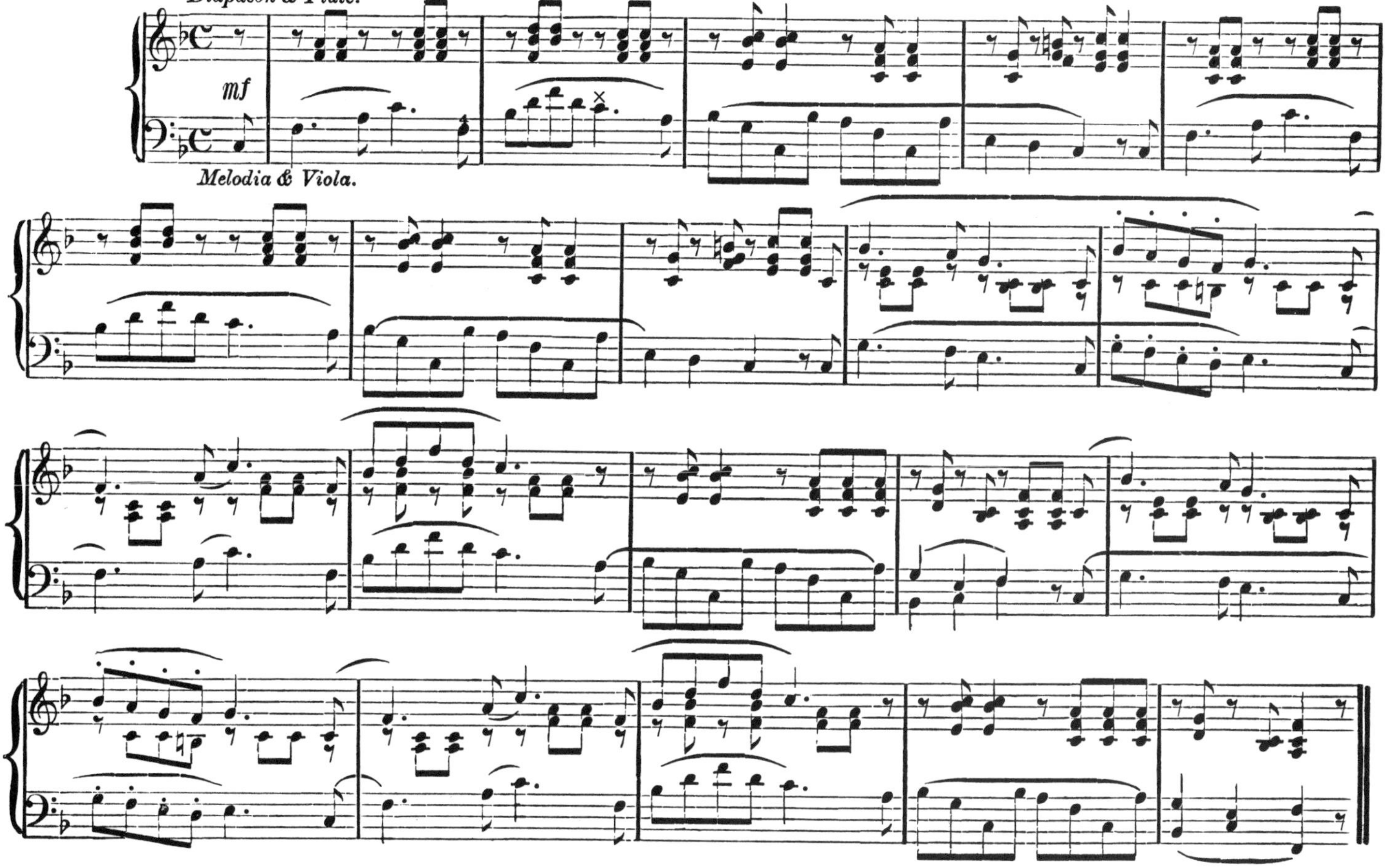

SCHUMANN.

mf

Melodia & Viola.

This 1878 Instruction and Music book is considered to be better than most that were prevalent in this period, because specific recommendations are made as to stops and their proper use.

LA DAME BLANCHE.

BOIELDIEU.

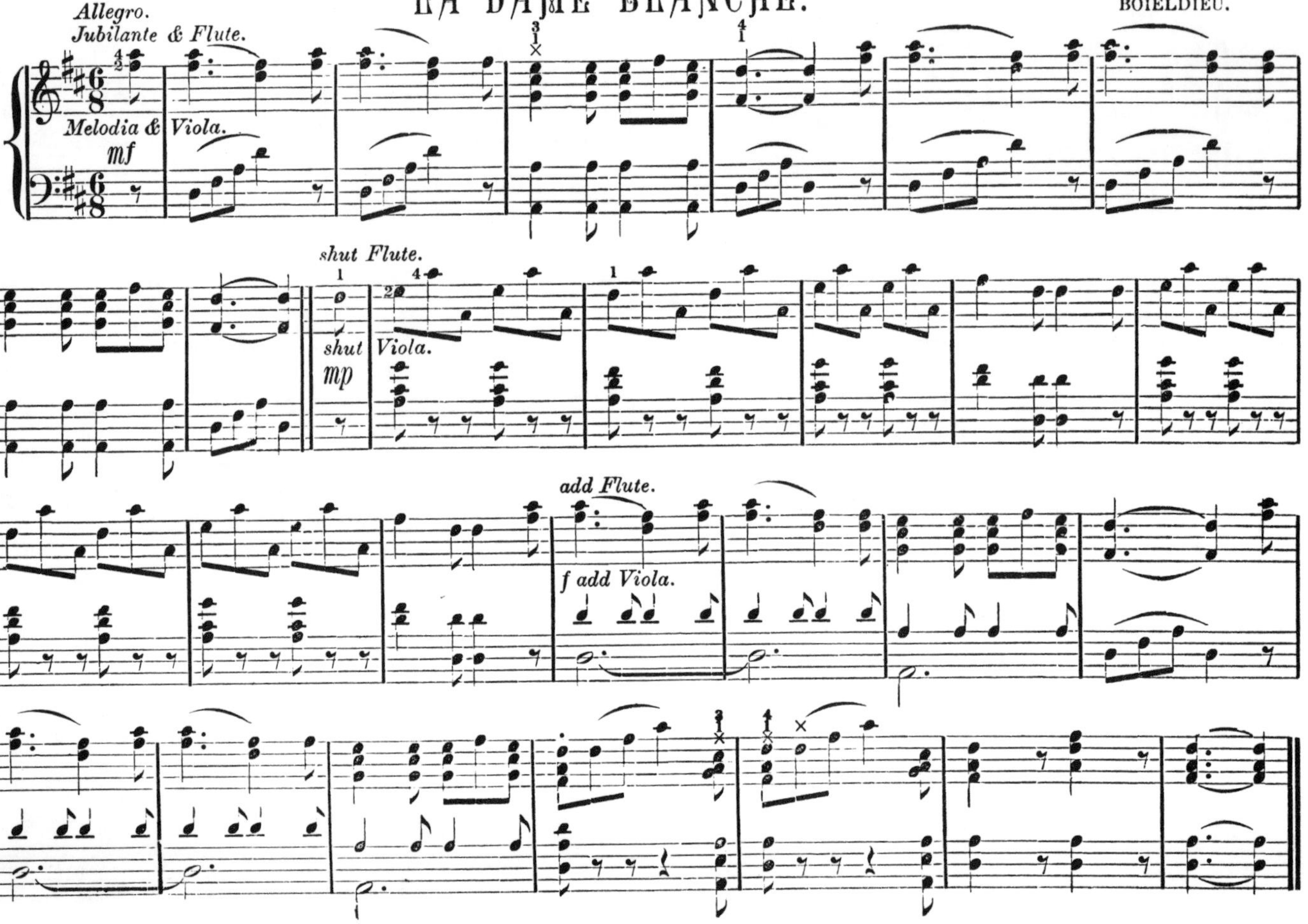
Allegro.
Jubilante & Flute.
Melodia & Viola.
mf
shut Flute.
shut
mp
Viola.
add Flute.
f add Viola.

NATIONAL AIRS.

AMERICAN.

STAR SPANGLED BANNER.

Maestoso.
p
Gr. Org.
Diapason.
Melodia.
f
ten.
ff
sfz

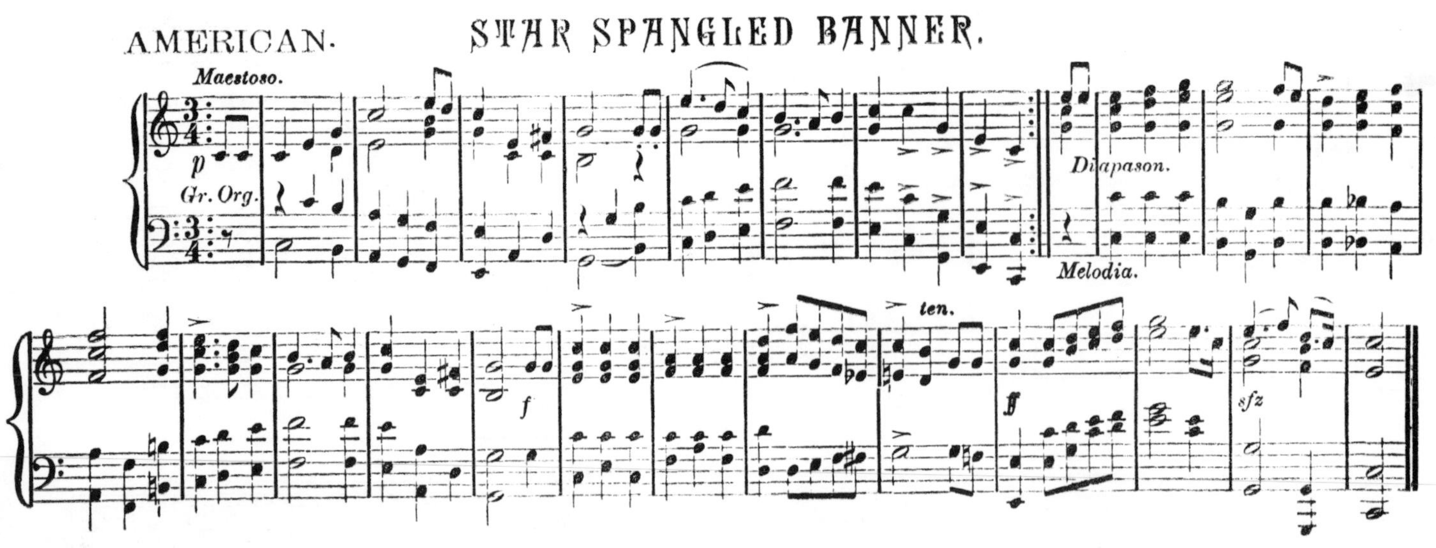

ENGLISH.
GOD SAVE THE QUEEN.
Andante.
Diapason.
Melodia. mf
f add Flute.
add Viola.
ROMANZA.
E. B. P.
Andante con espress.
Diapason & Jubilante.
mp
Melodia.
add Flute.
cres.
add Viola.
f
rit.
mp
shut Flute & Jubilante.
a tempo.
shut Viola.
poco animato.
add Jubilante.
shut Melodia &
add Violetta.
mf
(Play an octave lower than written.)
Tempo 1.
ten.
poco rit.
a tempo.
add Melodia
shut Jubilante.
sf
p
dim. e rall. pp

AIR FROM LUCIA DI LAMMERMOOR.

THE ROSE.

NEW SALON ORGAN.

HEIGHT, 6 ft. 7 in.; LENGTH, 4 ft. 7 in.; DEPTH, 2 ft. 1½ in. WEIGHT, boxed, 700 lbs.

SPECIFICATIONS

SUB-BASS, ...16 ft. tone, very deep and powerful.	GAMBA, ...(Bass), 8 ft. tone, mellow and soft.
CLARIONET, ...(Treble), 16 " strong and characteristic.	HAUTBOY, ... (Treble), 8 " strong and characteristic.
BOURDON, ...(Treble), 16 " strong, round and rich.	FLUTE, ...(Treble), 4 " brilliant and characteristic.
ROYAL JUBILANTE, (Treble), 16 " very fine solo stop.	VIOLETTA, ...(Bass), 4 " for accompaniment.
DIAPASON, ...(Treble), 8 " round and pipe-like.	CORNETTINO, ...(Bass), 2 " soft, string tone.
MELODIA, ...(Bass), 8 " round and pipe-like.	CORNET ECHO, ..(Bass), 2 " very soft—echo effect.
DULCIANA, ...(Treble), 8 " mellow and soft.	HARP ÆOLIENNE, (Bass), 2 " imitative, unique, charming.

ACCESSORIES.

HARMONIQUE, ...nearly doubles the power and brilliancy.	I. FORTE, ...swells right hand.
GRAND ORGAN (Pedal), draws full power of the Organ.	II. FORTE, ...swells left hand.
VOX HUMANA, ...tremulous effect.	KNEE SWELL (Right), ...opens swells from middle C up.
	KNEE SWELL (Left), ...opens swells from middle C down.

THE 100,000TH ORGAN.

STYLE 900.

We have the pleasure of presenting herewith Specifications and Description of our new SALON ORGAN. We have no hesitation in pronouncing this the finest Reed Organ yet manufactured. In its marvellous qualities of tone, it is simply unapproachable; and in its unique and tasteful Case, introducing the highest ideal of architectural design, it is without a rival.

Its characteristic voicing is the result of years of study and experiment, both in the construction of the Action and in the Voicing of the Reeds.

With this Organ, one skilled in its use has at his command a whole orchestra; and with reeds so quick to respond to the lightest and most delicate touch, the finest and most classical music can be produced with wonderful and delighting effect.

We invite especial attention to the HARP ÆOLIENNE. Subjected as it is to absolute control by the use of the Knee-Swell, the beautiful, dreamy and entrancing melody of the Æolian Harp is imitated with astonishing fidelity.

Special examination of the CLARIONET, HAUTBOY and FLUTE, is also invited. It is very customary among manufacturers to attach the names of different musical instruments to their stops, with no regard to their *characteristics of tone;* but in this Organ the performer can introduce either stop with the assurance that the special musical effect desired will be secured.

Estey was very proud of the fact that all their instruments were numbered consecutively, and not assigned arbitrarily so as to make production appear larger than it actually was. (see page 46).

The 100,000th organ is shown here as it was promoted in the 1881 catalog. This instrument is still in existence, in the private collection of Bob and Diane Yates of Glenshaw, Pennsylvania, and is shown in the pictorial section of this book on page 147 - But the actual case design differs.

1886.

ESTEY COTTAGE ORGAN.

Height, 5 ft. 6 in.; Length, 4 ft. 2 in.: Depth, 1 ft. 7½ in.; Weight (boxed), 325 lbs.

Style 5. One Two and one-half Octave Set of *Diapason Reeds*, and one Two and one-half Octave Set of *Melodia Reeds*, making one complete Five Octave Set of eight feet reeds, specially adapted for singing by one person, or for sweet *home* music. It also contains one Two and one-half Octave Set of *Flute Reeds*, and one Two and one-half Octave Set of *Viola Reeds*, making one complete Five Octave Set of four feet reeds, so-called, which adds much power and brilliancy to the organ. *Nine Stops:*

Diapason, Flute, Melodia, Viola, Dulciana, Dolce, Vox Humana, I. Forte II. Forte.

ESTEY CHAPEL ORGAN.

STYLE 140 (FRONT).

The Chapel Organ here illustrated is the lowest priced organ in our Chapel system. We have made the price exceptionally low in order to place the instrument within the reach of the humblest church or other organization. Two full Five Octave Sets of *Reeds* with *Vox Humana*, &c.

Nine Stops: Diapason, Vox Jubilantè, Melodia, Viola, Dulciana, Dolce, Vox Humana, I Forte, II. Forte.

Style 143. Same as Style 140. *Sub-Bass* and *Octave Coupler. Eleven Stops.*

Style 148. Two full Five Octave Sets and one Two and one-half Octave Set of Reeds, with *Sub-Bass*, and *Coupler.*

Twelve Stops: Diapason, Flute, Vox Jubilante, Melodia, Viola, Dulciana, Dolce, Sub-Bass, Harmonique, Vox Humana, I. Forte, II. Forte.

STYLE 140 (BACK).

Height, 4 ft. 3 in ; Length, 4 ft. 7 in.; Depth, 2 ft.; Weight (boxed), 320 lbs.

ESTEY CHURCH ORGAN.

Length, 4 ft. 11 in. (with Side Blower attached 6 ft. 1 in.); Depth, 2 ft. 9 in. (with Pedals attached, 4 ft.) Height, 5 ft.; Weight (boxed), 925 lbs.

Style 89. About five hundred of our Two Manual and Pedal Organs have been sold the world over, and have given the best of satisfaction. The specification below presents a most desirable organ in a solid substantial and reliable casing.

Five Octaves of *Flute Reeds*, Five Octaves of *Diapason Reeds*, Two and one-half Octaves of *Principal Reeds*, Two and one-half Octaves of *Dulciana Reeds*, Two and one-half Octaves of *Clarionet Reeds*, Two and one-half Octaves of *Violetta Reeds*, Two and one-half Octaves of *Cremona Reeds*, Two and one-half Octaves of *Gamba Reeds*, Two and one-half Octaves of *Bourdon Reeds*, Two and one-half Octaves of *Delicante Reeds*, the *Vox Humana, Manual Coupler and a full scale of Thirty Pedal Reeds*, with all desirable accessories.

ESTEY
PARLOR ORGAN.

The Parlor Organ shown on the opposite page, is really a most desirable instrument and can but commend itself most effectively to every one. By a comparison of its dimensions with others it will readily be seen, that this organ is in no sense diminutive, and we assure the reader that the material and workmanship is first-class. The Case is not as expensive as some, but it is certainly very attractive and salable.

Style 50. One Two and one-half Octave Set of *Diapason Reeds;* one Two and one-half Octave Set of *Vox Jubilante Reeds*; one Two and one-half Octave Set of *Melodia Reeds;* one Two and one-half Octave Set of *Viola Reeds;* with *Vox Humana, Grand Organ*, &c. *Nine Stops:*

Diapason, Vox Jubilante, Melodia, Viola, Dulciana, Dolce, Vox Humana, I. Forte, II. Forte.

Style 52. Same as style 50, with addition of *Treble Coupler and Bass Coupler. Eleven Stops.*

Style 53. Same as style 50, with the addition of *Harmonique Coupler*, and one octave of heavy *Manual Sub-Bass Reeds. Eleven Stops.*

Style 58. One Two and one-half Octave Set of *Diapason Reeds*, one Two and one-half Octave Set of *Flute Reeds*, one Two and one-half Octave Set of *Vox Jubilante Reeds*, one Two and one-half Octave Set of *Violetta Reeds*, one Two and one-half Octave Set of *Melodia Reeds*, one Two and one-half Octave Set of *Viola Reeds*, one Octave of *Manual Sub-Bass*, with *Harmonique Coupler, Vox Humana*, &c., &c. *Thirteen Stops:*

Diapason, Flute, Vox Jubilante, Melodia, Viola, Violetta, Dolce, Dulciana, Sub-Bass, Harmonique, Vox Humana, I. Forte, II. Forte.

ESTEY
PARLOR ORGAN.

Height, 6 ft. 2 in.; Length, 4 ft. 4½ in.; Depth, 1 ft. 11 in.; Weight (boxed), 380 lbs.

It is a source of satisfaction to the manufacturers of the Estey Organ that such a large number of the instruments made by them during the last forty years (more than 171 000) are *to-day* rendering most excellent service.

ESTEY
PHILHARMONIC CHAPEL ORGAN.

STYLE 430 (FRONT).
Height, 4 ft. 5 in.; Length, 4 ft. 2 in.; Depth, 1 ft. 11 in.; Weight (boxed), 380 lbs.

Every Estey Organ is made with thoroughness throughout, and with especial reference, to durability.

We invite special attention to the description of the Philharmonic Organs on the sixth and fourteenth pages of this Catalogue.

STYLE 430 (BACK.)

ESTEY
PHILHARMONIC CHAPEL ORGAN.

The Chapel Organ illustrated on the seventh or opposite page, marks a new departure in Organs for this purpose.

CASE. Modest in appearance but really elegant; solid Black Walnut, low top, open back, substantial.

ACTION. Specially adapted to develop the marvelous depth of tone not otherwise attainable. Simple and effective, not liable to get out of order.

BELLOWS. Constructed with exceptionally large capacity.

TONE. Both in quality and power far in advance of anything heretofore produced. Depth and richness combined with that sonorous quality so long looked for in Reed Organs.

THE ORGAN itself as a whole is destined to become very popular, and we confidently expect a very large demand.

Style 430. One Five Octave Set of *Philharmonic Diapason Reeds*, one Two and one-half Octave Set of *Vox Jubilante Reeds*, one Two and one-half Octave Set of *Viola Reeds*, one Octave of *Manual Sub-Bass Reeds*, with the *Vox Humana* and *Harmonique Coupler. Ten Stops.*

Style 432. One Five Octave Set of *Philharmonic Diapason Reeds*, one Two and one-half Octave Set of *Flute Reeds*, one Two and one-half Octave Set of *Viola Reeds*, one Two and one-half Octave Set of *Clarionet Reeds*, one Two and one-half Octave Set of *Bourdon Reeds*, one Octave of extremely powerful *Manual Sub-Bass Reeds*, with the *Harmonique Coupler, Vox Humana*, &c. *Thirteen Stops.*

For a medium grade of Organ for the home, we confidently recommend the Drawing Room Style, to the cut of which, on the adjoining page, we invite examination. Of generous proportions and graceful in its contour, it is a most desirable instrument. We furnish a large variety of Actions, with their respective complement of Reeds, in this case, but can only enumerate below a few of the most popular styles.

Style 15. One Two and one-half Octave Set of *Diapason Reeds*, one Two and one-half Octave Set of *Vox Jubilante Reeds*, one Two and one-half Octave Set of *Melodia Reeds*, one Two and one-half Octave Set of *Viola Reeds*, with *Vox Humana*. *Nine Stops:*

Diapason, Vox Jubilante, Melodia, Viola, Dolce, Dulciana, Vox Humana, I. Forte, II. Forte.

(Six Octave Organ this style, No. 30.)

Style 17. Same as Style 15, with *Harmonique*. *Ten Stops.*

(Six Octave Organ this style, No. 32.)

Style 18. Same as Style 15, with *Sub-Bass* and *Harmonique*. *Eleven Stops.*

(Six Octave Organ this style, No. 33.)

Style 28. One Two and one-half Octave Set of *Diapason Reeds*, one Two and one-half Octave Set of *Flute Reeds*, one Two and one-half Octave Set of *Vox Jubilante Reeds*, one Two and one-half Octave Set of *Violetta Reeds*, one Two and one-half Octave Set of *Melodia Reeds*, one Two and one-half Octave Set of *Viola Reeds*, one Octave of *Manual Sub-Bass*, with addition of *Harmonique Coupler* and *Vox Humana*. *Thirteen Stops:*

Diapason, Flute, Violetta, Vox Jubilante, Melodia, Viola, Dolce, Dulciana, Sub-Bass, Harmonique Coupler, Vox Humana, I. Forte, II. Forte.

(Six Octave Organ this style, No. 38.)

ESTEY
DRAWING ROOM ORGAN.

Height, 6 ft. 6 in.; Length, 4 ft. 4 in.; Depth, 1 ft. 11 in.; Weight (boxed), 390 lbs.

☞ Beauty, Utility and Durability are the desiderata in Reed Organs.

The Estey Organ is and has always been preeminent in each, and stands to-day without a successful rival.

ESTEY
CHANCEL ORGAN.

Style 330 (Front).
Height, 4 ft. 8 in.; Length, 4 ft. 7 in.; Depth, 2 ft. 3 in.; Weight (boxed), 425 lbs.

☞ This *Chancel Organ* is a special production of the *Mess. Estey & Company*, and is protected by U. S. patents Nos. 9,958 and 190,843 and all parties engaged in manufacturing or selling similar organs are doing so in violation of these patents, and consequently are liable under the law.

That the *Estey Organ Company* are pioneers in the line of Church, Chapel or Chancel Organs may be *inferred* from the fact that upwards of *nine thousand Organs of this kind alone* have been manufactured by them up to this time.

Style 330 (Back).

ESTEY
CHANCEL ORGAN.

For many years the chief reliance of the average country church was the Æolian, Melodeon or Seraphine—small in compass, limited in capacity and unsatisfactory in many ways.

These crude instruments were in time succeeded by the "Cottage Organ," different in construction, more convenient, and with enlarged capacity. Hundreds, perhaps thousands of these found their way into public places, and "served well their day and generation." With the advent of the Moody and Sankey movement, however, and the well-nigh universal use of a Reed Organ as an accompaniment to singing in public meetings, came the demand for an organ of larger scope, so designed that the player could face the audience and not be hidden by the instrument. Through various evolutions therefore has come the Chancel Organ—which for capacity, grace and richness of design and thorough mechanical construction has no equal.

Style 330. Two full Five Octave Sets of Reeds, with *Vox Humana, Sub-Bass, Octave Coupler,* &c. *Eleven Stops:*

Diapason, Vox Jubilante, Melodia, Viola, Dolce, Dulciana, Sub-Bass, Vox Humana, Harmonique Coupler, I. Forte, II. Forte.

Style 331. Three full Five Octave Sets of Reeds with *Vox Humana, Sub-Bass, Octave Coupler, Grand Organ, Knee Swell,* &c. *Thirteen Stops:*

Diapason, Flute, Vox Jubilante, Violetta, Melodia, Viola, Dolce, Dulciana, Sub-Bass, Vox Humana, Harmonique Coupler, I. Forte, II. Forte.

Style 334. Five Octaves of *Diapason-Melodia Reeds*, Five Octaves of *Flute-Viola Reeds*, Five Octaves of *Clarionet-Bourdon Reeds*, Two and one-half Octaves of *Wald Flute Reeds*, (brilliant), Two and one-half Octaves of *Cornettino Reeds* (beautiful effects), One Octave of extremely powerful *Manual Sub-Bass Reeds*, the *Harmonique Coupler*, with *Vox Humana*, &c. *Fifteen Stops.*

ESTEY
TRIUMPH ORGAN.

Height, 6 ft. 6 in.; Length, 4 ft. 4 in.; Depth, 1 ft. 11 in.; Weight (boxed,) 390 lbs.

We call attention to our warranty which accompanies every instrument. It covers a period of *five years* from the date of manufacture, but instances are by no means rare where, although the warranty had expired before, we have made good our terms. Five years is a long enough period, however, to *warrant* goods.

ESTEY
TRIUMPH ORGAN.

In no line of Cases has the Estey Organ Company achieved greater success than in the "High Backs," so called.

To the artistic eye the attempts of many manufacturers in this line, are simply torturing. There seems to be a design to get together an incongruous mass of moldings, turnings, bits of thin lumber, &c., &c., built one upon another, to secure height alone, with apparently never a thought of grace or beauty.

It would, we think, well repay the intending purchaser to look well to the construction of these articles, for in many instances they are "fearfully and wonderfully made."

On the contrary the "Estey" is, from the original design to the finished organ, in the hands of experienced artisans whose whole motive is to produce the Best.

Style 155. One Two and one-half Octave Set of *Diapason Reeds*, one Two and one-half Octave Set of *Vox Jubilante Reeds*, one Two and one-half Octave Set of *Melodia Reeds*, One Two and one-half Octave Set of *Viola Reeds*, with *Vox Humana*. *Nine Stops*.

Six Octave Organ this style, No. 170.

Style 157. Same as style 155, with *Harmonique*. *Ten Stops*.

Six Octave Organ this style, No. 172.

Style 158. Same as Style 155, with *Sub-Bass* and *Harmonique*. *Eleven Stops*.

Six Octave Organ this style, No. 173.

Style 168. One Two and one-half Octave Set of *Diapason Reeds*, one Two and one-half Octave Set of *Flute Reeds*, one Two and one-half Octave set of *Vox Jubilante Reeds*, one Two and one-half Octave Set of *Violetta Reeds*, one Two and one-half Octave Set of *Melodia Reeds*, one Two and one-half Octave Set of *Viola Reeds*, one Octave of *Manual Sub-Bass*, with addition of *Harmonique Coupler* and *Vox Humana*. *Thirteen Stops*.

Six Octave Organ this style, No. 178.

ESTEY
PHILHARMONIC ORGAN.

Height, 3 ft. 9 in.; Length, 5 ft.; Depth, 2 ft. 5 in.; Weight (boxed), 480 lbs.

But little space is left us in which to present the merits of our new Philharmonic Organ. For those who can enjoy the privilege of seeing and hearing it, no commendatory words are needed. We wish however, to say emphatically, that no other one-manual organ equals it in power and carrying capacity. It is a marvel and marks an epoch in the Reed Organ industry.

The Case, Bellows, Action, Reeds, Blowing Mechanism, Voicing, Tuning and Finishing all combine to produce an Organ far in advance of the best organ hitherto made.

Style 100. Two and one-half Octaves of *Basset* (16 ft.) *Reeds*, Two and one-half Octaves of *Choral* (8 ft.) *Reeds*, Two and one-half Octaves of *Diapason* (8 ft.) *Reeds*, Two and one-half Octaves of *Flute* (4 ft.) *Reeds*, Two and one-half Octaves of *Bourdon* (16 ft.) *Reeds*, Two and one-half Octaves of *Melodia* (8 ft.) *Reeds*, Two and one-half Octaves of *Viola* (4 ft.) *Reeds*, one Octave of very heavy *Manual Sub-Bass Reeds*, with *Coupler*, *Vox Humana*, &c., &c. *Fifteen Stops*.

The back is nicely finished, and a large space left comparatively free for the exit of the tone.

ESTEY
ACCLIMATIZED ORGAN.

Height, 3 ft. 3 in.; Length, 3 ft. 7 in.; Depth, 1 ft. 12 in.; Weight (boxed), 360 lbs.

Style 200. The *Acclimatized Organ* is especially designed and constructed to endure hard usage and the *severe climatic tests of tropical countries*.

Until the advent of the *Estey Acclimatized Organ* the introduction of a musical instrument into India and similar countries was extremely hazardous, and but very few were willing to take the risk.

Hundreds already sold are bearing constant testimony to their perfect trustworthiness.

No organ is constructed with more care even to the minutest detail than this.

The interior is furnished with one Two and one-half Octave set of *Diapason Reeds*, one Two and one-half Octave Set of *Flute Reeds*, one Two and one-half Octave Set of *Vox Jubilante Reeds*, one Two and one-half Octave Set of *Violetta Reeds*, one Two and one-half Octave Set of *Melodia Reeds*, one Two and one-half Octave Set of *Viola Reeds*, with *Manual Sub-Bass*, *Harmonique Coupler*, and *Vox Humana*. *Thirteen Stops*.

ESTEY
GOTHIC ORGAN.

Length, 4 ft. 5½ in.; Depth, 2 ft.; Height, 4 ft. 11½in.; Weight (boxed), 425 lbs.

Style 604. Two Sets of Reeds. *Nine Stops.*
(**Six Octave, this style, No. 654**)

Style 605. Adds Coupler to Style 604. *Ten Stops.*
(**Six Octave, this style, No. 655.**)

Style 605½ Add Sub-Bass to Style 605. *Eleven Stops.*
(**Six Octave, this Style, No, 655½**)

Style 610. Three Sets of Reeds, with *Coupler* and *Sub-Bass. Thirteen Stops.*
(**Six Octave, this style, No. 660.**)

Style 612. Four Sets of Reeds, with *Coupler* and *Sub-Bass. Sixteen Stops.*

ESTEY
HARMONIC ORGAN.

Length, 4 ft. 8 in (with Blow-Lever attached, 5 ft. 9½ in.); Depth, 2 ft. 7 in.; Height, 4 ft. 3 in; Weight (boxed), 555 lbs.

Style 85. The Harmonic Organ combines very large bellows capacity, with great variety of tone, and augmented power, in a rich, appropriate and very substantial case

This organ is furnished with blowing-lever so that a second person can operate the bellows if desired.

The capacious dimensions of the case admit of large space for Air Chambers and thus secure a resonance not attained in organs of smaller proportions. It contains one Five Octave Set of *Diapason Reeds*, one Five Octave Set of *Flute Reeds*, one Three Octave Set of *Clarionet Reeds*, one Three Octave Set of *Vox Jubilante Reeds*, one Two Octave Set of *Violetta Reeds*, one Three Octave Set of *Wald Flute Reeds*, of great brilliancy, a very powerful Set of *Manual Sub-Bass Reeds*, the *Vox Humana*, and the *Harmonique Coupler. Fourteen Stops.*

Diapason, Melodia, Flute, Viola, Violetta, Vox Jubilante, Clarionet, Wald Flute, Sub-Bass, Vox Humana, Harmonique Coupler, Melodia Forte, Wald Flute Forte, Flute Forte.

ESTEY
GRAND SALON ORGAN.

Style 900.
Height, 6 ft. 7 in.; Length, 4 ft. 7 in.; Depth, 2 ft. 1½ in.; Weight (boxed), 700 lbs.

Style 910.
Height, 6 ft. 7 in.; Length, 4 ft. 7 in.; Depth, 2 ft. 7 in.; Weight (boxed), 785 lbs.

Forty years of active connection with organ manufacturing have yielded a valuable experience.

This experience and knowledge of the possibilities in the art are available to the public through the medium of the Estey Organ.

ESTEY
GRAND SALON ORGAN.

Since the advent of the Peerless Salon Organ, it has so far as we know stood without a rival in its own special sphere. It is needless to speak of it in detail. Our reputation being a sufficient guarantee of its solid worth. Condensed description is appended.

Style 900.
18 STOPS.

SPECIFICATIONS:

SPEAKING STOPS.

Sub-Bass,		16 ft. tone,	very deep and powerful.
Clarionet,	(Treble).	16 "	strong and characteristic.
Bourdon,	(Treble),	16 "	full, round and rich.
Royal Jubilante,	(Treble),	16 "	very fine solo stop.
Diapason,	(Treble),	8 "	round and pipe-like.
Melodia,	(Bass),	8 "	round and pipe-like.
Dulciana,	(Treble),	8 "	mellow and soft.
Gamba,	(Bass),	8 "	mellow and soft.
Hautboy,	(Treble),	8 "	strong and characteristic.
Flute,	(Treble),	4 "	brilliant and characteristic.
Violetta,	(Bass),	4 "	for accompaniment.
Cornettino,	(Bass),	2 "	soft, string tone.
Cornet Echo,	(Bass),	2 "	very soft—echo effect.
Harp Æolian,	(Bass),	2 "	imitative, unique, charming

ACCESSORIES:

Accessory	Function
Grand Organ (Pedal),	draws full power of the Organ.
I. Forte,	draws swells right hand.
II. Forte,	draws swells left hand.
Harmonique,	nearly doubles the power and brilliancy.
Knee Swell (Right),	opens swells from middle C up.
Knee Swell (Left),	opens swells from middle C down.
Vox Humana.	

Style 910. Of same general design as Style 900, but
23 STOPS. with enlarged case.

ADDITIONAL SPECIFICATIONS.

Barytone	(Treble),	32 ft. tone,	extraordinary power.
Sub-Bourdon,	(Treble),	32 "	rich solo stop.
Basset,	(Bass),	16 "	rich and pervading.
Bassoon,	(Bass),	16 "	very powerful.
Wald Flute	(Treble),	2 "	very brilliant.

ESTEY
CATHEDRAL ORGAN.

The Cathedral Organ, specifications of which may be found below, represents the acme of Reed Church Organ Building.

Power, Expression and Delicacy of Touch are distinguishing features in this Organ.

Style 912.
18 STOPS.

SPECIFICATIONS:

GREAT MANUAL (5 OCTAVES, C SCALE).

Bourdon, ... 16 ft. Bass.
Melodia, ... 8 ft. Bass.
Violetta, ... 4 ft. Bass.
Royal Jubilante, ... 16 ft. Treble.
Clarionette, ... 16 ft. Treble.
Diapason, ... 8 ft. Treble.
Flute, ... 4 ft. Treble.
Vox Jubilante, ... 8 ft. Treble.

SWELL MANUAL (5 OCTAVES).

Gamba, ... 8 ft. Bass.
Cornet Echo, ... 2 ft. Bass.
Cornettino, ... 2 ft. Bass.
Harp Æolian, ... 2 ft. Bass.
Dulciana, ... 8 ft. Treble.
Bourdon, ... 16 ft. Treble.
Wald Flute, ... 2 ft. Treble.

PEDAL CLAVIER (2½ OCTAVES).

Double Diapason Pedals, ... 16 feet.

MECHANICAL.

Vox Humana. Knee Swell. Manual Coupler.

PEDAL MOVEMENTS.

Grand Organ. Pedal Coupler. Pedal Forte.

ESTEY CATHEDRAL ORGAN.
(WITH PIPE TOP.)

Length, 5 ft. (with Blower, 6 ft. 2 in.); Depth, 2 ft. 9 in. (with Pedals, 4 ft. 2 in.); Height, 9 ft.; Weight (boxed), 1070 lbs.

Style 915. Full description and specifications of this Organ may be found on pages 20 and 21.

"Code names" make an interesting study today. Before the telephone became universal, telegraphy was used to transact much business. Since telegrams were charged for by the word, merchandisers would establish single "code" words which could convey an entire message and thus reduce communication costs.

ESTEY
CATHEDRAL ORGAN.

Length, 5 ft. (with Blower, 6 ft. 2 in.); Depth, 2 ft 9 in. (with Pedals, 4 ft. 2 in.); Height, 5 ft.; Weight (boxed), 805 lbs.

The above Organ can be had with a magnificent Pipe Top if desired.

Attention is invited to the illustration of the same (Style 915) on the twenty-third page.

PRICE CURRENT.

STYLE.	CODE.	PRICE.
5	Gaudiness,	$ 160
15	Gentiles,	205
17	Gestures,	225
18	Geyser,	245
28	Giantess,	275
30	Gifted,	235
32	Gigantic,	255
33	Gimlet,	275
38	Giraffe,	315
50	Globular,	182
52	Glorified	202
53	Gracefully,	222
58	Gloomy,	252
85	Fallible,	475
89	Falsetto,	1,000
100	Gondola,	500
140	Glaciers,	190
143	Gladiator,	230
148	Gladsome,	250
155	Glycerine,	230
157	Glucose,	250
158	Goddess,	270
168	Goodness,	300
170	Gooseberry,	260
172	Gooseneck,	280
173	Goosequill,	300
178	Gordian,	340
200	Feature,	310
330	Flowery,	275
331	Fluency,	315
334	Fortress,	370
430	Godsend,	245
432	Godship,	290
604	Forefather,	250
605	Frenzy,	270
605½	Frescoed,	290
610	Forefront,	320
612	Freshet,	360
654	Foregoing,	280
655	Fretful,	300
655½	Fretwork.	320
660	Forehanded,	360
900	Footsteps,	650
910	Friar,	800
912	Glandular,	1,350
915	Glaringly,	1,500

Copyright, 1886, by ESTEY ORGAN CO., Brattleboro, Vt.

The Estey Organ Works.

WE HAVE seriously considered the advisability of omitting from this Catalogue all allusion to our Manufactory, and of confining ourselves simply to a description of the products. Inasmuch, however, as this Catalogue will reach the hands of new inquirers, who will be as much interested as their predecessors in the establishment, whence emanates the "Leading Organ of the World," we give below condensed sketch of this, the *most extensive* Reed Organ Works on the Globe.

They are beautifully situated on a plateau overlooking the village of Brattleboro. After adverse experiences both by fire and flood, Messrs. ESTEY & Co. purchased a large tract of land, and proceeded to erect thereon strong, substantial factories, from thirty to forty feet in width, and one hundred feet long, with accomodations for more than six hundred employees.

Besides the eight main factories, there are seven others of nearly equal magnitude, besides the immense Brick Dry Houses, constructed on a new plan, the invention of MR. FULLER, of the Company, and accommodating more than 100,000 feet of lumber.

The immense PACKING AND STORE HOUSE contains 15,000 feet of flooring! With the very large variety of organs made necessary by so wide a range of taste among customers all over the world, it is necessary to carry a very large stock of organs to serve customers promptly.

The FIRE PROOF ENGINE AND BOILER HOUSE, (36x80 feet) contains seven large boilers of three hundred and fifty horse power, furnishing steam for the Corliss Engine, and for heating.

Watchmen constantly on duty day and night visit every floor of each building once an hour. Their visits and the time of each visit are recorded on a dial in the office.

From the OFFICE goes out a net work of Telephones, Speaking Tubes and Electric Bells, bringing into instantaneous communication with headquarters all parts of the establishment.

A very interesting little sketch of a trip through this establishment will be mailed gratis, on application.

A few Important Points!

- The "Estey" is the **STANDARD** by which salesmen seek to sell their (inferior) organs. "Just as good as the Estey" is heard on every hand, but unconsciously every use of that argument is a compliment to and a recognition of the proud position occupied *alone* by the Estey Organ.
- The great reputation enjoyed by the Estey Organ is very largely due to their **"TONE."** This has always been their distinguishing feature, but wonderful strides have been made during the last ten years.
- **PERFECTION OF MATERIAL** is absolutely necessary to the durability and satisfactory working of an organ. In the various commodities that go to make up an organ, the Estey Company always use only the best. People of whom we buy say "We don't see why this, and this, won't answer your purpose. None of your competitors would think of rejecting it, and they will certainly take it all." So we select the best for our own use and let them dispose of the balance to others.
- **PERFECTION IN DETAILS** is a prominent feature of the Estey Organ. Constant and unremitting care is exercised by skilled inspectors, all experts in their different branches.
- Much might be said of the *Cases*, elegant, tasteful, substantial, well built, unique; of the *Reeds*, made of silver-brass of secret mixture found only in the Estey Organ; of the *Bellows*, with best paneled stock, Bessemer steel springs, the best coated rubber cloth; of the *Stop Action*, perfect in its working, with its metallic parts all coated with copper to prevent rust and soiling; of the superior quality of felts, leather and carpets; in short, pages might be filled with items, interesting and truthful, connected with the manufacture of Estey Organs, but proofs of this kind are not needed in order to establish the fact that the Estey Organ leads the World!

We call especial attention to the custom quite prevalent now-a-days among some Organ houses, of taking an arbitrary number (say 50,000) as a basis, and then rapidly increasing their numbers, as their neighbors outstrip them in actual manufacture, so that these signal numbers like the above are often reached **ON PAPER** by such jumps, before the slower, but equally certain steps, of **LEGITIMATE** numbering.

The 1886 catalog which appears here on pages 40 through 46, still features designs which are of substantial and heavy character. In subsequent catalogs note that the newer case designs are "lighter" and much less "massive" in their details. Note that the description above talks about eight main factories, perhaps suggesting that the company took over the two referred to earlier, or perhaps constructed them in this period. The pictures in this book all show eight, lined up like tenpins!

ORGANS.

PIERCY & CO., Sole Agents,

TROY AND ALBANY.

Ketterlinus. Phila. & New York

New Portable Organ.

(IN CHERRY—ACCLIMATIZED.)

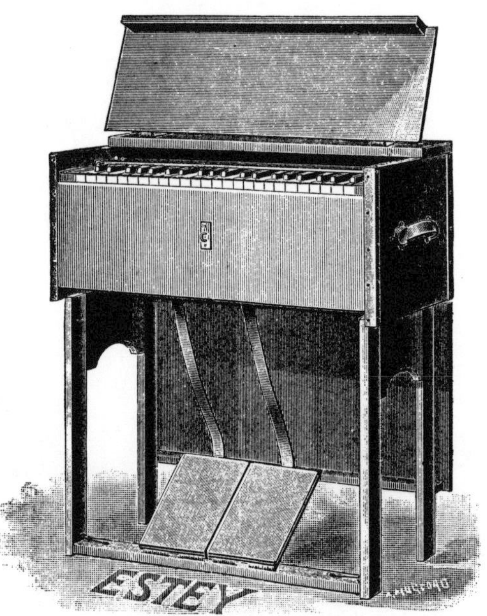

(OPEN)

(CLOSED)

STYLE 1. Open Register.

One Set of Reeds. 3½ Octaves. With Knee Swell.

DIMENSIONS.

OPEN.		CLOSED.	
Height . . .	2 feet 9 inches.	Height . . .	1 foot 1 inch.
Width . . .	2 feet 4 inches.	Width . . .	2 feet 4 inches.
Depth . . .	1 foot 4 inches.	Depth . . .	1 foot 6 inches.

Weight . . . . 65 pounds.

NEW PARLOR MODEL.

Height, 5 feet 7 inches; Length, 4 feet 4 inches; Depth, 1 foot 7¾ inches; Weight (boxed), 315 pounds.

STYLE 1520. 9 Stops.

2 COMPLETE SETS OF REEDS.

BASS.		TREBLE.	
Melodia	8	Diapason	8
Dolce	8	*Dulciana*	8
Viola	4	Vox Jubilante (*Solo*)	8

Forte I. Forte II.

Vox Humana.

Estey

NEW DRAWING ROOM ORGAN.

STYLE 1730. 9 Stops.

2 COMPLETE SETS OF REEDS.

BASS.		TREBLE.	
Melodia	8	Diapason	8
Dolce	8	*Dulciana*	8
Viola	4	Vox Jubilante (*Solo*)	8

Forte I. Forte II.

Vox Humana.

(Six-Octave Organ, this Style, No. 1770.)

STYLE 1733. 11 Stops.

2 1-5 SETS OF REEDS, WITH COUPLER.

BASS.		TREBLE.	
Melodia	8	Diapason	8
Dolce	8	*Dulciana*	8
Viola	4	Vox Jubilante (*Solo*)	8
Sub-Bass	16	Octave Coupler.	

Forte I. Forte II.

Vox Humana.

(Six-Octave Organ, this Style, No. 1773.)

STYLE 1732. 11 Stops.

2 SETS OF REEDS, WITH COUPLERS.

BASS.		TREBLE.	
Melodia	8	Diapason	8
Dolce	8	*Dulciana*	8
Viola	4	Vox Jubilante (*Solo*)	8
Bass Coupler.		Treble Coupler.	

Forte I. Forte II.

Vox Humana.

(Six-Octave Organ, this Style, No. 1772.)

STYLE 1738. 13 Stops.

3 1-5 SETS OF REEDS, WITH COUPLER.

BASS.		TREBLE.	
Melodia	8	Diapason	8
Dolce	8	*Dulciana*	8
Violetta	4	Vox Jubilante (*Solo*)	8
Viola	4	Flute	4
Sub-Bass	16	Octave Coupler.	

Forte I. Forte II.

Vox Humana.

(Six-Octave Organ, this Style, No. 1778.)

STYLE 1749. 15 Stops.

3 1-2 AND 1-5 SETS OF REEDS, WITH COUPLER.

BASS.		TREBLE.	
Melodia	8	Diapason	8
Dolce	8	*Dulciana*	8
Viola	4	Flute	4
Cornettino	2	Vox Jubilante (*Solo*)	8
Cornet Echo	2		

Harp Eolienne (*Bass*) . . . 2

Sub-Bass	16	Octave Coupler.	

Forte I. Forte II.

Vox Humana.

(Not furnished in Six Octaves.)

GRAND ORGAN AND KNEE SWELL TO ALL STYLES.

NEW DRAWING ROOM ORGAN.

DIMENSIONS.

Height, 6 feet 9¾ inches; Length, 4 feet 6½ inches; Depth, 1 foot 10¾ inches. Weight (boxed), 420 pounds.

VERY HANDSOME PIPE TOP FURNISHED WHEN ORDERED.

Estey

NEW TRIUMPH ORGAN.

STYLE 1830. **9 Stops.**

2 COMPLETE SETS OF REEDS.

BASS.		TREBLE.	
Melodia	8	Diapason	8
Dolce	8	*Dulciana*	8
Viola	4	Vox Jubilante (*Solo*)	8

Forte I. Forte II.

Vox Humana.

(Six-Octave Organ, this Style, No. 1870.)

STYLE 1832. **11 Stops.**

2 SETS OF REEDS, WITH COUPLERS.

BASS.		TREBLE.	
Melodia	8	Diapason	8
Dolce	8	*Dulciana*	8
Viola	4	Vox Jubilante (*Solo*)	8
Bass Coupler.		Treble Coupler.	

Forte I. Forte II.

Vox Humana.

(Six-Octave Organ, this Style, No. 1872.)

STYLE 1833. **11 Stops.**

2 1-5 SETS OF REEDS, WITH COUPLER.

BASS.		TREBLE.	
Melodia	8	Diapason	8
Dolce	8	*Dulciana*	8
Viola	4	Vox Jubilante (*Solo*)	8
Sub-Bass	16	Octave Coupler.	

Forte I. Forte II.

Vox Humana.

(Six-Octave Organ, this Style, No. 1873.)

STYLE 1838. **13 Stops.**

3 1-5 SETS OF REEDS, WITH COUPLER.

BASS.		TREBLE.	
Melodia	8	Diapason	8
Dolce	8	*Dulciana*	8
Violetta	4	Vox Jubilante (*Solo*)	8
Viola	4	Flute	4
Sub-Bass	16	Octave Coupler.	

Forte I. Forte II.

Vox Humana.

(Six-Octave Organ, this Style, No. 1878.)

STYLE 1849. **15 Stops.**

3 1-2 AND 1-5 SETS OF REEDS, WITH COUPLER.

BASS.		TREBLE.	
Melodia	8	Diapason	8
Dolce	8	*Dulciana*	8
Viola	4	Flute	4
Cornettino	2	Vox Jubilante (*Solo*)	8
Cornet Echo	2		

Harp Eolienne (*Bass*) . . . 2

Sub-Bass	16	Octave Coupler.	

Forte I. Forte II.

Vox Humana.

(Not Furnished in Six Octaves.)

NEW TRIUMPH ORGAN.

(PIPE TOP.)

DIMENSIONS.

Height, 7 feet; Length, 4 feet 6 inches; Depth, 1 foot 10½ inches.

Weight (boxed), 450 pounds.

Can furnish this exceedingly handsome Pipe Top with all Triumph Styles.

NEW CHANCEL ORGAN.

STYLE 557. 11 Stops.

2 SETS OF REEDS, WITH COUPLERS.

BASS.		TREBLE.	
Melodia	8	Diapason	8
Dolce	8	*Dulciana*	8
Viola	4	Vox Jubilante (*Solo*)	8
Bass Coupler.		Treble Coupler.	

Forte I. Forte II.

Vox Humana.

STYLE 558. 11 Stops.

2 1-5 SETS OF REEDS, WITH COUPLER.

BASS.		TREBLE.	
Melodia	8	Diapason	8
Dolce	8	*Dulciana*	8
Viola	4	Vox Jubilante (*Solo*)	8
Sub-Bass	16	Octave Coupler.	

Forte I. Forte II.

Vox Humana.

STYLE 563. 12 Stops.

2 1-2 AND 1-5 SETS OF REEDS, WITH COUPLER.

BASS.		TREBLE.	
Melodia	8	Diapason	8
Dolce	8	*Dulciana*	8

Vox Jubilante (*Solo*) . . . 8

Viola	4	Flute	4
Sub-Bass	16	Octave Coupler.	

Forte I. Forte II.

Vox Humana.

Estey

NEW CHANCEL ORGAN.

DIMENSIONS.

Height, ... 4 feet 3 inches.

Width, ... 4 feet 5 inches.

Depth, ... 1 foot 11 inches.

Weight (boxed), 360 pounds.

DIMENSIONS.

Height, ... 4 feet 3 inches.

Width, ... 4 feet 5 inches.

Depth, ... 1 foot 11 inches.

Weight (boxed), 360 pounds.

Compare this model with the Chancel organ on page 42. Not only is it lighter in appearance, but the weight is given as 65 pounds less, when boxed. It is not clear why the catalog designer saw fit to put all the dimensions and weight down twice on the same page, unless he was trying to fill space as present-day book publishers do with picture captions!

New Students' Pedal Organ.

One Manual Organ.

STYLE 323.

Three Sets of Reeds, with Full Pedal Scale (30 Notes)—Thirteen Stops.

BASS.		TREBLE.	
Melodia	8	Diapason	8
Violetta (*Soft*)	4	Vox Jubilante (*Solo*)	8
Viola	4	Flute	4

PEDAL CLAVIER.

Double Diapason	16	Double Dulciana (*Soft*)	16

MECHANICAL.

Octave Coupler. Knee Swell.
Vox Humana. Hand Side Blow-Lever.

PEDAL MOVEMENTS.

Grand Organ. Pedal Swell.
Pedal Coupler. Manual Swell.

Two Manual Organ.

STYLE 340.

SWELL MANUAL.

BASS.		TREBLE.	
Dolce	8	Dulciana	8
Viola	4	Flute	4

GREAT MANUAL.

Bourdon	16	Clarionet	16
Melodia	8	Diapason	8

PEDAL CLAVIER (2 1-2 OCTAVES.)

Double Diapason	16	Double Dulciana (*Soft*)	16

MECHANICAL.

Octave Coupler. Knee Swell.
Vox Humana. Manual Coupler.
Hand Side Blow-Lever.

PEDAL MOVEMENTS.

Grand Organ. Pedal Swell.
Pedal Coupler. Manual Swell.

With Each of the Above Styles an Organ Bench is Included.

New Students' Pedal Organ.

DIMENSIONS.

Length, 4 feet 8½ inches (with Blow-Lever, 5 feet 8¼ inches);
Depth, 2 feet 7½ inches (with Pedals, 4 feet 2 inches);
Height, 4 feet 4½ inches;

Weight (boxed), One Manual, 595 pounds; Two Manuals, 640 pounds.

PIPE TOP FURNISHED WHEN ORDERED.

Evidently Estey saw a chance to get some of the educational market, as this is one of the earliest references to a "Students" Organ. The idea must have been a good one, for various organs with the term "student" in their names appear from time to time hereafter throughout the years.

Estey New Philharmonic Organ.

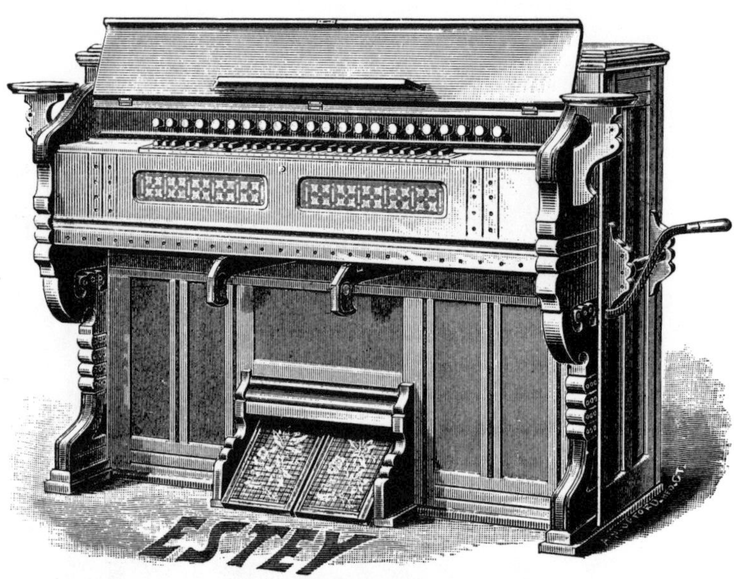

Height, 3 feet 9 inches; Length, 5 feet 5 inches (with Blow-Lever, 6 feet 3 inches); Depth, 2 feet 4 inches.
Weight (boxed), 545 pounds.

The New Philharmonic Organ is specially designed for large halls, concert rooms, conservatories of music and churches.

The vast improvements made in the construction of Organs have reached their highest realization, so far as power and breadth of tone are concerned, in this Organ.

The case is massive and elegant, and is constructed in such a manner as to afford great resonance.

The back is nicely finished, and a large space left comparatively free for the exit of the tone.

While great power will result from the use of the Organ in any position, the most satisfactory results will be obtained when the organist faces the audience.

As will be seen, the names of the stops are not materially altered from the regular styles, but in each instance largely augmented tone is produced.

STYLE 110.

BASS.		TREBLE.	
Bourdon	16	Basset	16
Melodia	8	Diapason	8
Dolce	8	*Dulciana*	8
Viola	4	Flute	4
Viola-Dolce	4	*Flute d'Amour*	4
Sub-Bass	16	Choral	8

STYLE 112.

BASS.		TREBLE.	
Bourdon	16	Basset	16
Melodia	8	Diapason	8
Dolce	8	*Dulciana*	8
Viola	4	Flute	4
Viola-Dolce	4	*Flute d'Amour*	4
Cornettino	2	Choral	8
Cornet Echo	2	Regal	8
Harp Eolienne	2	*Vox Jubilante*	8
Sub-Bass	16		

MECHANICAL.—(Alike in both.)

Bass Coupler. Treble Coupler. Vox Humana. Hand Side Blower.
Forte I. Forte II. Grand Organ (Knee). Grand Swell (Knee).

BEAUTIFUL PIPE TOP FURNISHED WHEN DESIRED.

New Philharmonic Organ.

(PIPE TOP.)

DIMENSIONS.

Height, 8 feet 2 inches; Length, 5 feet 5½ inches; Depth, 2 feet 4 inches.
Weight (boxed), 820 pounds.

New Drawing Room Organ.

(PIPE TOP.)

DIMENSIONS.

Height, 6 feet 10½ inches; Length, 4 feet 6 inches; Depth, 1 foot 11 inches.
Weight (boxed), 425 pounds.

This beautiful Pipe Top furnished with any Drawing Room Styles.

Cathedral Organ.

(WITH PIPE TOP.)

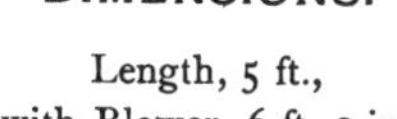

DIMENSIONS.

Length, 5 ft.,
(with Blower, 6 ft. 2 in.)

Depth, 2 ft. 9 in.
(with Pedals, 4 ft. 2 in.)

Height, 9 ft.

Weight (boxed), 1070 lbs.

The massive features of this case design, shown in a smaller illustration in the 1886 catalog, contrast with the slightly more crisp lines of others in 1890 suggesting that perhaps some of these were left ''in stock'', and were poor movers. It also appears here on page 74, from the 1895 catalog. In the latter it is Style 912; in the former, 915.

PRICE CURRENT.

STYLE.	CODE.	PRICE.
1	Fabian	$125
85	Fallible	475
89	Falsetto	1,000
110	Grasping	600
112	Grassplot	700
185	Gramercy	440
200	Feature	310
322	Gradual	480
340	Grammar	600
555	Grisette	190
557	Gristmill	210
558	Groaning	230
563	Grossness	250
568	Groundless	260
605	Frenzy	270
605½	Frescoed	290
610	Forefront	320
612	Freshet	360
655	Fretful	300
655½	Fretwork	320
660	Forehanded	360
808	Groveling	245
818	Grumblers	290
828	Guerdon	335
900	Footsteps	650
910	Frier	800
912	Glandular	1,350
1520	Hardihood	160
1630	Harvest	182
1632	Hatchets	202
1638	Hatbrush	252
1670	Hatband	212
1672	Hatbox	232
1678	Hatred	292

STYLE.	CODE.	PRICE.
1730	Haymakers	$205
1732	Hazardous	225
1733	Headland	245
1738	Healthful	275
1749	Heartsick	310
1770	Heedless	235
1772	Heiress	255
1773	Heirlooms	275
1778	Helmets	315
1830	Henchmen	230
1832	Herbage	250
1833	Herbalist	270
1838	Herculean	300
1849	Hermit	335
1870	Heroism	260
1872	Herrings	280
1873	Hesitating	300
1878	Hickory	340

PIPE TOP ORGANS.

STYLE.	CODE.	PRICE.
85	With Pipe Top	$625
89	" " "	1,200
110	" " "	760
112	" " "	860
185	" " "	590
340	" " "	750
610	" " "	440
910	" " "	925
912	" " "	1,550
1738	" " "	325
1838	" " "	350

TESTIMONIALS.

From A. FREYER, Organist of the Protestant Ch. and Professor at the Conservatory in Warsaw.

Among the many Harmoniums with which I have become acquainted during the many years I have been a teacher on the Harmonium and Organ (literally a life-time) I have *not seen any to equal* the ESTEY COTTAGE ORGAN.

The character of the tone is so beautiful and sympathetic that it does not, like other instruments, affect and weaken the nervous system. The supply of wind (air) is always sufficient; the intonation perfect, and the touch easy and certainly *superior to any* I know. Added to this is their solid and beautiful workmanship, and an elegant and attractive exterior so that NOTHING *is lacking*.—WARSAW, June, 1875.

From Rev. G. W. COAN, (Twenty-five years Missionary to Persia,) stationed at Oroomiah.

Mr. PARMELEE, of Erzroom, took our ESTEY Organ out with him TWELVE YEARS ago. After his return to America we sent to Trebizonde for it. It was brought again over the mountains, SIX HUNDRED MILES ON HORSEBACK, and was seven months reaching Oroomiah. But with all this rough treatment, and subsequent constant use it has kept in perfect tune—not a reed has failed—and NO PART HAS EVER NEEDED REPAIRS—save only the pedal carpets and straps, although our climate is a very dry and trying one to cabinet work.

From O. KADE, Musical Director to His Royal Highness the Grand Duke, and Leader of the Court Church Choir, at Schwerin, in Mecklenburg.

The Harmonium or Cottage Organ No. 40, of J. ESTEY & Co. in America, distinguishes itself from all other similar instruments by its fullness, beauty and truly Organ-like character of tone, and for home as well as Church purposes I most heartily recommend it.

From LOUIS GROSSMANN, the Great Composer, Virtuoso and Organist, in Warsaw, Poland.

The Cottage Organs of ESTEY & Co. in Brattleboro, I consider the most beautiful instruments of their kind. I have often played them in ensemble pieces and heard them in orchestral concerts, amalgamated with the most diversified instruments, and found that the round, full and beautiful tone, in spite of its soft, never harsh sounding quality, always predominated.

The sound of the ESTEY instruments is in strict imitation of a Church Organ, and one can play, even with a sixteen feet register, compound and close harmony, without (as it is the case in other Harmoniums) causing a confusion of sounds.

These instruments are well adapted, on account of their tried solidity, for *Churches*, *Seminaries*, *Conservatories* and *Theatres*, as well as for the most elegant *Salons*.

From W. B. LONHURST, late Presenter and Organist of St. Augustine College Chapel, Canterbury, England.

There is sweetness of tone in the reeds which I never found equaled in any other instrument. This marvellous delicacy will gain for them a very extensive appreciation. Their Organs stand first in the musical world, and great praise is due Messrs. ESTEY & Co. for bringing them to such a pitch of perfection.

From the world-renowned Prima Donna PAULINE LUCCA.

I have heard the beautiful COTTAGE ORGANS of Messieurs J. ESTEY & Co., of Brattleboro, and was astonished at the FULL, NOBLE, and SWEET tone of these instruments, which resembles so much the Pipe Organ, and which I have never found in any other American Organ or Harmonium. PAULINE LUCCA.

AIX-LA-CHAPELLE, Feb. 9, 1876.

From ADOLPH PROSNITZ, Professor at the Imperial Conservatory, in Vienna.

I have, with pleasure, become acquainted with ESTEY & Co.'s excellent Harmoniums, whose soft, noble tone and modulating capacity secures for them a prominent place among instruments of this kind.

From JOSEPH FOERSTER, Professor at the Imperial Conservatory and Choir Master at St. Adalbert, in Prague.

The Cottage Organs of J. ESTEY & Co. exhibited at the warerooms of the Imperial Court Purveyor, V. MICKO, in Prague, excel in a delicate and, in all passages, well balanced tone and in the marked characteristics of the Registers, and are, as the Organ representing instruments for all musical works of a serious style, highly recommendable. The exterior is very tasteful.

From Prof. AUGUST WILHELMIJ, the celebrated Violinist, in London, England.

I herewith testify with great pleasure to the celebrated Organ manufacturers, Messrs. J. ESTEY & Co., of Brattleboro, Vt., U. S. A., that their Organs are fine (beautiful) beyond comparison; I rate them above similar instruments of any other manufacturers that I have seen. The tone (sound) is full, round and noble; the touch exceedingly light and easy; the tune of the different registers specific and distinct, and the whole construction of blameless solidity.

ESTEY
ORGAN CO.
ESTEY
ORGANS
ESTABLISHED
1846
BRATTLEBORO,
VERMONT, U.S.A.

Style A case.

FIVE OCTAVES.

Style A 30. **$190.** Code—Implement.	Two full five octave set of Reeds with Grand Organ, Knee Swell, Vox Humana, etc., etc. NINE STOPS.
Style A 32. **$210.** Code—Imperial.	Adds Octave Couplers to A 30. ELEVEN STOPS.
Style A 33. **$230.** Code—Imposing.	Adds Octave Coupler and Sub-Bass to A 30. ELEVEN STOPS.
Style A 38. **$260.** Code—Impressive.	Three full five octave sets of Reeds, with Vox Humana, Octave Coupler, Sub-Bass, Grand Organ, Knee Swell, etc. THIRTEEN STOPS.

SIX OCTAVES.

Style A 72. **$240.** Code—Incense.	Two full six octave sets of Reeds, with Grand Organ, Knee Swell, Octave Couplers, Vox Humana, etc. ELEVEN STOPS.
Style A 78. **$300.** Code—Income.	Three full six octave sets of Reeds, Vox Humana, Octave Coupler, Sub-Bass, Grand Organ, Knee Swell, etc. THIRTEEN STOPS.

A VERY convenient music pocket has been provided in these organs directly back of the upright fretwork which supports the music while playing.

Go where you will there is this to be heard of the Estey Organ whether from those who have purchased and used or those who have dealt in them or even their fair-minded competitors, viz: "There is no better instrument made than the Estey."

It is and has been for years the standard by which other organs are judged and this very fact proves the excellent judgment of the great purchasing public as well as the high position of the organ. Make a note of this!

Style A Case.

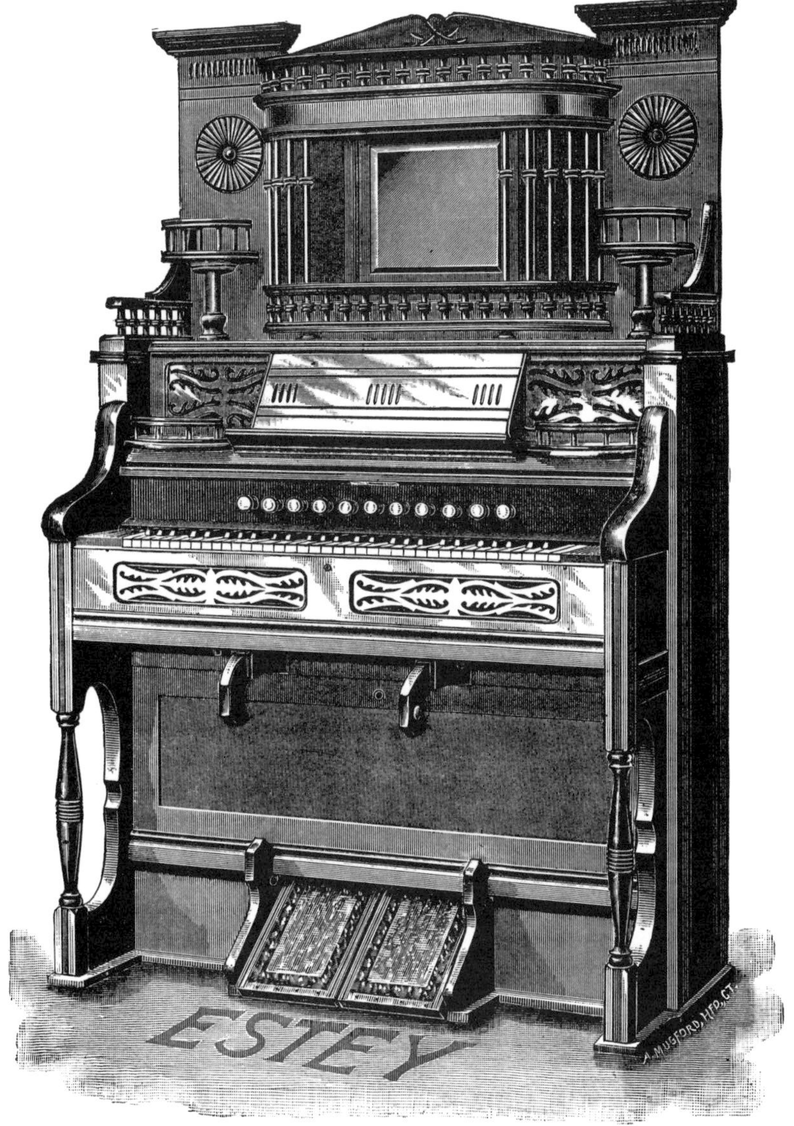

Height, 5 ft. 11 in.; Length, 3 ft. 10 in.; Depth, 1 ft. 11 in. Weight (boxed), 400 lbs.

THE first to bring out organs distinctively chaste in design, we take this opportunity to call attention to the above case. Every line and every appointment is of the first order and must commend itself to every purchaser.

An exceedingly popular style.

All these organs are furnished with center mirrors—nice bevel plate.

☞ Furnished in Quartered Oak, highly polished, if desired.

Style E case.

FIVE OCTAVES.

Style E 30. **$215.** Code—Laborer.	Two full five octave sets of Reeds with Grand Organ, Knee Swell, Vox Humana, etc. NINE STOPS.
Style E 32. **$235.** Code—Laconic.	Two full five octave sets of Reeds, with Octave Couplers, Grand Organ, Knee Swell, Vox Humana, etc. ELEVEN STOPS.
Style E 38. **$285.** Code--Lagoon.	Three full five octave sets of Reeds, Vox Humana, Octave Coupler, Sub-Bass, Grand Organ, Knee Swell, etc. THIRTEEN STOPS.
Style E 53. **$340.** Code—Lambkin.	Four and one-fifth sets of Reeds (including the wonderful Harp Æolienne) with Sub-Bass, Octave Coupler, etc. SIXTEEN STOPS.

SIX OCTAVES.

Style E 72. **$265.** Code—Lamplight.	Two full six octave sets of Reeds, with Grand Organ, Knee Swell, Octave Couplers, Vox Humana, etc. ELEVEN STOPS.
Style E 78. **$325.** Code--Lancets.	Three full six octave sets of Reeds, with Vox Humana, Octave Coupler, Sub-Bass, Grand Organ, Knee Swell, etc. THIRTEEN STOPS.

IT took a little time for this design to "strike" the public but *it is there now* and the demand for an organ of this grade has surprised even the manufacturer.

Demand is the only true index of popularity and judged by this standard it has a phenomenal future.

Convenient receptacle for sheet music underneath the center music support. Elegant bevel mirror plate in every organ.

Style E case.

Height, 6 ft. 1 in.; Length, 3 ft. 10 in.; Depth, 1 ft. 11 in. Weight (boxed), 405 lbs.

Furnished also in Quartered Oak.

Style Z Case.

FIVE OCTAVES.

Style Z 32.
$250.
Code—Joyfully.

One five octave set of Diapason-Melodia Reeds, one two and one-half octave set of Vox Jubilante Reeds, one two and one-half octave set of Viola Reeds, with Treble and Bass Couplers, Knee Swell, Vox Humana, etc. Eleven Stops.

Style Z 38.
$300.
Code—Judicial.

One five octave set of Diapason-Melodia Reeds, one five octave set of Flute-Viola Reeds, one two and one-half octave set of Vox Jubilante Reeds, one two and one-half octave set of Violetta Reeds (very soft for accompaniment), with Harmonique Coupler, Sub-Bass, Vox Humana, etc. Thirteen Stops.

Style Z 53.
$355.
Code—Justice.

One five octave set of Diapason-Melodia Reeds, one five octave set of Flute-Viola Reeds, one two and one-half octave set of Vox Jubilante Reeds, one two and one-half octave set of Bourdon Reeds, one two and one-half octave set of Cornettino Reeds, one two and one-half octave set of Cornet Echo Reeds, the beautiful Harp Æolienne, Manual Sub-Bass, Octave Coupler, Vox Humana, etc. Sixteen Stops.

☞Other styles (interiors) furnished to order.

Not Furnished in Six Octave Case.

From EVERETT J. EVANS, Band Master U. S. Steamship "Franklin."

After a rigid test allow me to add to your list of recommendations my name. The Estey Organ you sent me is without doubt the finest organ manufactured in this country or any other. The tone is grand; and the effect from the knee swells is something grand. The rich, heavy bass and harmonious treble can never be surpassed.

Portsmouth, Va.

From REV. B. F. CLARKSON, Pastor of Harford Avenue M. E. Church.

Will you please pardon me for intruding myself upon you for a moment or two? While listening to my little daughter this afternoon as she sat playing the organ, I was impressed with the sweetness and richness of its tone. I remember, too, that for eighteen years this organ has been in use in my home. To the best of my knowledge it has never been tuned or repaired in any way. It is a marvel of sweetness after many years of service. I purchased this organ eighteen years ago and feel that you ought to know how long and well it has served us.

I write this on my own volition, and at the solicitation or request of no one. I write simply to have you know how well the Estey Organ has stood the raps of eighteen years in the parsonage of a Methodist preacher, and the rough shaking of removals from circuit to circuit, from charge to charge.

Baltimore, Md.

Style Z CASE.

HEIGHT, 6 ft. 6½ in.; LENGTH, 3 ft. 9½ in.; DEPTH, 1 ft. 11 in. WEIGHT (boxed), 425 lbs.

Beautiful bevel mirror plate and elegant finish throughout.

FROM G. C. HALLIDAY.

I have had one of your organs for fourteen years. During that time I have played at least three pieces per day, making a total of 15,330 pieces which I have produced on the organ. The organ is almost as good to-day as it was the day it left the factory.

MT. GILEAD, OHIO.

The testimonial from Mr. Halliday suggests that he was a person for meticulous detail, with a statistical bent as well! One is left wondering if maybe upon playing piece Number 15,331 something went wrong with the instrument.

Style 1387.

NEW SCHOOL MODEL.

HEIGHT, 3 ft. 11 in.; DEPTH, 1 ft. 7 in.; LENGTH, 4 ft. 6 in. WEIGHT (boxed), 280 lbs.

Style 1387.
$160.
Code—Honorary.

One full five octave set of Diapason Reeds, one three octave set of Vox Jubilante Reeds, with Octave Couplers, Forte Stops, Knee Swell, etc. NINE STOPS.

Diapason, *Vox Jubilante*, *Melodia*, *Dolce*, *Dulciana*, *I. Forte*, *II. Forte*, *Treble Coupler*, *Bass Coupler*.

A VERY attractive organ—specially adapted to Sunday School Rooms, small Chapels and Lodge Rooms. Full, rich tone; case well finished; capacious bellows; very satisfactory instrument.

FROM REV. HOWARD F. DOWNS, Pastor M. E. Church.

It is with pleasure that I give my unqualified approval of the Estey Organs. After a number of years of experience, having used both Parlor and Chapel styles, and compared them with those of other makers, I deem the "Estey" the best in sweetness and richness of tone, in durability and other general qualities. I always recommend the "Estey" to those wanting a thoroughly first-class and reliable instrument.

LAUREL, MD.

FROM W. J. McKINNEY, Pastor Monument St. M. E. Church.

It gives me pleasure to say that we have had one of your Estey Parlor Cabinet Organs in use for fourteen years, and the tone is as pure and sweet to-day as when it first came from the factory. In my mother's home is an Estey Organ that has been in use about seventeen years, and so far as I know, has never been tuned or repaired, and is still in daily use and in fair condition. I cheerfully give you this voluntary testimonial.

BALTIMORE, MD.

Style 185 CASE.

NEW HARMONIC.

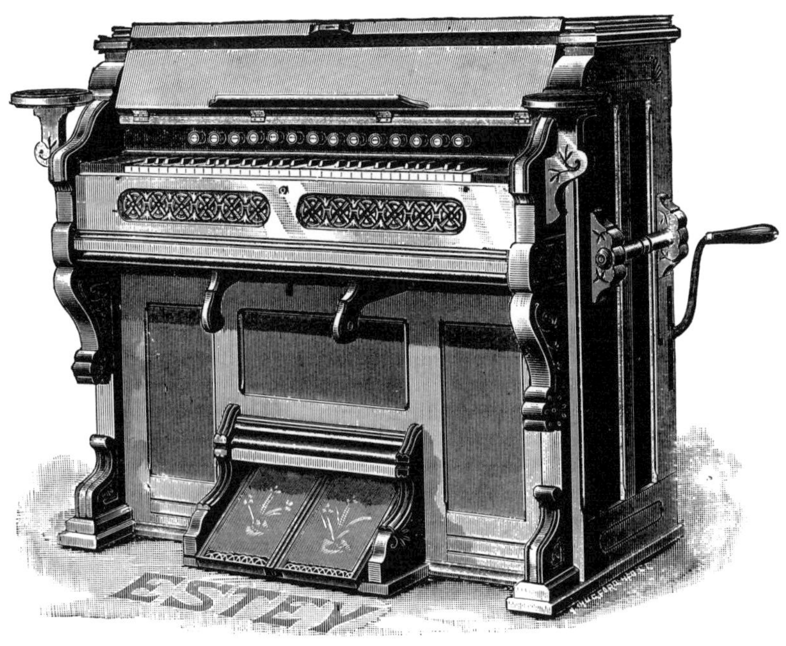

LENGTH, 4 ft. 8 in., (with Handle attached, 5 ft. 10 in.); DEPTH, 2 ft. 7 in.; HEIGHT, 4 ft. 3 in. WEIGHT (boxed), 555 lbs.

THIS Organ though plain in exterior finds favor with many churches and other organizations where its quiet elegance is in harmony with the surroundings.

The interior of this instrument, or the "music," so to speak, is specially noteworthy and is the most powerful in the series of organs containing the regular Estey reeds and action.

This style is furnished either in Walnut or Quartered Oak.

Style 185.
$475.
Code—Gramercy.

The New Harmonic Organ contains one five octave set of Diapason-Melodia Reeds, one five octave set of Flute-Viola Reeds, one three octave set of Clarionet Reeds, one three octave set of Vox Jubilante Reeds, one two octave set of Violetta Reeds, with a very powerful Manual Sub-Bass, the improved Vox Humana, Harmonique Coupler, Forte Stops, etc. FOURTEEN STOPS.

Style 1900 CASE.

PHILHARMONIC CHURCH ORGAN.

ALL these styles are furnished with the wonderful **Estey Philharmonic Reeds**, and special action and bellows, thus securing that phenomenal tone which is the delight of the customer and the envy of competitors.

A few styles are described below, but other interiors are furnished to order.

Style 1933.
$280.
Code—Highness.

Two full five octave sets including the **Estey Philharmonic Reeds** with Vox Jubilante, Manual Sub-Bass, Vox Humana, Octave Coupler, etc. TWELVE STOPS.

Style 1938.
$315.
Code—Highway.

Three full sets, including the **Estey Philharmonic Reeds,** Action and Bellows, with full Manual Sub-Bass, improved Vox Humana, Octave Coupler, etc. FOURTEEN STOPS.

Style 1950.
$365.
Code—Hindered.

One five octave set of Diapason-Melodia Reeds, one five octave set of Flute-Viola Reeds, one three octave set of Clarionet Reeds, one three octave set of Vox Jubilante Reeds, one two octave set of Violetta Reeds, with very powerful Manual Sub-Bass Reeds, in the **Estey improved Philharmonic Church Organ Action,** with capacious Bellows, Octave Coupler, Vox Humana, etc. SIXTEEN STOPS.

Style 1962.
$385.
Code—Huzza.

This organ is very similar to Style 1950, but it has in addition a three octave set of Wald Flute Reeds of wonderful brilliancy, which is found very serviceable in leading large choruses.

FROM WARREN CHOATE, Sec'y Washington Grove Camp Meeting.

The Philharmonic Estey Organ which you sent to Washington Grove at my request has given entire satisfaction. It led the singing in the open air Tabernacle meetings during the Yatman series of meetings, being of great assistance to the choir and aiding the large congregations of people very effectively. It is very easy to play and has such a clear leading tone that we could not get along without it. It will be used for the Camp meetings and will I am sure do the same good work there.

WASHINGTON, D. C.

FROM D. S. HOLLINGSHEAD, Organist 1st Presbyterian Church.

It is with great pleasure that I testify to the superiority of the Estey Philharmonic Organ. During the continuance of the meetings of the Rev. Jones and Small I served an engagement as organist, using this Organ exclusively.

While possessing ample power to fill the vast building, in which five or six thousand persons were congregated, its stop-work is so contrived that the most beautiful and delicate effects are obtainable. No trace of the *reediness*—so common to organs of other makes—is apparent. The bellows work so admirably that *crescendo* and *diminuendo* effects require no exertion whatever. In short, this organ is an ideal instrument, approaching perfection more nearly than any other of which I have any knowledge.

BALTIMORE, MD.

Style 1900 CASE.

Philharmonic Church Organ.

HEIGHT, 4 ft. 6½ in.; DEPTH, 2 ft.; LENGTH, 4 ft. 6½ in.

WEIGHT (boxed), 390 lbs.

THESE organs (described on the opposite page) are furnished in Black Walnut or Quartered Oak cases and are beautifully polished giving to them an exceeding richness and elegance.

FROM J. WRIGHT NICOLS, Organist Christ P. E. Church.

Allow me to express my thorough satisfaction with your new Estey Philharmonic Organ, which I have played with a great deal of pleasure. It is immeasurably superior to anything I have ever seen or heard in reed organs, and is vastly more effective than many small pipe organs. I can recommend it to churches and schools where a fine-toned, powerful instrument is needed.

BALTIMORE, MD.

Organs built for church and institutional environments frequently were fitted with ornamental backs in place of the plain, unfinished features of home instruments. This is because they were less apt to be placed against a wall, and the maker wished such congregations to be treated to ornamental beauty in all directions and also to hear the sound through the grille-work at the back of the case.

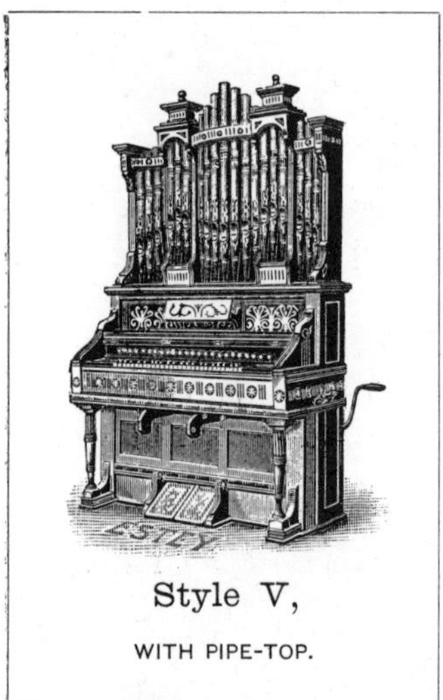

Style V,
WITH PIPE-TOP.

Style 110,
WITH PIPE-TOP.

Style 2000.
WITH PIPE-TOP.

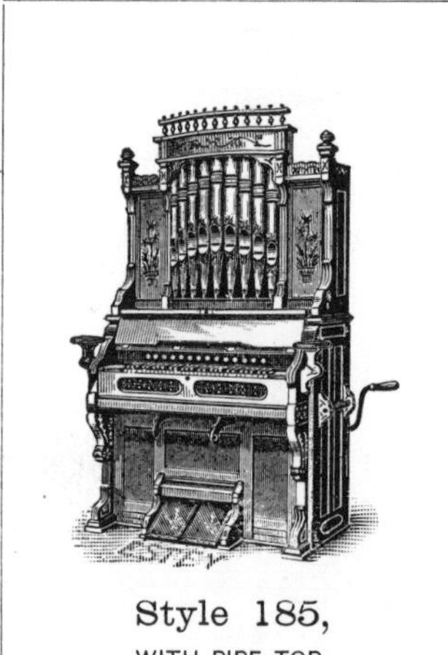

Style 185,
WITH PIPE-TOP.

Style 912,
WITH PIPE-TOP.

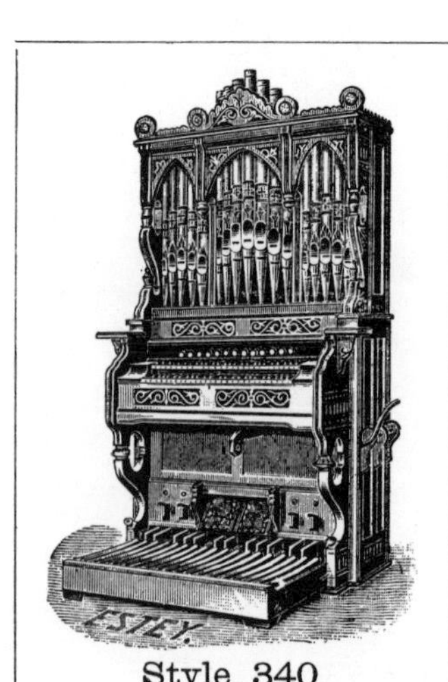

Style 340
WITH PIPE-TOP.

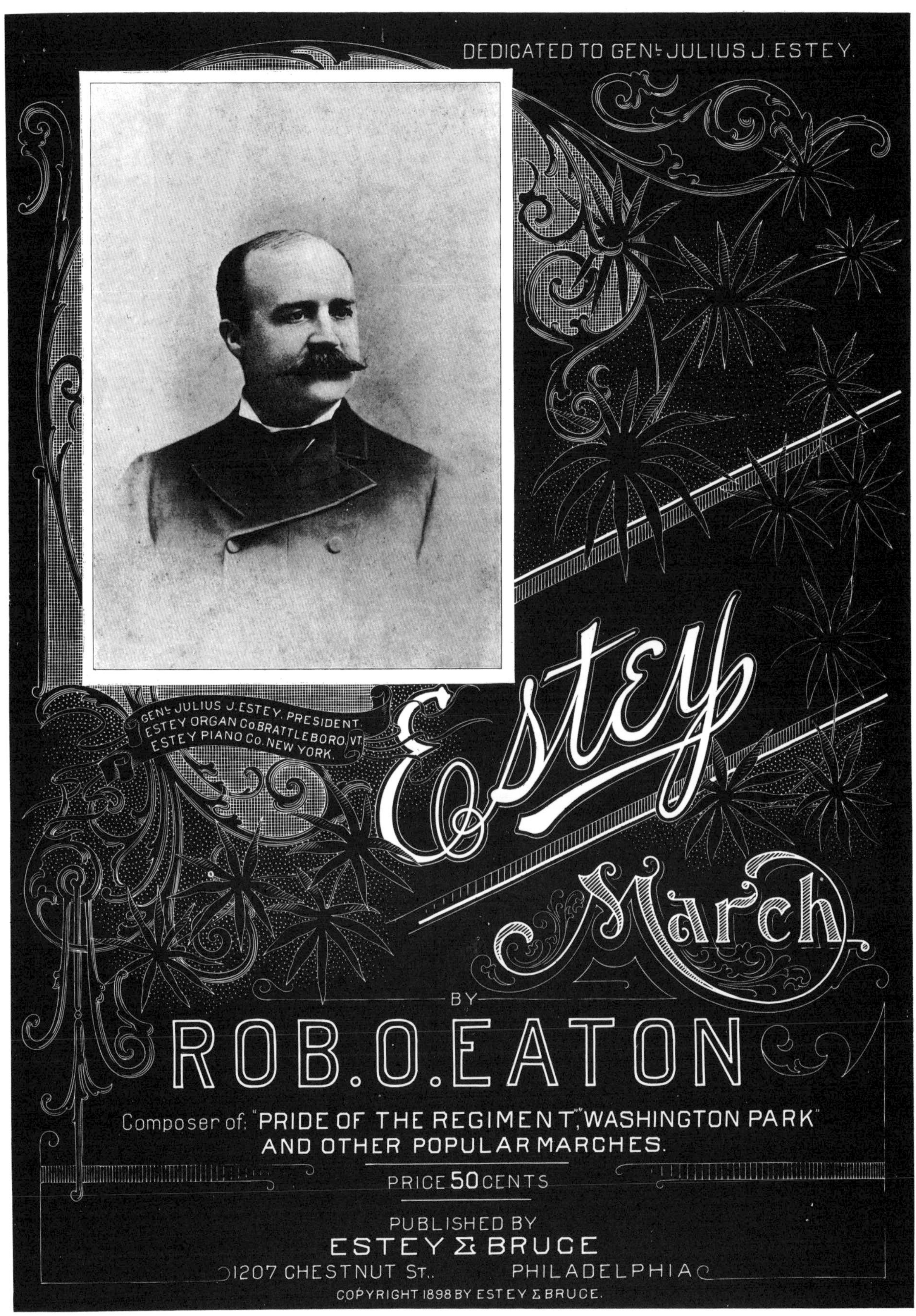
DEDICATED TO GENL. JULIUS J. ESTEY.
GENL. JULIUS J. ESTEY, PRESIDENT.
ESTEY ORGAN Co. BRATTLEBORO, VT.
ESTEY PIANO Co. NEW YORK.
Estey
March
BY
ROB. O. EATON
Composer of: "PRIDE OF THE REGIMENT", "WASHINGTON PARK"
AND OTHER POPULAR MARCHES.
PRICE 50 CENTS
PUBLISHED BY
ESTEY & BRUCE
1207 CHESTNUT St., PHILADELPHIA
COPYRIGHT 1898 BY ESTEY & BRUCE.

THE ESTEY MARCH.

R. O. EATON.

Copyright 1898 by Estey & Bruce.

The Estey March. 2.

THE NATION'S PRIDE!

ESTEY
ORGANS=PIANOS

During the past half-century, over **325,000** of these Famous Instruments have been made and sold, and the oldest of these are still giving satisfactory service. Can there be a better recommendation?

THE ESTEY ORGANS

have always been noted for their beautiful and exclusive designs of casings and their great variety of reed combinations. This Season's productions are in advance of all competition.

CHURCH AND PARLOR CASES

Prices, $25. to $1000.

THE ESTEY PIANO

is strictly "up-to-date" in every particular. It is made of the very best material; built on thoroughly scientific principles by the highest paid and most skillful piano makers—there is nothing slighted, nothing overlooked from start to finish.

IT IS A PERFECT PIANO

Prices, $300 to $1000.

In purchasing an ESTEY, either Organ or Piano, you secure the protection of a name which through a half century has been a guarantee against dissatisfaction.

EASY MONTHLY PAYMENTS

PIANOS—$10 to $25 down; $7 to $10 Monthly.
ORGANS—$5 to $10 down; $5 Monthly.

SEND FOR OUR LATEST DESCRIPTIVE CATALOGUE.

Estey

ORGAN AND PIANO
WAREROOMS,
1207 Chestnut St., Philadelphia.

PIANOS AND ORGANS TO RENT.

A BRIEF DESCRIPTION OF THE STOPS IN USE IN ESTEY ORGANS

Speaking Stops

NAME	PITCH	CHARACTERISTICS
Bourdon	16 ft.	Full and round
Choral	8 ft.	Bright and forceful tone
Clarinet	16 ft.	Resembles the Clarinet in quality
Corno	16 ft.	Combination of horn and reed tone. Made only in large scale Philharmonic Reeds. Used in larger models
Diapason	8 ft.	Foundation set of reeds by which others are tuned. Used more generally than any other stop. Round, full tone
Dulciana	8 ft.	Voiced soft. Combination of Flute and string tone
Flute	4 ft.	Brilliant, but not reedy. Generally used in combination
Flute d'Amour	4 ft.	Very soft and smooth tone; for accompaniment and echo effects
Harp Aeolienne Vox Celeste	2 ft. 4 ft. 8 ft.	Closely resembles the tone produced by the vibration of the strings of an Æolian Harp. Made with two reeds for each note. Equally satisfactory in playing harmony or used as accompaniment
Melodia	8 ft.	Voiced to give as near as possible a soft wood Flute tone. In strength less than Diapason
Oboe	8 ft.	Reed tone in character. Closely reproducing the orchestral instrument of same name
Salicional	8 ft.	Delicate, soft tone, similar to Dulciana but voiced with more string tone than Dulciana
Sub-Bass	16 ft.	*Bass.* Powerful and resonant
Trumpet	8 ft.	Very strong, open tone
Violetta	4 ft.	Similar in character to Flute, but voiced with less strength
Vox Jubilante	8 ft.	Its name "Voice Jubilant" will indicate its character; very effective as solo, and, when used in combination with other stops, imparts a peculiar brilliance to all. Effect obtained by using two reeds for each note
Wald Flute Violina	2 ft.	Very clear and penetrating. Used almost entirely with Full Organ

Pedal Stops

NAME	PITCH	CHARACTERISTICS
Pedal Bourdon	16 ft.	As big and round a tone as can be secured with a reed
Pedal Dulciana	16 ft.	Voiced soft to just give the suggestion of pedal set. Soft enough to use with softest set on either manual

Mechanical Stops

NAME	USES
Balanced Swell	*In Two-Manual Models* Pedal so constructed as to open all the swells or shutters and will remain at any given point if desirable to release the foot
Forte	Stop opens swells and augments the tone
Knee Swell	Gives same effect as Forte, only more gradual if desired
Grand Organ	Brings into use all the sets of reeds in the organ without the necessity of drawing a stop
Octave Coupler	So constructed that when any key is depressed its octave above or below is also depressed, thereby causing both to sound simultaneously
Swell to Great	Connecting the two manuals so that when a key on the lower (Great) manual is depressed it also depresses the corresponding key of the upper (Swell) manual
Swell to Pedals Great to Pedals	So connecting the manuals that when the pedal is depressed its corresponding key in the manual is depressed and also responds
Tremolo	A revolving fan, placed just back of the reeds, which, when set in motion, imparts to the tone a thrilling wave-like effect

The Construction of the Estey Organ

THE Century Dictionary, which may safely be presumed to be unbiased in its definitions, says that the organ is the most complicated and the noblest of musical instruments. Anyone who has ever heard a real musician at a real organ will readily agree that it is the noblest of all means that mankind has yet devised of producing harmonious sounds, and anyone who has ever tried to build a perfect organ will just as heartily agree that it is a most complicated instrument. That is why such consummate skill, such careful thoroughness, such infinite pains and such conscientious faithfulness to detail, are necessary to the production of a good organ—an instrument worthy the name. That is the secret of Estey superiority, that the reason why magnificent success has crowned our efforts. That is why a cheap organ can never be satisfactory.

Materials

In building the Estey organ the first step is the selection of the proper materials and at no point in the whole process of manufacturing the organ is greater care exercised than right here. Being the largest organ builders in the world, buying the largest quantities of organ materials, the Estey Company naturally has "first pick" of the world's supply of materials of this kind, and we are freely accused of being very "fussy" and "cranky" about what we accept. Well, maybe we are; but in over eighty years we have never yet used anything but the choicest lumber, free from all defects and thoroughly seasoned in the most approved manner, and all other materials to match; and we do not think we shall begin at this late day to use "seconds" or anything showing the slightest defect.

We keep in our lumber sheds and dry kilns a constant supply of more than two million feet of lumber. In the factory every piece is carefully and critically examined before it is used. We know it is right—good enough to bear the Estey name and the Estey life-time guarantee.

The Craftsmen

But good intentions and good materials alone will not make a perfect organ. We must have workmen with brains stored with knowledge of organ building; fingers skilled in their craft; consciences devoted to good work. We are particularly fortunate in this respect. No one has ever gone through the Estey factory without being forcibly impressed by the stamp of men at work there; not boys, nor little girls, nor careless, cheap labor of any kind; but men of ability and skill, who are making their craft almost a profession; many of them the heads of families, with beautiful homes in Brattleboro.

There are many gray-haired men at work today in the Estey factory who have been working there for fifty years, and in all that time they have never been hurried or told to "let it go at that," or pushed beyond the limit of the best and most careful work.

They have understood that the only thing asked of them was that they maintain and, if possible, improve the high quality of the Estey.

Naturally in all these years of work the men have been gaining ground. They have become a little more skillful month by month. They have learned the fine art of catching the peculiarities and the ways of the wind among the reeds, and it is they who make the sweet-toned Estey possible.

The Factory

But even the best workmen must have tools and facilities for their work, or they will fail of the great results. Here, again, the Estey factory leads the world. It is the largest organ factory in existence; it has the most complete equipment and better facilities for turning out high-grade work than has any other organ factory. This is, of course, an advantage to you, for it assures you that no part of the Estey organ you are going to buy has been neglected or slighted because of lack of means to produce the best results. And note particularly that every part of the Estey organ, from the smallest to the greatest, is made in the Estey factory under our personal supervision, so that we know it is right and can guarantee it with a clear conscience.

In our immense plant—see photographic view (on page 15), which represents it as it actually is and not as some artist dreamed we would like to have it—we have 250,000 square feet of floor space, and more modern, labor-saving machinery, a greater number of skilled workmen, and more of what some folks call "old maidish" exactness, than you will find in any two or three other organ factories combined. We have spared no expense in providing our workmen with the best of facilities for cutting down and keeping down the cost of manufacture.

But there we have stopped.

We have not tried to do with a machine that which ought to be done by hand—the part calling for skill of fingers, judgment of mind, the final touch, the human element—which no machine can replace. So, while you have every advantage of every labor-saving machine that it is possible to use in building the Estey, you have it without sacrificing in the least the high quality that has made the Estey the world's standard organ. The care, the thoroughness with which the Estey is made, impress the visitor as a strange contrast to the slap-dash, hurrah-boys, shove-her-along, haphazard, happy-go-lucky, rule-o'-thumb methods that are followed in factories building "cheap" organs. But the difference in methods of work is no greater than the difference in products.

Which kind of organ do you want?

The best procurable materials;

The most skilled and conscientious workmen;

The largest and best equipped factory in the world;

Over eighty years' experience;

All backed by a steadfast determination to maintain and increase the Estey reputation.

Do you wonder that the Estey organ is still the world's favorite?

The third and fourth generations of Esteys are now building the Estey organ. In his day Jacob Estey, the founder, was proud of the product of his factory; proud of his facilities and equipment; proud of the reputation the organ had already attained. But the present factory, the present output, and the Estey reputation today, far surpass his fondest dream. To maintain that prestige and reputation is almost a religion with the present generations. When you buy an Estey organ you can be absolutely sure that every dollar of your money has gone into the instrument in better quality.

Details of Construction

ALL organ builders must, as a matter of course, construct their organs on the same general principles, just as all steam engines or watches or pianos are made after the same general plan. The difference between a good and a poor organ does not lie in some special device which is used in one and not in the other; nor in some general principle which one utilizes and the other ignores, but in the skill and ingenuity with which the different parts are assembled and in the thoroughness and care with which they are made.

Organ building, then, almost more than any other craft, becomes a matter of personality. It is almost one of the fine arts, for the builder builds himself into the organ; it is a product of his personality and individuality. It may be of interest, therefore, to you as a purchaser of the Estey organ, to know something of the details of its construction. Of course the general principles are well understood. In the reed organ the sound is produced by vibrations of thin, metallic tongues, or reeds, under the influence of a current of air.

The value of the organ, the sweetness of the tone, the harmony—the general effect of the playing—all depend upon the skill and care with which these various parts are made and adapted to the work required of them. Carelessness and slip-shod methods are fatal to the best results.

The modern organ is in reality a combination of a number of organs; that is, it is made up of a number of sets of reeds, each reed in each set varying in pitch, but all the reeds in each set having the same quality of tone. Each set of reeds is technically known as "a stop," though in ordinary use the term stop is applied to the knob or lever which controls the mute covering that set of reeds. By pulling out a given stop you raise the mute and admit the air to the set of reeds controlled by that stop. If you pull out two stops the air is admitted to two sets of reeds, and so on. Now, when you press down a key it serves to open a little valve under the reed corresponding to the key in each set of reeds in the organ. These little valves open into what is called the wind-chest under the sounding board, from which the air has been exhausted by the bellows. The wind-chest being a vacuum, a current of air immediately rushes through the reeds whose corresponding valves have been opened—the tongues of the reeds vibrate, and a musical tone is produced.

The necessary parts of the interior of such an organ are:

1. *The Bellows,* or the "lungs of the organ," which create the current of air that acts upon the reeds.
2. *The Reeds,* which produce the sound and determine the tone.
3. *The Action,* including the KEYS and STOPS with their various appurtenances, which, if properly made, give the player absolute control of the instrument.

Fig. 1. The Bellows

The Bellows

Without going into great detail, we desire to call attention to the superior construction of some of the more important parts of the Estey organ. The lungs of an organ are, naturally, as important as any part of the whole instrument. We feel safe in saying that the over eighty years' experience and the hundreds of experiments we have made, have enabled us to avoid the mistakes so many manufacturers make in this part of the organ, and to produce a bellows that will last a lifetime.

The foundation or woodwork of the bellows is made of three-ply—that is, three different thicknesses of wood, glued together, the grain of one piece running across the grain of the piece next to it. The white strips showing the intake holes covered, are of the finest quality of sumac-tanned sheepskin. Possibly less expensive leather would do for this purpose—indeed, most manufacturers use a cheaper leather—but this sheepskin keeps a soft, pliable condition for years and years, while a less perfectly tanned leather would become hard and crack and crumble after five or ten years' service. The same care is exercised in selecting the cloth for the bellows. It has an extra heavy coating of rubber and will last a lifetime. It is made especially for the Estey organ and costs a great deal more than the ordinary rubber cloth used in ordinary organ bellows.

The wind is distributed in such a manner as to insure perfect and prompt response. To avoid accidents, due to too great suction of wind, we have installed in all our bellows an automatic escape-valve, which opens when the bellows are exhausted.

The Reeds

The sweet tone that has always been so characteristic of the Estey organ is largely due to the care and pains taken in making the reeds. We have perfected the art of reed-making. We make our own reeds, because we cannot find in the whole world better reeds. If we could, we are not too proud to take off our hat to the man who makes them and pay him his price for them.

But they are not made.

For years the metal used in the Estey reeds, especially for the tongues, has been of a special composition—a formula which has been jealously guarded. Its action and tone quality are such as we have been unable to produce by any other alloy. But it is not in the metal alone that the Estey's superiority consists. It is even more in the making of the reeds.

The reed is in reality made by special automatic machinery that stamps, moulds and grooves the plate, forms the tongue and rivets it to the plate with a delicacy and rapidity that makes it the envy of every organ and reed manufacturer in the country. The reeds come from the machine in a condition which many manufacturers would consider "good enough," but in the Estey factory the process of reed perfecting has not yet begun. "Good enough" for the Estey is another way of spelling perfection.

After an inspection by an expert to see that they are mechanically perfect, the reeds are passed to the cleaning and voicing department, where delicate fingered women with accurate ears, clean and polish them and then voice and pitch them by filing a little here and scraping a little there. The tongue must fit in the groove of the plate with the accuracy of the most delicate parts of a watch. In its vibrations it must not touch either side of the groove and yet it must just escape touching. In this department the reed tongue is also curved—the quality of tone depending upon the delicate curve given the tongue.

Next, the reeds pass to the tuning department, where the expert tuners place them in the organ, voicing and harmonizing them, seeing that the reeds of each set have the proper quality of tone, the proper volume of tone. They fit them into the reed cells in which they belong so that, if necessary, not only the reed may be corrected, but even the shape of the cell changed in order to secure an absolutely perfect tone.

With the organ in perfect tune, pitched right, it would seem that perfection had been reached, and yet the organ must be passed upon by the corrector—a past master of organ tuning—whose chief concern is that every organ shall come up to the Estey standard of tone quality—that it shall have that "sweet tone" which made the Estey famous. It is to him that we owe the fact of the absolute uniformity of the Estey product.

The Action

This action rests upon the *Foundation Board,* and consists of the *Sounding Board,* the *Reed Cell Board,* the *Swells* and *Couplers,* the *Keys* and the *Stop Action.*

The Foundation Board

This is in reality the foundation of the organ, and like the foundation of a house, the dependent point of construction. Upon it rest the wind-chest, the sounding board, the reed cells, and, in fact, the entire mechanism—or "action," as it is technically termed—of the organ. How important, then, that it should be right in every particular. In the Estey organ, the foundation board is made of the highest grade three-ply stock that our lumber buyers can secure in the country's best lumber markets. The bellows is attached to the foundation board from below as well as strongly braced to the sides of the case.

The Sounding Board

The Sounding Board (shown in Fig. 2) corresponds to the top of a violin, and on it depends the resonance of the organ's tone. In the Estey it is made of quarter-sawed old growth spruce of the highest grade, free from knots and stains, straight grained and seasoned until it is drier even than the proverbial "tinder." The care we use here not only prevents the sounding board from cracking, checking or warping, but also has much to do with giving the Estey its full, resonant tone. The sounding board is securely fastened to the foundation board by long screws. The intervening space forms the air-tight chamber called the wind-chest.

There are little apertures made just above the sounding board, one for each reed in the organ, through which the current of air passes from the reed into the wind-chest. These openings are covered by valves, little strips of clear white pine, held in place by springs. The Estey valves are covered with the highest grade of felt and soft white leather and carefully made that there may be no possibility of their twisting or warping. Should they warp in the least they would allow a continuous singing or ciphering of the reeds above them, and, of course, ruin the effect of any playing. The little wire springs which hold these valves in place are made of the best nickeled brass wire and will not rust or corrode in any climate.

We use as much care in selecting the wood for the sounding boards in the Estey organs as do the makers of violins for their highest priced instruments. Clear spruce will not do. It must be absolutely perfect. And if the readers of this booklet could know how difficult it is to get stock sufficiently good for this purpose and the price that we are obliged to pay, they would be surprised. Mahogany is one of the highest priced woods, and yet the price we pay for spruce for Estey sounding boards is nearly as much as one would pay for the best mahogany. We use only New England spruce, old growth and quarter-sawed. It must be absolutely clear of sap, and in order to secure this we accept only absolutely perfect stock. This shows the care we take in details to give the Estey organ purest tone and to insure its being a perfect musical instrument.

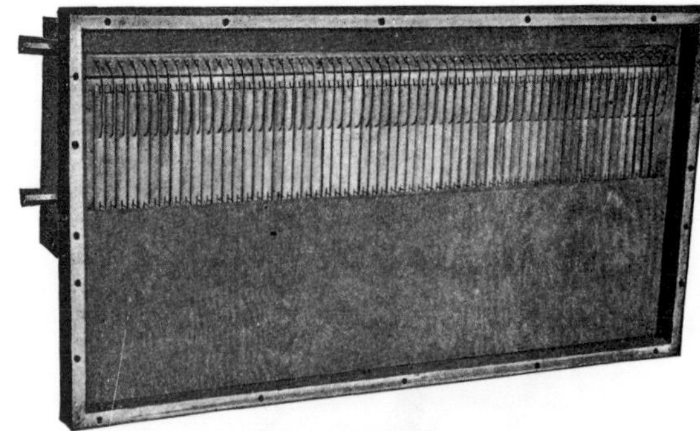

Fig. 2. The Sounding Board

Reed Cells

On top of the sounding board is placed the reed cell board, as shown in Fig. 3. This reed cell board in the Estey is always an absolutely perfect piece of wood, free from all knots, stains and imperfections of any kind. It is thoroughly dried so that it does not shrink or swell and thus bind on the reeds or allow them to rattle. In it are cut the little chambers, or grooved cells, of various sizes and shapes, in which are placed the reeds.

Here is an illustration of the painstaking manner in which we proceed in the manufacture of these reed cell boards, in order to obtain the best tonal results:

We cut the openings of the cells of different heights, varying according to the size of the reeds. Our experts who observe the quality of tone of each set of reeds, its volume and shading, as well as the sound of each separate note, determine, by fine measurements based upon scientific principles, the shape, height and depth of each cell. The measurements determined upon by these experts are followed rigidly, so much so that the tools employed in cutting these little apertures, or reed cells, are ground by our machinists to the thousandth of an inch. It is through these cells that the current of air rushes over the reed, causing the tongue of the reed to vibrate.

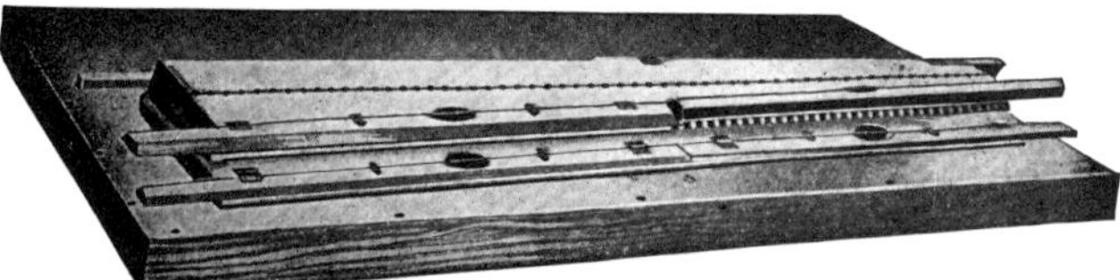

Fig. 3. Reed Cell Board

The cells containing brass reeds correspond to the pipes of a pipe organ. The cells for each set of reeds are covered by mute strips, controlled by the stops above the keyboard, which shut off the wind from all the cells and reeds excepting those belonging to the set the organist wishes to employ. In illustration, Fig. 3, one mute strip is opened, showing the cells—the others are closed.

The reeds, when they are placed in the cells, do not rest directly upon the board, but fit into little grooves—like a drawer in a slide—of the exact size of the reed; an exact fit being necessary to prevent the reed from rattling.

We take another extra precaution in the Estey reed cells to prevent all possibility of a leak. Just at the opening of the cell we cut a slight groove and fit into it a small piece of felt, firmly gluing it in place. This acts as a cushion under the heel of the reed, giving it a slight upward pressure and holding it firmly in place.

The mute strips are fastened with little brass hinges and are held in place by nickeled wire springs, protected by piece of felt, as shown in the illustration, both to prevent them from wearing the wood and to render them absolutely noiseless. This is only another of the hundred "little things"—the "old maidish" fussiness of which we are accused—that go to make the sum total of Estey excellence.

The Swells and Couplers

In Fig. 4 are shown the octave couplers (the bent wires) which connect each valve with the valve of the corresponding note—an octave higher in the treble and an octave lower in the bass—thus doubling the volume of sound; the swell, or shutter, operated by the knee, which makes possible the crescendo effect, and the pitman rods, or little trackers that operate the valves, in place, ready for the keys.

To insure absolute uniformity of size and distance of the little holes in which the tracker pins move, we had made in our own factory a machine that bores the entire set of sixty-one holes in an action at one motion. In drilling a hole through wood little particles are shown on two sides of the hole, which when exposed to dampness swell and might grip the little wooden plungers.

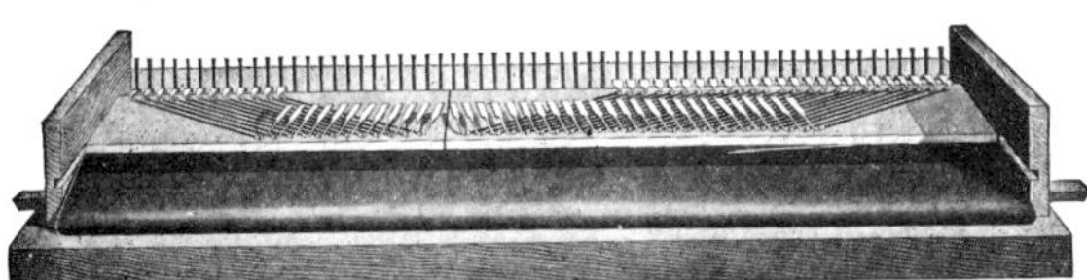

Fig. 4. Octave Couplers

We prevent such possibility by burning these holes with a white hot iron, which sears the hole and forever eliminates this otherwise possible annoyance.

Made of the best procurable material; properly made by hand, by veterans in the craft; properly set and properly regulated, the key action of the Estey is as nearly perfect as it is possible for human skill to produce.

The Keys and Key Frame

The keys of the Estey (shown in Fig. 5, added to the action) are made in the Estey factory, and are not purchased at haphazard from a key manufacturer. This is in keeping with the Estey policy of being sure that everything about the Estey organ is exactly right.

The keys are made of the finest quality white basswood, free from stain or discoloration of any kind. We are so particular on this point that to prevent the running of sap and consequent staining of the wood, we make the keys from boards that are sawed when the log is frozen.

The keys are covered with highly polished, extra thick, first quality fiberloid.

The frame which holds the pins for the keys is made of a semi-hard wood that can be dried against all possibility of swelling and shrinking. This is of the greatest importance, as the key pins must always be held in exactly the same position, else the frame creeps forward or backward and binds on the pins, causing the keys to stick or give them slow action.

The holes for the pins are bored, the pins placed in position and then driven to their place by an automatic machine that has more than human accuracy and seems, almost, to have human intelligence. The most skilled workman could hardly bore a series of holes at exactly—to a hair's breadth—the same distance apart; certainly he could not strike two successive blows with a

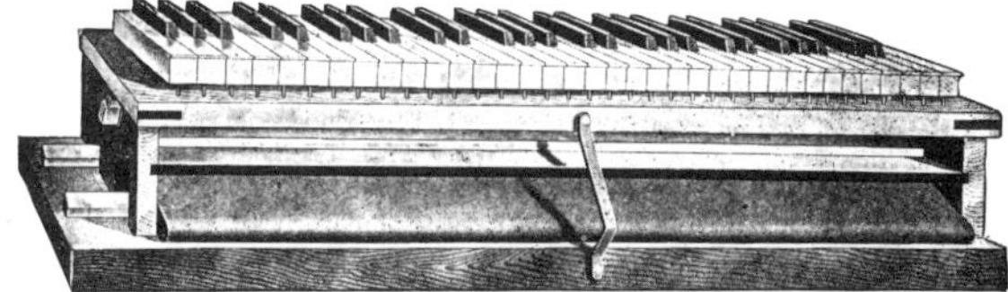

Fig. 5. Keys and Key Frame

hammer with exactly the same force; but this automatic machine, built especially for the Estey factory, places the pins in the frame with microscopic uniformity. This accuracy has much to do with the perfect touch and uniformity of the Estey organ.

The Stop Action

The action of the organ, ready to set into the case, is shown in Fig. 6, with the stop board in place. Unquestionably the stop action of the Estey organ is the most simple, the most accurate and the freest from noise of all methods yet employed in organ

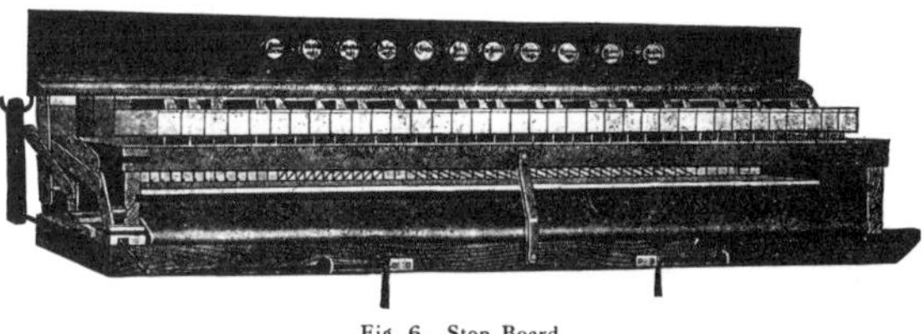

Fig. 6. Stop Board

building. Little slides of hard maple connect coppered wire with the mute strips or stops over the different sets of reeds, as shown on the left side of the illustration. This construction is the result of years of experience and experimenting and has proved itself to be the most practical method of stop action.

Simplicity of Stop Action

We quoted one of the dictionaries a few pages back, to the effect that the organ is the most complicated as well as the noblest of all musical instruments. It is, indeed, a complex instrument, but from that very fact rises much of the Estey's triumph. Its simplicity has overcome much of the instrument's complexity.

Note in Fig. 7—showing the action in the case viewed from the back—the

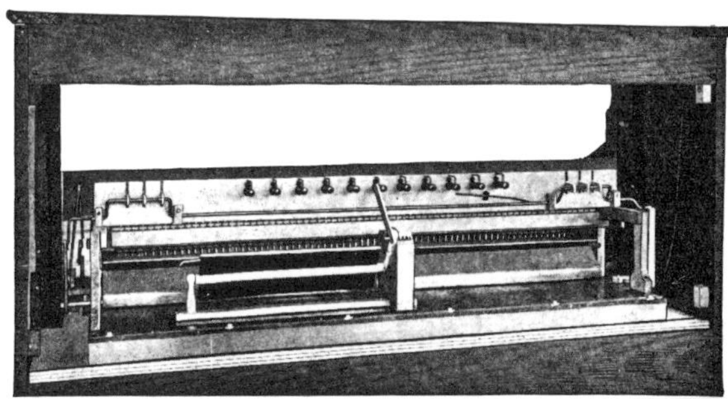

Fig. 7. Estey Action (From the Back)

perfect simplicity and freedom from complicated parts. The illustration also shows, directly in the center, the little box enclosing the tremolo wheel. When the Tremolo stop ("Vox Humana") is drawn, the fan revolves and gives a very pleasing effect to the treble reeds. In the Estey this is effective for the front as well as the back reeds.

The Case

As good an instrument as the Estey organ deserves a handsome case, and we provide it. Our cabinet work is not excelled by that of the finest furniture. And the purchaser can rest assured that he is getting exactly what the specifications call for. If the description specifies walnut case, *it is* walnut; where the specification is for oak, we use the finest grade of white oak, and in others, where the purchaser does not want to go to the expense of a full walnut case, we make a walnut finish. This latter case is made of birch, a hard wood, stained to represent walnut. It really is a perfect reproduction of a beautiful dark walnut. In any case, you are sure of getting exactly what is specified in plain terms. We use no shoddy materials of any kind, inside or outside the Estey. Our mirrors are of the finest quality of plate glass. The carpet on the pedals is first quality, and from start to finish, the furnishing of an Estey is the best that money can buy.

We have by no means touched on every feature of the Estey construction, but have simply pointed out a few of the essentials of a good organ—the things you should be most particular about in buying an organ.

The Estey Organ

A BRIEF DESCRIPTION OF SEVERAL OF THE STYLES OF ORGANS WHICH ARE MOST SOUGHT FOR

1903

A Record Unparalleled!

THREE HUNDRED AND FORTY THOUSAND ESTEY ORGANS MANU-FACTURED AND SOLD

ESTEY ORGAN COMPANY

BRATTLEBORO, VERMONT, U. S. A.

Style 8
Case

Length, 3 feet 8 inches. Height, 3 feet 4 inches. Depth, 1 foot 6 inches. Weight (boxed), 230 pounds.

Style 8. Two full sets of Reeds and Couplers.

CODE
Faltereth.

Bass.		**Treble.**	
Melodia,	8 ft.	Diapason,	8 ft.
Viola,	4 ft.	Vox Jubilante,	8 ft.
Bass Coupler.		Treble Coupler.	

An *Estey* organ at such a price that the smallest school or other organization need not stagger at the cost.

Of course "*Estey*" on the nameboard is sufficient guarantee because, no matter what the price, if that magic name is there the organ is all right!

Furnished in American Oak case.

Style 9
Case

Height, 75 inches. Length, 45½ inches. Depth, 20⅛ inches. Weight (boxed), 360 pounds.

Style 91.

CODE:
Gladsome (Walnut).
Heliotrope (Oak).

CONTENTS.

Two full sets of Reeds of five octaves each, with Treble and Bass Couplers, Knee Swell, Grand Organ, Tremolo, etc. ELEVEN STOPS.

RECAPITULATION.

Bass.		Treble.
Melodia,		Diapason,
Dolce,		*Dulciana*,
Viola,		Vox Jubilante,
Bass Coupler,		Treble Coupler,
I Forte,		II Forte,
	Vox Humana.	

Always specify whether Oak or Walnut Case is wanted.

A neat, refined and comparatively inexpensive organ. The demand is flattering and denotes attractiveness in the organ itself, and satisfied purchasers as well.

Style 10 Case

Length, 3 feet 10 inches. Height, 6 feet 4 inches. Depth, 1 foot 10 inches. Weight (boxed), 350 pounds.

Style 101. Five Octaves.

CODE:
Glaciers (Walnut).
Heirlooms (Oak).

CONTENTS.

Two full sets of Reeds of five octaves each, with Treble and Bass Couplers, Knee Swell, Grand Organ, Tremolo, etc. ELEVEN STOPS.

RECAPITULATION.

Bass.		Treble.
Melodia,		Diapason,
Dolce,		*Dulciana*,
Viola,		Vox Jubilante,
Bass Coupler,		Treble Coupler,
I Forte,		II Forte,
	Vox Humana.	

Always specify whether Oak or Walnut Case is wanted.

A rich looking and beautifully finished organ, suited to any cottage. The musical combinations are, as usual in Estey Organs, well chosen and best adapted to home use.

Style 20 Case

Length, 3 feet 10 inches. Height, 6 feet 11 inches. Depth, 1 foot 10 inches. Weight (boxed), 375 pounds.

Style 201. Five Octaves.

CODE:
Gladiator (Walnut).
Heedless (Oak).

Style 271. Six Octaves.

CODE:
Glasspaper (Walnut).
Heiress (Oak).

CONTENTS.

Two full sets of Reeds of five or six octaves each, with Treble and Bass Couplers, Knee Swell, Grand Organ, Tremolo, etc. ELEVEN STOPS.

RECAPITULATION.

Bass.	Treble.
Melodia,	Diapason,
Dolce,	*Dulciana*,
Viola,	Vox Jubilante,
Bass Coupler,	Treble Coupler,
I Forte,	II Forte,

Vox Humana.

Always specify whether Oak or Walnut Case is wanted.

Furnished both in Five and Six Octaves. This is one of our best sellers and is having a splendid demand. The case is bold and striking but in the best of taste. Every purchaser is delighted and glad to show it to his friends.

Style 40 Case

Length, 3 feet 10 inches. Height, 6 feet 7 inches. Depth, 1 foot 9 inches. Weight (boxed), 350 pounds.

Style 401. Five Octaves.
CODE:
Glaucoma (Walnut).
Opponent (Oak).

Style 471. Six Octaves.
CODE:
Glassiness (Walnut).
Opportune (Oak).

CONTENTS.

Two full sets of Reeds of five or six octaves each, with Treble and Bass Couplers, Knee Swell, Grand Organ, Tremolo, etc. ELEVEN STOPS.

RECAPITULATION.

Bass.	Treble.
Melodia,	Diapason,
Dolce,	*Dulciana*,
Viola,	Vox Jubilante,
Bass Coupler,	Treble Coupler,
I Forte,	II Forte,

Vox Humana.

Always specify whether Oak or Walnut Case is wanted.

This beautiful organ is furnished both in Five and Six Octaves. Many wish to play piano music and the larger compass assists the player very materially. The case is richly embellished with tasteful ornamentation.

Style N Case. Five-Octave Styles.

Style N 32.

CODE:
Gaiters (Walnut).
Offerton (Oak).
11 Stops.

Two five-octave sets of Reeds, with Divided Couplers.

Knee Swell and Grand Organ (Knee).

Bass.		Treble.	
Melodia, . . .	8 ft.	Diapason, . .	8 ft.
Dolce, . . .	8 ft.	*Dulciana*, . .	8 ft.
Viola, . . .	4 ft.	Vox Jubilante, .	8 ft.
Bass Coupler,		Treble Coupler,	
I Forte,		II Forte,	

Vox Humana.

Style N 38.

CODE:
Glitter (Walnut).
Officer (Oak).
13 Stops.

Three five-octave sets of Reeds, with one octave of Manual Sub-Bass Reeds and Octave Coupler.

Knee Swell and Grand Organ (Knee).

Bass.		Treble.	
Melodia, . . .	8 ft.	Diapason, . .	8 ft.
Dolce, . . .	8 ft.	*Dulciana*, . .	8 ft.
Viola, . . .	4 ft.	Flute, ...	4 ft.
Violetta (soft), .	4 ft.	Vox Jubilante, .	8 ft.
Sub-Bass, . .	16 ft.	Octave Coupler,	
I Forte,		II Forte,	

Vox Humana.

Style N 47.

CODE:
Glimpse (Walnut).
Official (Oak).
14 Stops.

Four five-octave sets of Reeds, with one octave of Manual Sub-Bass Reeds and Octave Coupler.

Knee Swell and Grand Organ (Knee).

Bass.		Treble.	
Melodia, . . .	8 ft.	Diapason, . .	8 ft.
Dolce, . . .	8 ft.	*Dulciana*, . .	8 ft.
Viola, . . .	4 ft.	Flute, . . .	4 ft.
Harp Æolienne,	2 ft.	Vox Jubilante, .	8 ft.
Sub-Bass, . .	16 ft.	Bourdon, . .	16 ft.
Vox Humana,		Octave Coupler,	
I Forte.		II Forte.	

Six-Octave Styles.

Style N 72.

CODE:
Globard (Walnut).
Omnibus (Oak).
11 Stops.

Two six-octave sets of Reeds, with Divided Couplers.

Knee Swell and Grand Organ (Knee).

Bass.		Treble.	
Melodia, . . .	8 ft.	Diapason, . .	8 ft.
Dolce, . . .	8 ft.	*Dulciana*, . .	8 ft.
Viola, ...	4 ft.	Vox Jubilante, .	8 ft.
Bass Coupler,		Treble Coupler,	
I Forte,		II Forte,	

Vox Humana.

Style N 78.

CODE:
Girondist (Walnut).
Omnipotent (Oak).
13 Stops.

Three six-octave sets of Reeds, with one octave of Manual Sub-Bass Reeds and Octave Coupler.

Knee Swell and Grand Organ (Knee).

Bass.		Treble.	
Melodia, . . .	8 ft.	Diapason, . .	8 ft.
Dolce, . . .	8 ft.	*Dulciana*, . .	8 ft.
Viola, ...	4 ft.	Flute, . . .	4 ft.
Violetta (soft), .	4 ft.	Vox Jubilante, .	8 ft.
Sub-Bass, . .	16 ft.	Octave Coupler,	
I Forte,		II Forte,	

Vox Humana.

Style N 79.

CODE:
Gladdened (Walnut).
Operatic (Oak).
14 Stops.

Four six-octave sets of Reeds, with one octave of Manual Sub-Bass Reeds and Octave Coupler.

Knee Swell and Grand Organ (Knee).

Bass.		Treble.	
Melodia, . . .	8 ft.	Diapason, . .	8 ft.
Dolce, . . .	8 ft.	*Dulciana*, . .	8 ft.
Viola, ...	4 ft.	Flute, . . .	4 ft.
Harp Æolienne,	2 ft.	Vox Jubilante, .	8 ft.
Sub-Bass, . .	16 ft.	Bourdon, . .	16 ft.
Vox Humana,		Octave Coupler,	
I Forte.		II Forte.	

Style of Case shown on opposite page.

Style N
Case

Height, 6 feet 4 inches. Length, 3 feet 9 inches. Depth, 1 foot 11 inches. Weight (boxed), 380 pounds.

Always specify whether Walnut or Quartered Oak Case is desired.

For description of Interiors see opposite page.

Style FF Case. Five-Octave Styles.

Style FF 32. Two five-octave sets of Reeds with Divided Couplers.

CODE:
Garland (Walnut).
Obviously (Oak).
11 Stops.

Knee Swell and Grand Organ (Knee).

Bass.		Treble.	
Melodia, . . .	8 ft.	Diapason, . . .	8 ft.
Dolce, ...	8 ft.	*Dulciana*, . . .	8 ft.
Viola, ...	4 ft.	Vox Jubilante, .	8 ft.
Bass Coupler,		Treble Coupler,	
I Forte,		II Forte,	
Vox Humana.			

Style FF 38. Three five-octave sets of Reeds, with one octave of Manual Sub-Bass Reeds and Octave Coupler.

CODE:
Gifted (Walnut).
Obtruding (Oak).
13 Stops.

Knee Swell and Grand Organ (Knee).

Bass.		Treble.	
Melodia, . . .	8 ft.	Diapason, . . .	8 ft.
Dolce, ...	8 ft.	*Dulciana*, . . .	8 ft.
Viola, ...	4 ft.	Flute, ...	4 ft.
Violetta (soft), .	4 ft.	Vox Jubilante, .	8 ft.
Sub-Bass, . . .	16 ft.	Octave Coupler,	
I Forte,		II Forte,	
Vox Humana.			

Style FF 47. Four five-octave sets of Reeds, with one octave of Manual Sub-Bass Reeds and Octave Coupler.

CODE:
Garter (Walnut).
Occasional (Oak).
14 Stops.

Knee Swell and Grand Organ (Knee).

Bass.		Treble.	
Melodia, . . .	8 ft.	Diapason, . . .	8 ft.
Dolce, ...	8 ft.	*Dulciana*, . . .	8 ft.
Viola, ...	4 ft.	Flute, ...	4 ft.
Harp Æolienne, .	2 ft.	Vox Jubilante, .	8 ft.
Sub-Bass, . . .	16 ft.	Bourdon, . . .	16 ft.
Vox Humana,		Octave Coupler,	
I Forte.		II Forte.	

Six-Octave Styles.

Style FF 72 Two six-octave sets of Reeds with Divided Couplers.

CODE:
Gleaming (Walnut).
Oculist (Oak).
11 Stops.

Knee Swell and Grand Organ (Knee).

Bass.		Treble.	
Melodia, . . .	8 ft.	Diapason, . . .	8 ft.
Dolce, ...	8 ft.	*Dulciana*, . . .	8 ft.
Viola, ...	4 ft.	Vox Jubilante, .	8 ft.
Bass Coupler,		Treble Coupler,	
I Forte,		II Forte,	
Vox Humana.			

Style FF 78 Three six-octave sets of Reeds with one octave of Manual Sub-Bass Reeds and Octave Coupler.

CODE:
Glibly (Walnut).
Occupancy (Oak).
13 Stops.

Knee Swell and Grand Organ (Knee).

Bass.		Treble.	
Melodia, . . .	8 ft.	Diapason, . . .	8 ft.
Dolce, ...	8 ft.	*Dulciana*, . . .	8 ft.
Viola, ...	4 ft.	Flute, ...	4 ft.
Violetta (soft), .	4 ft.	Vox Jubilante, .	8 ft.
Sub-Bass, . . .	16 ft.	Octave Coupler,	
I Forte,		II Forte,	
Vox Humana.			

Style FF 79. Four six-octave sets of Reeds, with one octave of Manual Sub-Bass Reeds and Octave Coupler.

CODE:
Glimmering (Walnut).
Occiput (Oak).
14 Stops.

Knee Swell and Grand Organ (Knee).

Bass.		Treble.	
Melodia, . . .	8 ft.	Diapason, . . .	8 ft.
Dolce, ...	8 ft.	*Dulciana*, . . .	8 ft.
Viola, ...	4 ft.	Flute, ...	4 ft.
Harp Æolienne, .	2 ft.	Vox Jubilante, .	8 ft.
Sub-Bass, . . .	16 ft.	Bourdon, . . .	16 ft.
Vox Humana,		Octave Coupler,	
I Forte.		II Forte.	

Style of Case shown on opposite page.

Style FF
Case

Height, 6 feet 4 inches. Length, 3 feet 10 inches. Depth, 1 foot 11 inches. Weight (boxed), 400 pounds.

Always mention whether Walnut or Quartered Oak Case is desired.

For description of Interiors see opposite page.

Style C Case. Five-Octave Styles.

Style C 32. Two five-octave sets of Reeds, with divided Couplers.

CODE:
Linnet (Walnut).
Literature (Oak).
11 Stops.

Knee Swell and Grand Organ (Knee).

Bass.		Treble.	
Melodia, . . .	8 ft.	Diapason, . . .	8 ft.
Dolce, ...	8 ft.	*Dulciana*, . . .	8 ft.
Viola, ...	4 ft.	Vox Jubilante, .	8 ft.
Bass Coupler,		Treble Coupler,	
I Forte,		II Forte,	

Vox Humana.

Style C 38. Three five-octave sets of Reeds with one octave of Manual Sub-Bass Reeds and Octave Coupler.

CODE:
Linstock (Walnut).
Lithocarp (Oak).
13 Stops.

Knee Swell and Grand Organ (Knee).

Bass.		Treble.	
Melodia, . . .	8 ft.	Diapason, . . .	8 ft.
Dolce, ...	8 ft.	*Dulciana*, . . .	8 ft.
Viola, ...	4 ft.	Flute, ...	4 ft.
Violetta (soft), .	4 ft.	Vox Jubilante, .	8 ft.
Sub-Bass, . . .	16 ft.	Octave Coupler,	
I Forte,		II Forte,	

Vox Humana.

Style C 47. Four five-octave sets of Reeds, with one octave of Manual Sub-Bass Reeds and Octave Coupler.

CODE:
Liquefied (Walnut).
Lithology (Oak).
14 Stops.

Knee Swell and Grand Organ (Knee).

Bass.		Treble.	
Melodia, . . .	8 ft.	Diapason, . . .	8 ft.
Dolce, ...	8 ft.	*Dulciana*, . . .	8 ft.
Viola, ...	4 ft.	Flute, ...	4 ft.
Harp Æolienne, .	2 ft.	Vox Jubilante, .	8 ft.
Sub-Bass, . . .	16 ft.	Bourdon, . . .	16 ft.
Vox Humana,		Octave Coupler,	
I Forte.		II Forte.	

Six-Octave Styles.

Style C 72. Two six-octave sets of Reeds with Divided Couplers.

CODE:
Lirocone (Walnut).
Locations (Oak).
11 Stops.

Knee Swell and Grand Organ (Knee).

Bass.		Treble.	
Melodia, . . .	8 ft.	Diapason, . . .	8 ft.
Dolce, ...	8 ft.	*Dulciana*, . . .	8 ft.
Viola, ...	4 ft.	Vox Jubilante, .	8 ft.
Bass Coupler,		Treble Coupler,	
I Forte,		II Forte,	

Vox Humana.

Style C 78. Three six-octave sets of Reeds with one octave of Manual Sub-Bass Reeds and Octave Coupler.

CODE:
Listening (Walnut).
Loadstone (Oak).
13 Stops.

Knee Swell and Grand Organ (Knee).

Bass.		Treble.	
Melodia, . . .	8 ft.	Diapason, . . .	8 ft.
Dolce, ...	8 ft.	*Dulciana*, . . .	8 ft.
Viola, ...	4 ft.	Flute, ...	4 ft.
Violetta (soft), .	4 ft.	Vox Jubilante, .	8 ft.
Sub-Bass, . . .	16 ft.	Octave Coupler,	
I Forte,		II Forte,	

Vox Humana.

Style C 79. Four six-octave sets of Reeds with one octave of Manual Sub-Bass Reeds and Octave Coupler.

CODE:
Liquidate (Walnut).
Locality (Oak).
14 Stops.

Knee Swell and Grand Organ (Knee).

Bass.		Treble.	
Melodia, . . .	8 ft.	Diapason, . . .	8 ft.
Dolce, ...	8 ft.	*Dulciana*, . . .	8 ft.
Viola, ...	4 ft.	Flute, ...	4 ft.
Harp Æolienne, .	2 ft.	Vox Jubilante, .	8 ft.
Sub-Bass, . .	16 ft.	Bourdon, . . .	16 ft.
Vox Humana,		Octave Coupler,	
I Forte.		II Forte.	

Style of Case shown on opposite page.

Style C
Case

Height, 6 feet 8 inches. Depth, 1 foot 10 inches. Length, 3 feet 9 inches. Weight (boxed), 390 pounds.

Always mention whether Walnut or Oak Case is desired.

For description of Interiors see opposite page.

Style S Case. Five-Octave Styles.

Style S 32. Two five-octave sets of Reeds with Divided Couplers.

CODE:
Flames (Walnut).
Obeying (Oak).
11 Stops.

Knee Swell and Grand Organ (Knee).

Bass.		Treble.	
Melodia, . . .	8 ft.	Diapason, . . .	8 ft.
Dolce, ...	8 ft.	*Dulciana*, . . .	8 ft.
Viola, ...	4 ft.	Vox Jubilante, .	8 ft.
Bass Coupler,		Treble Coupler,	
I Forte,		II Forte,	
	Vox Humana.		

Style S 38. Three five-octave sets of Reeds, with one octave of Manual Sub-Bass Reeds and Octave Coupler.

CODE:
Flannel (Walnut).
Oblation (Oak).
13 Stops.

Knee Swell and Grand Organ (Knee).

Bass.		Treble.	
Melodia, . . .	8 ft.	Diapason, . . .	8 ft.
Dolce, ...	8 ft.	*Dulciana*, . . .	8 ft.
Viola, ...	4 ft.	Flute, ...	4 ft.
Violetta (soft), .	4 ft.	Vox Jubilante, .	8 ft.
Sub-Bass, . . .	16 ft.	Octave Coupler,	
I Forte,		II Forte,	
	Vox Humana.		

Style S 47. Four five-octave sets of Reeds, with one octave of Manual Sub-Bass Reeds and Octave Coupler.

CODE:
Flatterers (Walnut).
Obliged (Oak).
14 Stops.

Knee Swell and Grand Organ (Knee).

Bass.		Treble.	
Melodia, . . .	8 ft.	Diapason, . . .	8 ft.
Dolce, ...	8 ft.	*Dulciana*, . . .	8 ft.
Viola, ...	4 ft.	Flute, ...	4 ft.
Harp Æolienne, .	2 ft.	Vox Jubilante, .	8 ft.
Sub-Bass, . . .	16 ft.	Bourdon, . . .	16 ft.
Vox Humana,		Octave Coupler,	
I Forte.		II Forte.	

Six-Octave Styles.

Style S 72. Two six-octave sets of Reeds, with Divided Couplers.

CODE:
Fleecy (Walnut).
Obliging (Oak).
11 Stops.

Knee Swell and Grand Organ (Knee).

Bass.		Treble.	
Melodia, . . .	8 ft.	Diapason, . . .	8 ft.
Dolce, ...	8 ft.	*Dulciana*, . . .	8 ft.
Viola, ...	4 ft.	Vox Jubilante, .	8 ft.
Bass Coupler,		Treble Coupler,	
I Forte,		II Forte,	
	Vox Humana.		

Style S 78. Three six-octave sets of Reeds, with one octave of Manual Sub-Bass Reeds and Octave Coupler.

CODE:
Fleeted (Walnut).
Obliterate (Oak).
13 Stops.

Knee Swell and Grand Organ (Knee).

Bass.		Treble.	
Melodia, . . .	8 ft.	Diapason, . . .	8 ft.
Dolce, ...	8 ft.	*Dulciana*, . . .	8 ft.
Viola, ...	4 ft.	Flute, ...	4 ft.
Violetta (soft), .	4 ft.	Vox Jubilante, .	8 ft.
Sub-Bass, . . .	16 ft.	Octave Coupler,	
I Forte,		II Forte,	
	Vox Humana.		

Style S 79. Four six-octave sets of Reeds, with one octave of Manual Sub-Bass Reeds and Octave Coupler.

CODE:
Flemings (Walnut).
Oblong (Oak).
14 Stops.

Knee Swell and Grand Organ (Knee).

Bass.		Treble.	
Melodia, . . .	8 ft.	Diapason, . . .	8 ft.
Dolce, ...	8 ft.	*Dulciana*, . . .	8 ft.
Viola, ...	4 ft.	Flute, ...	4 ft.
Harp Æolienne, .	2 ft.	Vox Jubilante, .	8 ft.
Sub-Bass, . . .	16 ft.	Bourdon, . . .	16 ft.
Vox Humana,		Octave Coupler,	
I Forte.		II Forte.	

Style of Case shown on opposite page.

Style S
Case

Height, 6 feet 8 inches. Length, 3 feet 10 inches. Depth, 1 foot 11 inches. Weight (boxed), 400 pounds.

Always mention whether Walnut or Oak Case is desired.

For description of Interiors see opposite page.

Style X Case

Height, 4 feet 6 inches. Length, 5 feet. Depth, 2 feet 2 inches. Weight (boxed), 400 pounds.

Style X 74. Seven and one-third Octaves Compass.

CODE:
Florid (Walnut).
Obelisk (Oak).
Macaroni (Mahogany).

Two full *seven and one-third* octave sets of Reeds with Divided Couplers.

The foundation Reeds—Diapason and Melodia—are in "open-register," so called, and the Vox Jubilante and Viola Reeds with the Treble Coupler and Bass Coupler are drawn by the Grand Organ Knee Lever, successively or simultaneously at the will of the player.

This organ can be furnished either in Black Walnut, Quartered Oak or with Mahogany finish.

Style G Case

Height, 9 feet 10 inches. Depth, 3 feet; with Pedals in position, 4 feet 6 inches. Length, 7 feet 7 inches; with Blow Lever, 8 feet 9 inches. Weight (boxed), 1800 pounds.

Style G 59. Always includes the Pipe Top.

CODE: Heroism. Furnished with Blow Lever. Furnished in specially selected Quartered Oak Casing.

The contents or interior is of exactly the same character and capacity as Style K 59

Style 301
Case

Length, 3 feet 10 inches. Height, 4 feet 1 inch. Depth, 1 foot 9 inches. Weight (boxed), 290 pounds.

Style 301.

CODE:
Gladly (Walnut).
Hellenic (Oak).
11 Stops.

SCHOOL ORGAN.

CONTENTS.

Two full sets of Reeds of five octaves each, with Treble and Bass Couplers, Knee Swell, Grand Organ, Tremolo, etc.

RECAPITULATION.

Bass.	Treble.
Melodia,	Diapason,
Dolce,	*Dulciana,*
Viola,	Vox Jubilante,
Bass Coupler,	Treble Coupler,
I Forte,	II Forte,

Vox Humana.

Always specify whether Oak or Walnut Case is wanted.

Case—Quartered Oak or Black Walnut.

Action—Excellent working; best material.

Bellows—Special construction; ample wind capacity.

Reeds—*Estey*, the best in the world.

Style R
Case

Length, 3 feet 10 inches. Height, 4 feet 4 inches. Depth, 1 foot 11 inches. Weight (boxed), 340 pounds.

Style R 32.

CODE:
Livery (Walnut).
Hellespont (Oak).
11 Stops.

Bass.		Treble.	
Melodia,	8 ft.	Diapason,	8 ft.
Dolce,	8 ft.	*Dulciana,*	8 ft.
Viola,	4 ft.	Vox Jubilante,	8 ft.
Bass Coupler,		Treble Coupler,	
I Forte,		II Forte,	
	Vox Humana.		

Two sets of Reeds, with Divided Couplers. Eleven Stops. Knee Swell and Grand Organ (Knee).

Style R 38.

CODE:
Logical (Walnut).
Helmets (Oak).
13 Stops.

Bass.		Treble.	
Melodia,	8 ft.	Diapason,	8 ft.
Dolce,	8 ft.	*Dulciana,*	8 ft.
Viola,	4 ft.	Flute,	4 ft.
Violetta (soft),	4 ft.	Vox Jubilante,	8 ft.
Sub-Bass,	16 ft.	Octave Coupler,	
I Forte,		II Forte,	
	Vox Humana.		

Three sets of Reeds, with Sub-Bass and Octave Coupler. Knee Swell and Grand Organ (Knee).

Six-octave organ of this design furnished with either action, when specially ordered.

Always specify whether Oak or Walnut Case is wanted.

Style H Case.

Style H 33. Two five-octave sets of Reeds with Octave Coupler and one octave of Sub-Bass Reeds.

CODE:
Farming (Walnut).
Henceforth (Oak).
11 Stops.

Knee Swell and Grand Organ (Knee).

Bass.		Treble.	
Melodia, . . .	8 ft.	Diapason, . . .	8 ft.
Dolce, ...	8 ft.	*Dulciana*, . . .	8 ft.
Viola, ...	4 ft.	Vox Jubilante, .	8 ft.
Sub-Bass, . . .	16 ft.	Vox Humana,	
I Forte,		II Forte,	
Octave Coupler.			

Style H 38. Three five-octave sets of Reeds with one octave of Manual Sub-Bass Reeds and Octave Coupler.

CODE:
Fantasia (Walnut).
Henchmen (Oak).
13 Stops.

Knee Swell and Grand Organ (Knee).

Bass.		Treble.	
Melodia, . . .	8 ft.	Diapason, . . .	8 ft.
Dolce, ...	8 ft.	*Dulciana*, . . .	8 ft.
Viola, ...	4 ft.	Flute, ...	4 ft.
Violetta (soft), .	4 ft.	Vox Jubilante, .	8 ft.
Sub-Bass, . . .	16 ft.	Octave Coupler,	
I Forte,		II Forte,	
Vox Humana.			

Style H 97. Four five-octave sets of Reeds, with one octave of Manual Sub-Bass Reeds and Divided Couplers. 257 Reeds.

CODE:
Fashion (Walnut).
Heraldic (Oak).
16 Stops.

Knee Swell and Grand Organ (Knee).

Bass.		Treble.	
Melodia, . . .	8 ft.	Diapason, . . .	8 ft.
Dolce, ...	8 ft.	*Dulciana*, . . .	8 ft.
Viola, ...	4 ft.	Flute, ...	4 ft.
Viola Dolce, . .	4 ft.	Vox Jubilante, .	8 ft.
Harp Æolienne, .	2 ft.	Choral, ...	8 ft.
Sub-Bass, . . .	16 ft.	Vox Humana,	
Melodia Forte,		Flute Forte,	
Bass Coupler.		Treble Coupler.	

The interiors indicated above are those most in demand for an organ of this size. Others may be added from time to time, but the three given cover the ground very thoroughly. If more capacity in reed-power is desired, it is advisable to introduce larger casings and bellows capacity.

The use of Philharmonic Reeds in this series of organs greatly increases their volume of tone.

Although the numbers given to the interiors (33, 38, etc.) are the same as used elsewhere in the catalogue, the reed boards are made upon a different scale entirely, and the tone-effects are far in the lead, owing to the construction of the reeds and their consequent surroundings.

Style of Case shown on opposite page.

The organ pictured on page 96 is what is known as a "piano-cased" organ. Since pianos were more expensive to build than reed organs, perhaps many buyers bought these styles in an attempt to enhance the prestige of their homes, yet still retain the musical beauty inherent in the organ's characteristic sounds.

Style H Case

Height, 4 feet 4½ inches. Depth, 2 feet 2 inches. Length, 4 feet 3 inches. Weight (boxed), 400 pounds.

Always specify whether Oak or Walnut Case is wanted.

For Description of Interiors see opposite page.

Style K
Case

Height, 5 feet 8 inches; with Pipe Top, 9 feet 8 inches. Depth, 2 feet 8 inches (with Pedals, 4 feet 2 inches). Length, 5 feet 9 inches; with Blow Lever, 6 feet 11 inches. Weight (boxed), 1125 pounds; Pipe Top adds 340 pounds.

Style K 59.

Without Pipe Top.
CODE:
Glycerine (Walnut).
Hereditary (Oak).

With Pipe Top.
CODE:
Guardian (Walnut).
Hermit (Oak).

A very attractive Pipe Top can be furnished, when desired, at a moderate advance in cost.

Furnished in Black Walnut or Quartered Oak casing.

For description of Interiors see opposite page.

Style K 59.

Philharmonic.

Two Manuals and Pedals. **Fifteen Stops.** **Ten Sets of Reeds.**

SPECIFICATIONS.

Manuals.

Five Octaves, CC to C^4, 61 notes.

Pedals.

Two and one-half Octaves, CCC to F, 30 notes.

Great Manual.

Clarionet,	16 ft., 61 notes.
Diapason,	8 ft., 61 notes.
Trumpet,	8 ft., 61 notes.
Salicional,	8 ft., 61 notes.

Swell Manual.

Bourdon,	16 ft., 37 notes.
Oboe,	8 ft., 61 notes.
Dulciana,	8 ft., 61 notes.
Flute,	4 ft., 61 notes.

Pedal Organ.

Open Diapason,	16 ft., 30 notes.
Stopped Diapason,	16 ft., 30 notes.

Total, 524 Reeds.

Couplers.

Swell to Great.
Octave Coupler (Great).
Great to Pedals.
Swell to Pedals.

Accessories.

Vox Humana. Wind Indicator. Organist's Bench. Hand Side Blower.

Pedal Movements.

Full Organ. Balanced Swell.

This organ is in touch with the latest developments in reed organ building, and is appropriate for churches or other public places.

The registers are complete in themselves and not divided as in single manual organs.

The pedal registers are of the full two and one-half octave scale, the same as the modern Pipe Organ.

It is furnished with the large scale Philharmonic Reeds, which approximate in quality of tone the Pipe Organ.

Style T Case

Height, 5 feet; with Pipe Top, 8 feet 10 inches. Length, 5 feet 2 inches; with Blow Handle, 6 feet 4 inches. Depth, 2 feet 7 inches; with Pedals, 4 feet 2 inches. Weight (boxed), 780 pounds; Pipe Top adds 280 pounds.

Always specify whether Walnut or Oak Case is desired.

For description of Interiors see opposite page.

Style T 58.

Two Manuals and Pedals. 15 Stops. 487 Reeds.

Without Pipe Top.
CODE:
Forerunner (Walnut).
Herbarium (Oak).

With Pipe Top.
CODE:
Foreseeing (Walnut).
Herculean (Oak).

SPECIFICATION.

Manuals.

Five Octaves, CC to C^4, 61 notes.

Pedals.

Two and one-half Octaves, CCC to F, 30 notes.

Great Manual.

Bourdon, ... 16 ft., 61 notes.
Clarionet, ... 16 ft., 37 notes.
Diapason, ... 8 ft., 61 notes.
Trumpet, ... 8 ft., 61 notes.

Swell Manual.

Dulciana, ... 8 ft., 61 notes.
Vox Jubilante, ... 8 ft., 37 notes.
Flute, ... 4 ft., 61 notes.
Harp Æolienne (two ranks), . . . 2 ft., 24 notes.

Pedal Organ.

Open Diapason, ... 16 ft., 30 notes.
Stopped Diapason, ... 16 ft., 30 notes.

Couplers.

Swell to Great.
Octave Coupler (Great).
Swell to Pedals.
Great to Pedals.

Accessories.

Vox Humana. Wind Indicator. Organist's Bench. Hand Side Blower.

Pedal Movements.

Full Organ. Balanced Swell.

This organ is designed for use in small churches, and s well adapted also to Lodge Rooms. As in Pipe Organs the registers or sets of reeds run throughout the keyboard instead of dividing as in the one-manual organs.

The design on the opposite page represents the Organ with Pipe Top, which adds moderately to the cost. By covering the Top the effect without it can be readily observed.

Style V Case

Length, 4 feet 11 inches; with Blow Handle, 6 feet 1 inch. Height, 4 feet 6 inches; with Pipe Top, 8 feet 4 inches. Depth, 2 feet 4 inches. Weight (boxed), 540 pounds; Pipe Top, 265 pounds additional.

Furnished either with or without the Pipe Top. In either case it is complete, as the Pipe Top is for appearance simply. For church use it certainly adds much to its impressiveness, and at the moderate advance in cost is often selected.

Always specify whether Oak or Walnut Case is wanted.

For description of Interiors see opposite page.

Style V Case.

Style V 57. 318 Reeds.

CODE:
Goodness (Walnut).
Happening (Oak).

Bass.		Treble.		Mechanical.	
Bourdon, ...	16 ft.	Bassett, ...	16 ft.	Bass Coupler,	Treble Coupler,
Melodia, ...	8 ft.	Diapason, . . .	8 ft.	Vox Humana,	Hand Side Blower,
Dolce, ...	8 ft.	*Dulciana*, . . .	8 ft.	I Forte,	II Forte,
Viola, ...	4 ft.	Flute, ...	4 ft.	Grand Organ,	Knee Swell,
Viol d'Amour, .	4 ft.	*Flute d'Amour*, .	4 ft.	Organist's Bench.	
Harp Æolienne, .	2 ft.	Choral, ...	8 ft.		
Sub-Bass, . .	16 ft.	Regal, ...	8 ft.		
		Vox Jubilante, .	8 ft.		

Style V 65. 392 Reeds.

CODE:
Gorgeous (Walnut).
Happily (Oak).

Bass.		Treble.		Mechanical.	
Bourdon, ...	16 ft.	Clarionet, . . .	16 ft.	Bass Coupler,	Treble Coupler,
Sub-Bass, . . .	16 ft.	Bassett, ...	16 ft.	Vox Humana,	Hand Side Blower,
Melodia, ...	8 ft.	Diapason, . . .	8 ft.	I Forte,	II Forte,
Dolce, ...	8 ft.	*Dulciana*, . . .	8 ft.	Grand Organ,	Knee Swell,
		Choral, ...	8 ft.	Organist's Bench.	
		Regal, ...	8 ft.		
		Vox Jubilante, .	8 ft.		
Viola, ...	4 ft.	Flute, ...	4 ft.		
Viol d'Amour, .	4 ft.	*Flute d'Amour*, .	4 ft.		
Harp Æolienne, .	2 ft.	Wald Flute, . .	2 ft.		

Into these organs are introduced the *special scale* Philharmonic Reeds. The reeds are not made like the ordinary organ reeds, but have wide tongues or vibrators which are mounted upon extra wide and extra heavy brass plates; the case also is made much longer than the regular organs, to receive the extended reed-board. The general effect of this aggregation of heavy-toned reeds is phenomenal.

Style of Case shown on opposite page.

Style L
Case

Length, 4 feet; with Blow Handle, 5 feet 2 inches. Height, 4 feet 3 inches. Depth, 2 feet 3 inches. Weight (boxed), 475 pounds.

Style L 97. 257 Reeds.

CODE:
Gracefully (Walnut).
Opposition (Oak).
16 Stops.

Bass.		Treble.	
Melodia,	8 ft.	Diapason,	8 ft.
Dolce,	8 ft.	*Dulciana,*	8 ft.
Viola,	4 ft.	Flute,	4 ft.
Viola Dolce,	4 ft.	Vox Jubilante,	8 ft.
Harp Æolienne,	2 ft.	Choral,	8 ft.
Sub-Bass,	16 ft.	Vox Humana,	
Melodia Forte,		Flute Forte,	
Bass Coupler.		Treble Coupler.	

Grand Organ (Knee) and Knee Swell.

This organ is furnished with Hand Side Blower, **Philharmonic Reeds,** Organist's Bench.

Pipe Top of excellent design can be had, when desired, at a reasonable advance in price.

Always specify whether Oak or Walnut Case is wanted.

Style O
Case

Length, 4 feet 6 inches. Height, 4 feet 1 inch. Depth, 2 feet 4 inches. Weight (boxed), 520 pounds.

Style O 94. C Scale.

CODE:
Diviner (Walnut).
Divulsions (Oak).
15 Stops.

SPECIFICATIONS.

Bass.		Treble.	
Corno,	16 feet, 24 notes.	Corno,	16 feet, 37 notes.
Trumpet,	8 feet, 24 notes.	Trumpet,	8 feet, 37 notes.
Diapason,	8 feet, 24 notes.	Diapason,	8 feet, 37 notes.
		Vox Jubilante,	8 feet, 37 notes.
Flute,	4 feet, 24 notes.	Flute,	4 feet, 37 notes.
Harp Æolienne (two sets),	2 feet, 24 notes.		
Sub-Bass,	16 feet, 13 notes.		

II Forte. Vox Humana. I Forte.

Bass Coupler. Treble Coupler.

The latest in Chapel Styles and immensely popular.

Large Philharmonic scale reeds, ample bellows, additional blow lever. Bound to be a leader!

ESTEY DUO-MANUAL ORGANS

It is a well-known fact that a splendid reed organ is far preferable to a cheap or very small pipe organ. For many years we have made a specialty of building the finest types of these instruments, putting into them the same careful, painstaking workmanship and the same high grade of materials that go into our finest pipe organs.

Hundreds have been installed in churches, lodges and fine residences. The number of Estey Duo-Manual Organs in use probably exceeds all other makes combined.

While containing many sets of reeds, the construction is simple, and every precaution is taken to avoid the necessity for frequent regulation found so often in other two-manual organs. Estey Duo-Manuals require practically no attention beyond occasional lubrication of the bellows shaft cranks.

The swell section is contained in an inverted chest directly above the swell keyboard, and wind is conducted by trunks at both ends of the action. Each swell key, operating its own valve, admits air to the reeds in the swell sets in the same manner that the great keys admit air to the reeds in the great organ. The construction is really two separate organs, eliminating the delicate and complicated levers formerly used.

Above this chest is the pedal section, operated by rods and fingers which pass from the pedal keyboard underneath the bellows and up the back of the case to the pedal reeds.

Any reed in the organ may be easily removed. The same is true of the valves in each section, should dust or some other foreign substance get into the organ and hold a valve open. All Duo-Manual Organs are furnished with a bellows composed of four lifters, or movable sections, operated by a shaft and rotary blowing handle. Where the organ is to be blown by the Orgoblo this handle may be removed. The Orgoblo, an electrically driven fan blower designed especially for Estey Organs, is described on page 14.

There is no place where an organ meets with such lack of care and such exposure to extremes as in the majority of churches. At the conclusion of the service the windows are closed and the church locked. During the week it remains unventilated, damp with condensation from the breath of many people, unprotected from sudden variations in temperature and humidity. Often a church organ is thought to be out of order when the only treatment needed is fresh air and possibly a little artificial heat.

In proof of this we can cite the case of a two-manual organ in a Maryland church several years ago. It had been exposed to unusual dampness, water standing constantly in the cellar directly under the instrument. We were condemned for faulty material and construction. At our suggestion the organ was returned to the factory. When it reached us, after a trip of about ten days in the hot summer weather, it was found to be in perfect playing condition. The thorough drying out that it got in shipment was all it needed.

We issue a booklet on "Care and Adjustment of Estey Two-Manual Organs and Suggestions as to the Use of Stops" which covers these questions thoroughly. We shall be glad to mail a copy on request.

Grand organ pedal on Models T, G and E is now placed at right of balanced swell pedal instead of at left as shown on illustrations. Studio Model now has Grand organ pedal placed at right of swell and great pedals.

All oak cases may be finished in any other shade than golden, also in walnut or mahogany finish, at an advanced price of course. Allow five weeks for delivery.

The Studio Model is not recommended for use in churches or other public places where volume is required. To meet that demand use Models T or G.

The weights given in catalog are based on the use of heavy boxes for foreign shipments. A lighter box is used on domestic shipments, thus reducing the weight.

A BRIEF DESCRIPTION OF THE STOPS AND THEIR PITCH IN USE IN DUO-MANUAL ESTEY ORGANS

MANUAL STOPS

NAME	PITCH	CHARACTERISTICS	NAME	PITCH	CHARACTERISTICS
Bourdon	16 ft.	Full and round	Melodia	8 ft.	Voiced to give a soft Wood Flute tone. In strength less than Diapason
Clarinet	16 ft.	Resembles the Clarinet			
Diapason	8 ft.	Foundation set of reeds by which others are tuned. Used more generally than any other stop. Round, full tone	Oboe	8 ft.	Reed tone, closely reproducing the orchestral instrument of same name
Dulciana	8 ft.	Voiced soft. Combination of Flute and string tone	Salicional	8 ft.	Delicate, soft tone, similar to Dulciana, but voiced with more string tone than Dulciana
Flute	4 ft.	Brilliant, but not reedy. Generally used in combination	Trumpet	8 ft.	Very strong, open tone
Vox Celeste	8 ft.	Closely resembles the tone of an Æolian Harp. Made with two reeds for each note. Equally satisfactory in playing harmony or used as accompaniment	Violetta	4 ft.	Similar in character to Flute, but voiced with less strength

PEDAL STOPS

NAME	PITCH	CHARACTERISTICS	NAME	PITCH	CHARACTERISTICS
Pedal Bourdon	16 ft.	Round, full tone. Sufficient for full organ	Pedal Dulciana	16 ft.	Voiced soft to give just the suggestion of pedal set. Soft enough to use with softest set on either manual

MECHANICAL STOPS

NAME	USES	NAME	USES
Balanced Swell	Pedal to open all swells or shutters. Will remain at any given point if desirable to release the foot	Swell to Great	Connecting the manuals so that when a key on the great manual is depressed it also depresses the corresponding key of the swell manual
"Grand" or Full Organ	Brings into use all the sets of reeds in the organ without the necessity of drawing a stop	Swell to Pedals Great to Pedals	So connecting the manuals that when the pedal is depressed its corresponding key in the manual is depressed and also responds
Octave Coupler	So constructed that when any key is depressed its octave above or below is also depressed, causing both to sound simultaneously	Tremolo	A revolving fan, placed just back of the reeds, which imparts to the tone a thrilling wave-like effect

STYLES G and T

for Special Locations

These organs, shown on the following four pages, represent the most modern development in the art of reed organ manufacture.

Styles T, G and E are equipped with large scale Philharmonic Reeds, found only in Estey Organs. The registers are not divided as in many single-manual instruments, but each is complete in itself. The pedal registers are full two and one-half octave scale, exactly as in the modern pipe organ.

The pipe tops are purely ornamental and have no musical value. Style T may be supplied with or without top as desired. Style G is always furnished with top, part of this space being used to contain the chest of large pedal reeds. In both styles, however, the height of tops may be reduced to meet space requirements, or increased by the use of additional paneling. We shall be glad to advise on any problem of this sort.

Pedals for foot blowing may be added at an extra cost, but are not recommended. They will operate only two of the four lifters on the bellows, and hence give a limited wind supply. A hand blower lever is furnished, which may be removed if the organ is to be blown by machine.

The Orgoblo, an electrically driven fan blower made expressly for Estey Organs, may be used where the blower can be installed in a basement or adjoining room. The Orgoblo is described on page 14.

THE ESTEY BLOWING MACHINE

may be installed on the floor beside the organ and is especially desirable for apartments or other places where it is not possible or convenient to cut walls or floors to install wind trunking, etc., as is necessary with fan blowers. It may be used with any Estey organ having a 4 lifter type of bellows with extending bellows shaft. Booklet giving full description mailed on request.

STYLE T

Code Name—Lactescent   With Pipe Top—Lacustrine

Furnished without pipe top unless otherwise ordered, in oak only. The standard finish is Dark Golden Oak, and other shades of oak to order at slightly advanced price. Rotary blow handle supplied, or arranged for electric blowing machine.

Action—61-15 stops. 10 sets of reeds
Manuals—Five octaves, CC to C4, 61 notes
Pedals—Concave radiating, two and one-half octaves, CCC to F, 30 notes

GREAT MANUAL		SWELL MANUAL	
Clarinet . . .	16 ft., 61 notes	Oboe	8 ft., 61 notes
Diapason . . .	8 ft., 61 notes	Salicional . .	8 ft., 61 notes
Dulciana . . .	8 ft., 61 notes	Flute	4 ft., 61 notes
Trumpet . . .	8 ft., 61 notes	Vox Celeste (2 ranks)	8 ft., 61 notes

PEDAL ORGAN

Pedal Bourdon . 16 ft., 30 notes   Pedal Dulciana . 16 ft., 30 notes

Total 548 reeds

COUPLERS

Swell to Great   Great to Pedals
Octave Coupler (Great)   Swell to Pedals

PEDAL MOVEMENTS

Full Organ   Balanced Swell

ACCESSORIES

Tremolo   Wind Indicator   Organist's Bench

Length—5 feet 7 inches; with blow handle, 6 feet 2 inches
Height—5 feet; with pipe top, 9 feet 7 inches
Depth—2 feet 7 inches; with pedals, 4 feet 3 inches
Weight—boxed, 940 pounds; pipe top adds 340 pounds
Case—106 cubic feet. Top, 57 cubic feet

STYLE T

STYLE G

Code Name—Halcyon

Furnished with pipe top only. Standard finish is Dark Golden Oak; other shades, of oak only, to order at slightly advanced price. Rotary blow handle furnished, or arranged for electric blowing machine.

Action—61-15 stops. 10 sets of reeds

Manuals—Five octaves, CC to C4, 61 notes

Pedals—Concave radiating, two and one-half octaves, CCC to F, 30 notes

GREAT MANUAL		SWELL MANUAL	
Clarinet . . .	16 ft., 61 notes	Oboe	8 ft., 61 notes
Diapason . . .	8 ft., 61 notes	Salicional . .	8 ft., 61 notes
Dulciana . . .	8 ft., 61 notes	Flute	4 ft., 61 notes
Trumpet . . .	8 ft., 61 notes	Vox Celeste (2 ranks)	8 ft., 61 notes

PEDAL ORGAN

Pedal Bourdon . 16 ft., 30 notes   Pedal Dulciana . 16 ft., 30 notes

Total 548 reeds

COUPLERS

Swell to Great   Great to Pedals
Octave Coupler (Great)   Swell to Pedals

PEDAL MOVEMENTS

Full Organ   Balanced Swell

ACCESSORIES

Tremolo   Wind Indicator   Organist's Bench

Length—6 feet 8 inches; with blow handle, 7 feet 3 inches
Height—9 feet 10 inches
Depth—3 feet; with pedals in position, 4 feet 6 inches
Weight—boxed, 1025 pounds; top adds 525 pounds
Case—130 cubic feet; top, 98 cubic feet

STYLE G

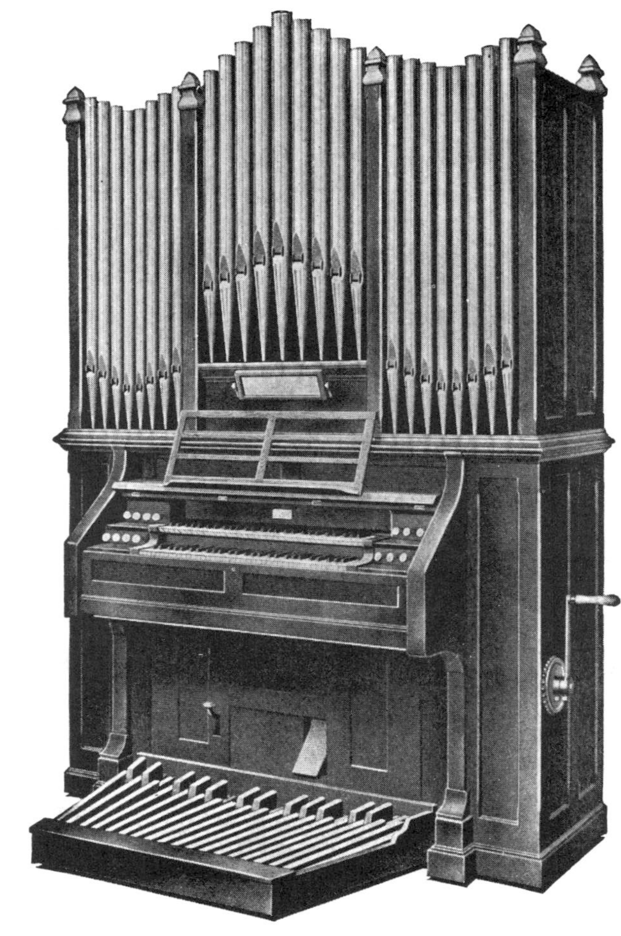

STYLE E

STYLE E

CODE NAME—Lipogram

This organ, although designed especially for students' practice, is well adapted to a small chapel or church and many have been installed for this purpose. The reeds are of large scale and the positions of pedals, stops, etc., are the same as in modern pipe organs. All necessary accessories are supplied for the convenience of the player.

The case is finished only in oak. The standard is Dark Golden Oak, but other shades may be ordered at a slightly advanced price. A rotary blow handle is supplied. Pedals for foot blowing may be added at an extra cost, or the organ may be arranged for electric blowing machine.

ACTION—54-11 stops. 6 sets of reeds
MANUALS—Five octaves, CC to C4, 61 notes
PEDALS—Concave radiating, two and one-half octaves, CCC to F, 30 notes

GREAT MANUAL		SWELL MANUAL	
Bourdon . . .	16 ft., 61 notes	Dulciana . . .	8 ft., 61 notes
Diapason . . .	8 ft., 61 notes	Flute	4 ft., 61 notes

PEDAL ORGAN

Pedal Bourdon . 16 ft., 30 notes   Pedal Dulciana* . 16 ft., 30 notes

COUPLERS

Swell to Great   Swell to Pedals
Octave Coupler   Great to Pedals

PEDAL MOVEMENTS

Full Organ   Balanced Swell

ACCESSORIES

Tremolo   Wind Indicator   Organist's Bench

Length—5 feet 2 inches; with blow handle, 5 feet 9 inches
Height—4 feet 4 inches
Depth—2 feet 8 inches; with pedals attached, 4 feet 2 inches
Weight—boxed, 790 pounds. Case, 85 cubic feet

* Not a separate set of reeds, but made by placing a shutter over the Pedal Diapason set.

STUDIO ORGAN

CODE NAME—Lateral

The design of this organ marks a new departure in reed organ consoles. There is neither action nor wind chest under the keyboard. These are built in the body of the instrument back of the keys, as in a pipe organ, thus affording the player free movement of the limbs. Not recommended for a church.

The voicing of the reeds is of the same fine quality as in all Estey Organs. The arrangement of stops given in the specification which follows we consider an ideal one, giving the greatest possible variety in solo stops as well as in stops that may be used for accompaniment. However, sets of different character or pitch can be substituted or the proportionate strength of the sets altered to please the individual taste.

The couplers, being mechanical, cannot be increased without adding weight to the touch and this is therefore not advised. Ample wind supply is provided by large size bellows, with four lifters and blow handle, and the organ may also be equipped with an electric blowing machine.

Stock finishes are dark mahogany or dark brown oak. Other finishes may be furnished on order.

ACTION—15 stops. 10 sets of reeds
MANUALS—Five octaves, CC to C4, 61 notes
PEDALS—Concave radiating, two and one-half octaves, CCC to F, 30 notes

GREAT MANUAL		SWELL MANUAL	
Diapason . . .	8 ft., 61 notes	Salicional . .	8 ft., 61 notes
Dulciana . . .	8 ft., 61 notes	Melodia . . .	8 ft., 61 notes
Clarinet . . .	16 ft., 61 notes	Oboe	8 ft., 61 notes
Violetta . . .	4 ft., 61 notes	Vox Celeste (2 ranks)	8 ft., 61 notes

PEDAL ORGAN

Pedal Bourdon . 16 ft., 30 notes   Pedal Dulciana . 16 ft., 30 notes

Total 548 reeds

COUPLERS

Swell to Great   Great to Great (4 ft.)
Swell to Pedal   Great to Pedal

ACCESSORIES

Grand or Full Organ   Balanced Great Pedal   Wind Indicator
Balanced Swell Pedal   Tremolo   Organist's Bench

Length—5 feet 9 inches. Height—5 feet 5 inches
Depth—3 feet 2½ inches; with pedals, 4 feet 6 inches
Weight—boxed, 1070 pounds. Case—135 cubic feet

STUDIO ORGAN

THE ORGOBLO

An Electrically Driven Fan Blower made Expressly for Estey Organs

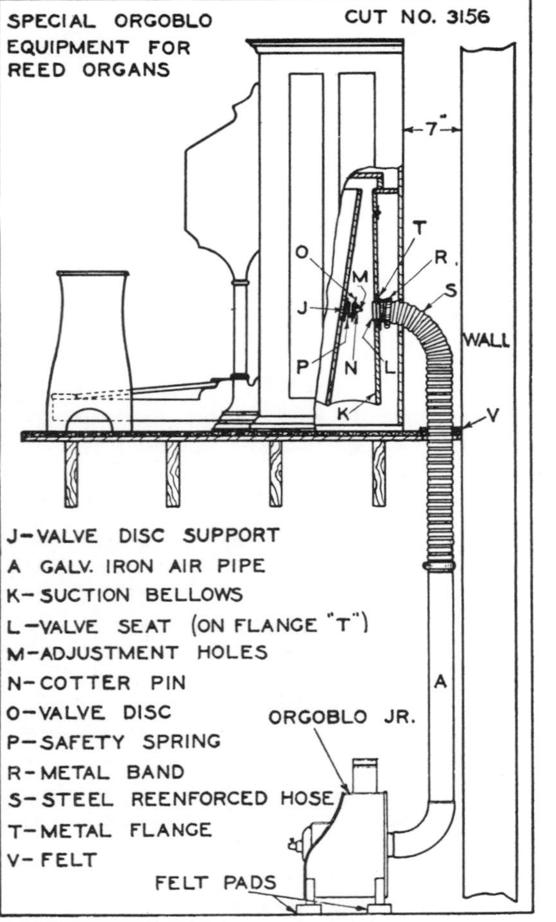

The Orgoblo provides a constant and ample wind supply wherever electric power is available, and does away with the tedious and inconvenient process of pumping by hand.

It is easy to install and requires no special wiring. It should be placed in the basement or some adjoining room, where the vibration of the fan will not be audible. A four-inch wind supply pipe connects with the organ through an opening made in floor or partition, care being also taken to see that the pipe itself does not come in contact with the latter.

A valve in the organ bellows automatically regulates the wind supply, so that no regulating chain from bellows to blower is required. The motor, which may be either alternating or direct according to the type of current furnished, is built into the machine and cannot be supplied separately. In case of failure of electric power an automatic damper allows pumping by hand.

A special booklet describing the Orgoblo in detail will be mailed on request.

STUDIO OF PROF. EDWARD P. KIMBALL

Assistant organist, Great Mormon Tabernacle, Salt Lake City, Utah

(Note the Studio Model installed)

CASE DESIGN 6

Actions
32
35

Length, 3 feet 8 inches. Height, 3 feet 11 inches. Depth, 1 foot 8 inches.
Average weight (boxed), 290 pounds. 30 cubic feet.

ESTEY SCHOOL ORGAN

Not furnished with finished back to match case. Back is stained black.

In Oak or Walnut Finish

Always specify whether Oak or Walnut Finish Case is wanted.

Code Word

	OAK	WALNUT FINISH
6-32,	Flood	Floral
6-35,	Fierce	Fife

There is an ever-increasing demand for small organs with power sufficient for school, vestry or other medium-sized halls. In this organ the problem is met most successfully by offering an instrument that has power as well as variety of tone.

CASE DESIGN 11

Actions
32
35

Length, 3 feet 8 inches. Height, 3 feet 11 inches. Depth, 1 foot 8 inches.
Average weight (boxed), 290 pounds. 30 cubic feet.

ESTEY SCHOOL ORGAN

With finished back to match case.

In Oak or Walnut Finish

Always specify whether Oak or Walnut Finish Case is wanted.

Code Word

	OAK	WALNUT FINISH
11-32,	Flotilla	Floridness
11-35,	Flourished	Flowery

When organ is to be placed where the organist faces the audience, the back of organ should be as carefully finished as the front. We have provided for this with our Style 11.

CASE
DESIGN
R

Actions
32
35
38
97

Length, 3 feet 10 inches. Height, 4 feet 4 inches. Depth, 1 foot 11 inches.
Average weight (boxed), 340 pounds. 39 cubic feet.

ESTEY CHAPEL ORGAN

Furnished with finished back to match case.

In Oak and Walnut
Always specify whether Oak or Walnut Case is wanted.

Code Word

	WALNUT	OAK		WALNUT	OAK
R-32,	Livery	Hellespont	R-38,	Logical	Helmets
R-35,	Loftily	Heiress	R-97,	Lodgment	Hilarity

One of the first requirements in an organ that is to be used as an accompanying instrument for the human voice, as in church and Sunday school services, is that it have ample sustaining quality. The special construction and extra large size of the bellows in this instrument make it preëminently one of the best to lead and sustain the congregational singing of church, chapel or lodge.

CASE
DESIGN
H

Actions
38
97
98

Length, 4 feet 4 inches. Height, 4 feet 1 inch. Depth, 2 feet 3¾ inches.
Average weight (boxed), 440 pounds. 53 cubic feet.

ESTEY CHURCH ORGAN

Furnished with finished back to match case.

In Oak or Walnut
Always specify whether Oak or Walnut Case is wanted.

Code Word

	WALNUT	OAK
H-38,	Fantasia	Henchman
H-97,	Fashion	Heraldic
H-98,	Fatty	Fawning

Pipe Top furnished when so ordered, or may be had at a later date. (See illustration on page 20.)

This organ is well adapted to use in smaller churches. Its range is from the full, rich Diapason to the remarkably sweet and delicate tones of the Æolienne Harp and Flute.

In architecture and interior construction it is the embodiment of the latest achievements in organ building.

Contains Philharmonic Scale reeds.

CASE DESIGN O

Actions 81 83

Length, 4 feet 10½ inches. Height, 4 feet. Depth, 2 feet 5½ inches.
Weight (boxed), 570 pounds. 63 cubic feet.

ESTEY PHILHARMONIC SCALE

Furnished with finished back to match case.

In Oak or Walnut

Always specify whether Oak or Walnut Case is wanted.

Pipe top never furnished unless specified in order. Finished back not furnished when pipe top is ordered.

Code Word

	Walnut	Oak
O-81,	Kopeck	Lottery
O-83,	Kyanite	Lamprey

Here we have combined delicacy and brilliancy with an unusual capacity for orchestral effect. Ample in power for large church. Its great variety of registration makes it one of the best reed organs for efficiently leading congregational singing or for chorus work.

Bench and hand blow lever furnished with every instrument of this style. Pipe top furnished when so ordered or may be had at later date. (See illustration on page 20.) Case is equipped with pedal support. A slight movement of the lever locks the pedals in place thus providing a firm rest for the feet when the hand blower is used.

ESTEY PHILHARMONIC ORGAN

This splendid organ is furnished with the patented "Philharmonic" (large scale) reeds, not to be found in other organs. The larger reeds require additional bellows capacity, which, in turn, necessitates a larger case.

Actions 81 and 83, therefore, can be furnished only in Case O. Action 83 is made on the double chest principle, a distinct advance in reed organ construction, an exclusive Estey feature.

Part of the secret, if any, in the delightfully clear, resonant tone of the Estey organ is due to our belief—and practice—in using ample sounding board. It is impossible to obtain real tone without ample sounding board. The double chest construction gives us a most generous supply, the main chest carrying but four full rows of reeds; sets in addition to these are placed in an inverted action directly over the keys.

The key itself is extra long and while it presses down on the usual little wooden rod opening the valve, admitting air to the sets in the main chest, the end of the key opposite the point where the fingers rest presses up in a similar manner and opens a valve in this second chest.

In short, the construction is really two separate organs, eliminating the delicate and complicated levers formerly used in large organs. Wind is conducted to the second chest by wind trunks at both ends of the action.

We are sometimes asked if these large organs can be supplied with transposing keyboard. The construction of Action 83, with the double chest and the necessary wind trunks, will not permit of a transposing keyboard. It may be added to O-81.

The large actions are always furnished with hand blow lever and may be ordered with an electrically driven blowing machine. See descriptions on pages 18 and 20.

We do not know of an organ, unless it be one of our two-manual organs, that can compare with this excellent model O.

Action 81. Five octaves, sixteen stops, two hundred and eighty-five reeds. Four full sets of reeds, including the double set of Harp Æolienne reeds and one set of seventeen heavy Sub-Bass reeds. This action contains the famous large scale Philharmonic reeds. Furnished only in case O.

Bass		Treble	
Diapason	8 ft.	Diapason	8 ft.
Dulciana	8 ft.	*Dulciana*	8 ft.
Flute	4 ft.	Flute	4 ft.
Vox Jubilante	8 ft.	Vox Jubilante	8 ft.
Harp Æolienne	2 ft.	Corno	16 ft.
Sub-Bass	16 ft.		
I Forte		II Forte	

Mechanical

Bass Coupler, Treble Coupler, Tremolo, Grand Organ, Knee Swell, Organist's Bench, Hand Side Blower

Action 83. Five octaves, sixteen stops, four hundred and seven reeds. Six full sets, including the double set of Harp Æolienne reeds and one set of seventeen heavy Sub-Bass reeds and octave couplers. This action contains the famous large scale Philharmonic reeds. Furnished only in case O.

Bass		Treble	
Diapason	8 ft.	Diapason	8 ft.
Flute	4 ft.	Flute	4 ft.
Vox Jubilante	8 ft.	Vox Jubilante	8 ft.
Harp Æolienne	2 ft.	Corno	16 ft.
Trumpet	8 ft.	Trumpet	8 ft.
Violina	2 ft.	Wald Flute	2 ft.
Sub-Bass	16 ft.		

Mechanical

Bass Coupler, Treble Coupler, Tremolo, Grand Organ, Knee Swell, Organist's Bench, Hand Side Blower

ESTEY ARTIST'S ORGAN

An organ in design and specification or contents appealing to those seeking the highest merit rather than elaborate decoration. Power has been given second consideration to quality or delicacy in voicing, although naturally the large number of reeds (440) produces a splendid full organ. Each set or "stop" being divided Bass and Treble permits delightful combinations for solo and accompaniment. The beautiful effect of a string sextet may be produced with organ, violin and 'cello, while full organ with swells closed gives an excellent reproduction of some distant cathedral organ. The shutter swells in back are most effective.

Found in the homes of music lovers and lovers of organ music.

While we have occasionally sold this particular model for small churches, we do not recommend it for such work. It is not made with the large scale Philharmonic reeds as used in our larger organs for churches and other public work.

Fan blower, electrically operated, may be supplied with this model.

CASE DESIGN Z

Height, 3 feet 9 inches. Length, 4 feet 6 inches. Depth, 2 feet 4 inches. Weight (boxed), 470 pounds. 51 cubic feet.

Action 56. Sixteen stops, six complete sets (or 7 1-5 rows) of beautifully voiced reeds

SPECIFICATIONS

Bass		Treble	
Diapason	8 ft.	Diapason	8 ft.
Oboe	8 ft.	Oboe	8 ft.
Vox Jubilante	8 ft.	Vox Jubilante	8 ft.
Flute	4 ft.	Flute	4 ft.
Harp Æolienne (two ranks)	4 ft.	Harp Æolienne (two ranks)	4 ft.
Clarinet	16 ft.	Clarinet	16 ft.
Sub-Bass (thirteen notes)	16 ft.		
Bass Coupler		Treble Coupler	

Tremolo

ARTIST'S ORGAN, Z-56

Furnished with finished back to match case.

Bench furnished with every instrument of this style.

IN DARK GOLDEN OAK, OR DARK WALNUT

Always specify whether Oak, or Walnut Case is wanted.

CODE WORD

	WALNUT	OAK
Z-56,	Zenith	Zerda

THE LATEST FOLDING ORGAN

STYLE JJ

Code Word
Style JJ, Folding

When open, the keyboard is 30 inches from the floor,
and the case stands 32 inches high.
When closed or collapsed, the case measures 33 inches long,
14 inches wide and 12 inches high.
Weight, 60 pounds (boxed, 100 pounds). 5 cubic feet.

Contains one full four-octave set of reeds, well voiced, ample wind power.

Portable, strong, durable, easily opened and closed.

Easily transported and always adequate.

Provided with strong leather handles for safe and easy moving.

A treasure for missionaries or traveling singers.

Furnished in Oak only.

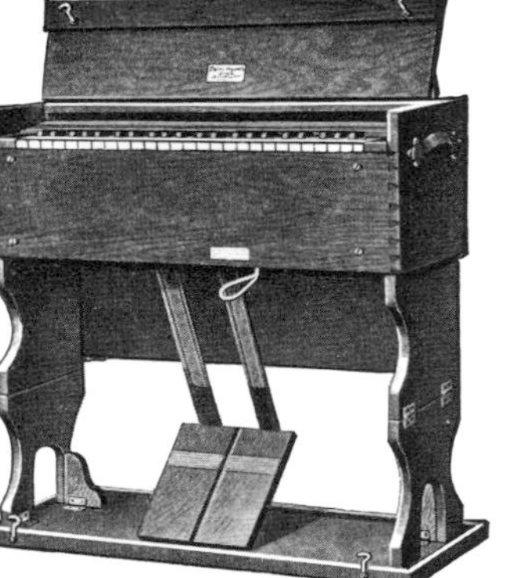

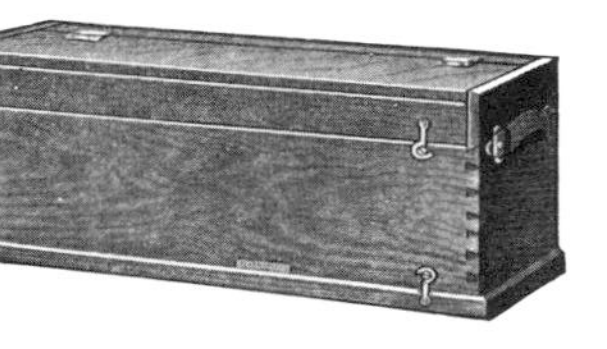

STYLE 2

STYLE 2, FOLDING ORGAN

Code Word
Style 2, Fabled

Length, 2 feet 9 inches. Height, open, 2 feet 9 inches.
Height, closed, 1 foot 2 inches. Depth, 1 foot 8 inches.
Weight, 70 pounds (boxed, 135 pounds).
9 cubic feet.

Organ contains two full four-octave sets of reeds and octave coupler.

This Folding Organ has proven its value and made for itself thousands of friends during the years it has been on the market.

The case is made of Oak, and is especially strong and well adapted for traveling purposes.

It can be readily opened or closed by one person and is secured firmly with strong hooks and screws.

For ordinary traveling no packing case whatever is required.

Great care is exercised in the manufacture of these organs throughout, waterproof glue, brass screws, coated wire, etc., being used to avoid the disastrous effects of tropical climates on wood and metal alike.

Hundreds have been sold and are giving splendid satisfaction and their record is certainly phenomenal.

Height, 32 inches. Length, 32 inches. Depth, 17 inches.
Weight (boxed), 95 pounds. 7 cubic feet.

THE NEW SCHOOL MODEL "C"

Code Word
Jocund

Contains one full four-octave set of reeds, 49 notes.

While the action in this organ is identical with the small models Estey has made for a score of years, features and improvements based on suggestions from Music Supervisors have been incorporated to make an ideal instrument for schools.

The front board is cut away to allow room for the knees under the keyboard. This facilitates pumping. The height of the organ is such that an ordinary chair serves perfectly instead of a special bench or stool.

The bellows capacity has been increased about fifty per cent, thereby insuring a perfect sustained tone. This, with special attention to voicing, provides a tonal quality unapproached by any other small organ, and equal to that of the most expensive large organ.

A double instead of single swell is incorporated. This means the control over volume of tone has been increased so the soft organ is quite enough for the childish voice and full organ is ample for accompaniment for forty or fifty voices.

This is not a folding organ. The legs and base are extremely rigid. Half-inch selected oak stock is used. The ends are panelled to eliminate warping and improve the appearance. Metal rods connect the pedals and bellows instead of a webbing which will not wear as long. Casters are provided. The standard finish is a dull waxed oak.

Style "C" is shipped knocked down. It can be set up for use in five minutes. Net weight, 65 pounds.

CASE DESIGN 17

Actions
32
35

Length, 3 feet 8 inches. Height, 6 feet. Depth, 1 foot 8 inches.
Average weight (boxed), 340 pounds. 36 cubic feet
Mirror size, 10 x 24 inches.

FIVE OCTAVES. IN WALNUT FINISH ONLY

CODE WORD

17-32. Firewood
17-35, Fireworks

Where quality is appreciated yet available amount is limited we have designed this moderate case so that anyone may afford to own an Estey Organ. Same quality of material used in this organ as in our more elaborate designs.

CASE DESIGN 18

Actions
32
35

Length, 3 feet 10 inches. Height, 6 feet 2 inches. Depth, 1 foot 8 inches.
Average weight (boxed), 370 pounds. 44 cubic feet.
Mirror size, 10 x 28 inches.

FIVE OCTAVES. IN OAK OR WALNUT FINISH
Always specify whether Oak or Walnut Finish Case is wanted.

CODE WORD

	WALNUT FINISH	OAK
18-32,	Frescoed	Fretful
18-35,	Freshman	Friendship

While over decoration has been avoided, there is sufficient to keep this design in exceedingly good taste.

ACTIONS OR INTERIORS

Furnished as described under the illustrations of different case designs

All organs tuned A 440 Pitch unless otherwise ordered.

Action 32.

Considered the ideal arrangement for two full sets of reeds.

Five octaves, eleven stops, one hundred and twenty-two reeds. Two full sets of reeds and octave couplers.

Bass		Treble	
Diapason	8 ft.	Diapason	8 ft.
Dulciana	8 ft.	*Dulciana*	8 ft.
Flute	4 ft.	Vox Jubilante	8 ft.
Bass Coupler		Treble Coupler	
I Forte		II Forte	

Tremolo

Action 35.

Five octaves, twelve stops, one hundred and eighty-four reeds. Two full sets of reeds with one double set of Harp Æolienne reeds of two and one-half octaves and octave couplers.

Bass		Treble	
Diapason	8 ft.	Diapason	8 ft.
Dulciana	8 ft.	*Dulciana*	8 ft.
Flute	4 ft.	Vox Jubilante	8 ft.
Harp Æolienne (two ranks)	2 ft.	Treble Coupler	
Bass Coupler		Tremolo	
I Forte		II Forte	

Action 38.

Five octaves, thirteen stops, one hundred and ninety-six reeds. Three full sets of reeds with one octave of Sub-Bass reeds and octave couplers.

Bass		Treble	
Diapason	8 ft.	Diapason	8 ft.
Dulciana	8 ft.	*Dulciana*	8 ft.
Vox Jubilante	8 ft.	Vox Jubilante	8 ft.
Flute	4 ft.	Flute	4 ft.
Sub-Bass	16 ft.	Treble Coupler	
Forte			
Bass Coupler		Tremolo	

Action 97.

Permits the greatest variety. Our leader.

Five octaves, sixteen stops, two hundred and fifty-seven reeds. Four full sets of reeds, including the double set of Harp Æolienne reeds and one octave of Sub-Bass reeds and octave couplers.

Bass		Treble	
Diapason	8 ft.	Diapason	8 ft.
Dulciana	8 ft.	*Dulciana*	8 ft.
Flute	4 ft.	Flute	4 ft.
Flute d'Amour	4 ft.	Vox Jubilante	8 ft.
Harp Æolienne (two ranks)	2 ft.	Choral	8 ft.
Sub-Bass	16 ft.	Tremolo	
I Forte		II Forte	
Bass Coupler		Treble Coupler	

Action 98.

In Case H only.

A Splendid Church Organ

Five octaves, eighteen stops, three hundred eighteen reeds, five sets of reeds, including the double set of Harp Æolienne reeds and one octave of Sub-Bass reeds and octave couplers.

Bass		Treble	
Bourdon	16 ft.	Bourdon	16 ft.
Diapason	8 ft.	Diapason	8 ft.
Dulciana	8 ft.	*Dulciana*	8 ft.
Flute	4 ft.	Flute	4 ft.
Flute d'Amour	4 ft.	Vox Jubilante	8 ft.
Harp Æolienne	2 ft.	Choral	8 ft.
Sub-Bass	16 ft.	Tremolo	
Forte I		Forte II	
Bass Coupler (down)		Treble Coupler (up)	

A WORD OF EXPLANATION

In describing the interiors or actions used in Estey Organs, where we specify two full sets, it means sets of reeds extending throughout the keyboard. Many manufacturers specify two full sets of *two and one-half octaves each*, but our method has always been to call a set of reeds a full set only when it extends throughout the keyboard; so the Estey Organ of *two full sets* is equal to most organs described as having *four sets*.

Please note that all actions are made only in five octaves, unless otherwise specified.

In order to simplify so far as possible the names of the stops and make it less confusing for the organist, we have for some time used the same name for stops in both Bass and Treble, viz., Diapason–Diapason, instead of Diapason–Melodia, Flute–Flute, instead of Flute–Viola. The number of sets of reeds will be found the same as well as the pitch of the particular set.

A SUGGESTION

We strongly recommend the actions containing the larger number of reeds. The small additional expense is more than offset by the variety of tonal effects made possible.

IMPORTANT NOTICE

Benches are not shipped with organs unless ordered. (Models O and Z excepted.)

We claim the privilege of making minor changes in case design or decoration to case without notice. No radical change, however, will be made without furnishing new illustration.

DUO-MANUAL ORGANS

We issue a separate catalog of Duo-Manual Organs showing five designs suitable for Churches, Schools, Residences, Lodge Rooms, etc., mailed on request.

TRANSPOSING KEYBOARD

The actions contained in cases Style 6, 11, R and H may be had, at an increase in price, with Transposing Keyboard, which enables the player to raise or lower the pitch with a single movement of the hand.

The idea of a Transposing Keyboard is not new, but it is only recently that it has been made practical and furnished at a price to make it easily procurable. It is most valuable for church and school work. Where the music may be written too high for the voices, slide the keyboard one key to the left —continue to play in the same key it is written—and you have lowered the pitch. The possibilities are practically unlimited, as the Transposing Keyboard permits playing in five different keys—two semitones each way.

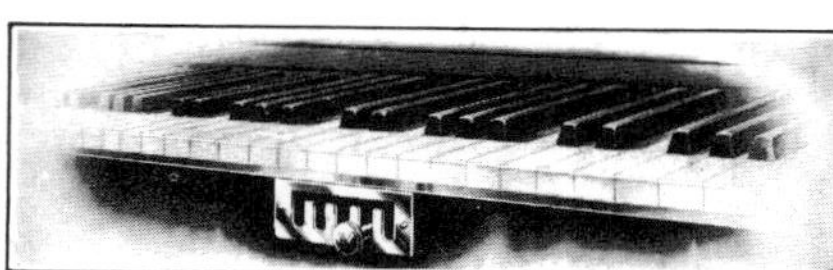

GOTHIC ORGAN

ESTEY ORGAN CORPORATION
Brattleboro, Vermont
U. S. A.

ACTIONS FOR THE GOTHIC ORGAN

ACTION 38

This action is rich in tone colors and has a surprising abundance of power. For ensemble singing it provides exceptionally fine accompaniment.

SPECIFICATION: Five octaves, fourteen stops, three sets of reeds with one octave of sub bass reeds, one hundred ninety-six reeds. The Dulciana is derived from the Diapason and the Flute d'Amour from the Flute. The Vox Jubilante reeds are tuned sharp and the stop draws the Vox Jubilante and the Diapason together.

BASS		TREBLE	
Diapason	8 ft.	Diapason	8 ft.
Dulciana	8 ft.	*Dulciana*	8 ft.
Vox Jubilante	8 ft.	Vox Jubilante	8 ft.
Flute	4 ft.	Flute	4 ft.
Flute d'Amour	4 ft.	*Flute d'Amour*	4 ft.
Sub Bass	16 ft.		

Bass Coupler Tremolo Treble Coupler

ACTION 97

The beautiful Harp Aeolienne is included in this specification, and the Diapason reeds are of the Philharmonic scale. This instrument has great power, and yet beauty and delicacy of tone.

SPECIFICATION: Five octaves, sixteen stops, four and one-half sets of reeds including the double set of Harp Aeolienne of two octaves, and one octave of sub bass reeds, two hundred eighty-one reeds. The Dulciana is derived from the Diapason, and the Flute d'Amour from the Flute. The Vox Jubilante reeds are tuned sharp and the stop draws the Vox Jubilante and the Diapason together.

BASS		TREBLE	
Diapason	8 ft.	Diapason	8 ft.
Dulciana	8 ft.	*Dulciana*	8 ft.
Choral	8 ft.	Choral	8 ft.
Flute	4 ft.	Flute	4 ft.
Flute d'Amour	4 ft.	*Flute d'Amour*	4 ft.
Harp Aeolienne	2 ft.	Vox Jubilante	8 ft.
Sub Bass	16 ft.		

Bass Coupler Tremolo Treble Coupler

ACTION 98

The Bourdon and Diapason are made from Philharmonic scale reeds, and the location of the cell boards gives unusually fine resonant qualities. For quality, variety and power, this action is unsurpassed.

SPECIFICATION: Five octaves, seventeen stops, five sets of reeds including the double set of Harp Aeolienne of two octaves, and one octave of sub bass reeds, three hundred eighteen reeds. The Dulciana is derived from the Diapason, and the Flute d'Amour from the Flute. The Vox Jubilante reeds are tuned sharp and the stop draws the Vox Jubilante and the Diapason together.

BASS		TREBLE	
Bourdon	16 ft.	Bourdon	16 ft.
Diapason	8 ft.	Diapason	8 ft.
Dulciana	8 ft.	*Dulciana*	8 ft.
Flute	4 ft.	Flute	4 ft.
Flute d'Amour	4 ft.	*Flute d'Amour*	4 ft.
Harp Aeolienne	2 ft.	Vox Jubilante	8 ft.
Sub Bass	16 ft.	Choral	8 ft.

Bass Coupler Tremolo Treble Coupler

SPECIFY CURRENT CHARACTERISTICS

The Gothic Organ

Up to now a reed organ of comprehensive specification has required a separate motor blower unit for the best musical results. A motor blower is not only expensive, but once the installation has been made the location of the organ is practically fixed.

Estey has developed an electrical blowing apparatus which is enclosed in the organ case, and which operates on the usual lighting currents. The organ may, therefore, be moved at will.

The Gothic organ is equipped with the electrical blowing apparatus. An expression pedal is provided which, an innovation in reed organ construction, gives a wider range from pianissimo to forte than has heretofore been possible. A grand organ pedal is also provided.

The Gothic organ is available in oak and walnut cases. The Bench has been especially designed to match the case.

The Gothic organ is intended for Churches, Chapels, Schools and Lodges where volume is essential, although the pleasing case design and fine finishes, together with effective volume control, recommend its use in the home.

Cable address, Estey Brattleboro

CODE

Action	*Oak*	*Walnut*
38	goal	gold
97	gong	good
98	goth	gown

SPECIFY CURRENT CHARACTERISTICS

Available in Oak and Walnut

Length 4 feet $4\frac{1}{2}$ inches, height 4 feet $\frac{3}{4}$ inches, depth 2 feet 2 inches. Average weight boxed for domestic shipment 400 pounds; export shipment 510 pounds. 54 cubic feet.

ESTEY ORGAN

We present a new two manual and pedal organ. Designed and built out of our experience of ninety-one years, we believe it to be a masterpiece of the organ builder's art. We offer it to you with a feeling of pride in our accomplishment and we feel sure that you will consider it as highly as we do.

The novelty of this new organ does not lie in unimportant changes in an old and familiar instrument. It is the result of a completely new and revolutionary conception. Not only does it embody new principles of design and construction, but most important it is a remarkable musical instrument.

ESTEY ORGAN CORPORATION
BRATTLEBORO, VERMONT
U.S.A.

SPECIFICATIONS

Great

1.	Diapason	8′	73 Reeds
2.	Dulciana	8′	73 Reeds
3.	Flute	4′	73 Reeds
4.	Trumpet	8′	73 Reeds

Swell

5.	Voix Celeste	8′	134 Reeds
6.	Melodia	8′	73 Reeds
7.	Violino	4′	73 Reeds
8.	Oboe	8′	73 Reeds

Pedal

9.	Bourdon	16′	44 Reeds
10.	Gedeckt from No. 9	16′	32 Notes
11.	Flute from No. 9	8′	32 Notes

Couplers

Great to Great 16′—4′ — Great to Pedal 8′
Swell to Great 16′—8′—4′ — Swell to Pedal 8′
Swell to Swell 16′—4′ — Great Unison "Off"
Swell Unison "Off"

Pedal Movements and Accessories

Balanced Expression Pedal — Balanced Crescendo Pedal
Tremolo — Bench — Music Rack — Motor — Blower

Outside Dimensions

Width 57½″ — Depth to back of bench 49⅞″
Depth of case 30⅝″ — Height 46⅜″

Approximate weight (packed) 1000 lbs.

Q. Is this instrument a pipe organ, a reed organ or an electrotone?

A. It is a reed organ.

Q. How does it differ from the conventional reed organ?

A. It differs from the conventional reed organ in quality, volume and variety of tone; in the type of key action, coupler action and stop action; in the method by which expression is controlled; in appearance; in ease of operation and in playability.

Q. Does the organ have an electric pick-up or amplifier?

A. No. And because the tone is not amplified it is true and without distortion throughout the range from Pianissimo to Fortissimo.

Q. But how is adequate volume secured without amplification?

A. An entirely new design of cell and soundboard construction produces not only adequate volume of tone, but also a quality and variety of tone never before heard in a reed organ.

Q. What type of key action and coupler action is used?

A. The key and coupler action are electro-pneumatic. The key action has a top resistance touch which remains constant regardless of the number of couplers in use.

Q. Are both intermanual and intramanual couplers provided?

A. Yes. The organ has standard pipe organ couplers, nine in number with two unison releases.

Q. What type of stop action is used?

A. The stop action is electro-pneumatic and is controlled by tilting tablets attractive in appearance and positive in operation.

Q. Are the manual keys, pedal keys, expression and crescendo pedals in proper relation to each other?

A. Yes. They are located in accordance with the recommendations of the American Guild of Organists.

Q. Does the instrument require frequent tuning?

A. It requires no tuning whatever.

Q. Do minor adjustments require the services of an expert familiar with a complicated mechanism?

A. No. Any first class organ service man can make all necessary adjustments.

Q. What is the approximate cost of operation?

A. Under normal playing conditions about three cents per hour will cover the cost of operation.

Q. Would it be possible to add Chimes to the organ?

A. Yes. Chimes can be added providing the necessary space is available.

Q. How large an auditorium will the organ adequately serve?

A. It will meet the requirements of a room of average acoustic properties seating approximately five hundred persons.

Q. In what finishes is the organ available?

A. In Walnut only.

Q. Is extra expense involved in the installation of the instrument?

A. No. The organ is entirely self-contained, and to make it ready for operation it is only necessary to plug the flexible cord into a convenient electric receptacle.

TONAL PERFECTION

The Virtuoso has those thrilling qualities of ensemble and solo which can be achieved only from natural tone sources. The Free Reed has long been accepted in its natural voice, as a tonal source rich in harmonics. Over one hundred exquisite and beautiful tonal combinations can be readily worked out from the manual voices and couplers. The Virtuoso lends itself ideally to the playing of the great music of all ages.

A symphony of perfection . . . truly a musical masterpiece.

CONSOLE APPOINTMENTS

The console appointments include both intra and inter manual couplers, a full 32-note pedal clavier, overhanging swell keys, proper positioning of balanced swell and crescendo pedals, and all details according to exact A. G. O. specifications. Only in the custom built pipe organ console will the organist find the Virtuoso counterpart.

An organist's dream . . . truly a musical masterpiece.

ELECTRO-MAGNETIC ACTION

The very same skills which Estey has perfected since the turn of the century in the magnificent structure of its pipe organs have been completely utilized in the incorporation of electric and magnetic principles found in the Virtuoso. These amazing features permit regular pipe organ key and stop actions. The Virtuoso is the first to unshackle the two manual reed organ from cumbersome mechanical couplers. The organist is now able to employ any and all couplers in effective combinations with complete playing ease.

Systematized knowledge that only Estey's experience can produce; the result . . . a musical masterpiece.

MAINTENANCE

Maintenance costs are negligible. Should minor adjustments become necessary, they can be effected by any service man. Reed organs which are given normal protection from the elements do not need retuning. Great grandmother's melodeon handed down through the years is the best possible testimonial in this regard. There are no tubes, resistors or condensers to be replaced. In fact there is no untried principle present in the Virtuoso.

THE ESTEY Virtuoso

THE TRIUMPH OF FIVE GENERATIONS

SPECIFICATIONS

Manual Compass CC to c4
Action: Electro-Magnetic
A. G. O. Standard Console and Pedal Board
Stop Tablets and Couplers over Swell Manual

Pedal Compass CCC to G
Pitch: A-440

GREAT ORGAN

1.	Diapason	8′	61 Reeds
2.	Dulciana	8′	61 Reeds
3.	Octave	4′	61 Reeds
4.	Trumpet	8′	61 Reeds
	Chimes (Prepared for)		

SWELL ORGAN

5.	Melodia	8′	68 Reeds
6.	Salicional	8′	68 Reeds
7.	Voix Celeste (T.C.)	8′	56 Reeds
8.	Violino	4′	68 Reeds
9.	Oboe	8′	68 Reeds
	Tremolo		

PEDAL ORGAN

10.	SubBass	16′	32 Reeds
11.	Gedackt (From #10)	16′	32 Notes
12.	Octave (Ext. #10)	8′	12 Reeds

COUPLERS

Great to Great	16′—4′
Swell to Great	16′—8′—4′
Swell to Swell	16′—4′
Great to Pedal	8′—4′
Swell to Pedal	8′—4′
Great Unison "Off"	
Swell Unison "Off"	

PEDAL MOVEMENTS AND ACCESSORIES

Balanced Expression Pedal, Balanced Crescendo Pedal, Bench with Compartment, Music Rack, Motor, Rectifier or Generator, Blower.

OUTSIDE DIMENSIONS

Width 57-½″ — Depth to back of Bench 49-⅞″
Depth of Case 30-⅝″ — Height 46-⅜″
Approximate Weight (packed) 1000 lbs.

Case in Dark Mahogany finish, with bench to match.

Height, 49 in. Length, 55 in. Depth, 29 in. With pedals attached, depth 44 in.
Gross weight, boxed, 780 lbs. Net weight 495 lbs., with bench, 540 lbs.
Measurement, 65 cubic feet.

THE ESTEY
STUDENT ORGAN

For years there has been a demand from organists, organ students, music schools and conservatories, for a two manual and pedal practice reed organ, conforming to pipe organ measurements, and so compactly built it could pass through an ordinary door and installation made in a room of limited size.

We have met that demand with the new Estey Student organ. The electrically driven blowing outfit is housed in the organ case, eliminating all piping and the cutting of floors and walls.

With the extension cord connected with the lighting circuit, plug in the back of the organ, turn on the switch, and the organ is ready to use. There being no fixed connection you can move the organ to any location desired, exactly as you would a piano.

This organ is not recommended for a church, or where volume or great tone variety is demanded.

SPECIFICATIONS

Action: 9 stops, 6 sets of reeds.
Manuals: Five octaves, CC to C4, 61 notes.
Pedals: A. G. O. Standard Concave Radiating, two and one-half octaves, CCC to F, 30 notes.

GREAT MANUAL	SWELL MANUAL
Great Diapason, 8 ft. . 61 notes	Swell Oboe, 8 ft. . . . 61 notes
Great Dulciana, 8 ft. . 61 notes	Swell Flute, 4 ft. . . . 61 notes

PEDAL ORGAN

Pedal Bourdon, 16 ft. . 30 notes	Pedal Bourdon, 8 ft. . 30 notes
Pedal Gedeckt, 16 ft.	Pedal Basso, 8 ft.

Total 304 reeds.

Swell to Great Coupler.	Balanced Swell Pedal.
Balanced Great Pedal.	Switch at treble end, connecting with motor.

(Use of the Swell to Great Coupler is optional. Naturally its use means a heavier touch of the keys.)

To operate motor, 110 voltage, 60 cycle, single phase, alternating current must be provided. Confer with us if other current in use.

*

ESTEY ORGAN COMPANY, INC.
Manufacturers
BRATTLEBORO, VERMONT, U. S. A.

BRANCH SALESROOMS

Boston: 31 St. James Ave., Park Square Bldg.
Chicago: 830 Lyon and Healy Bldg., Wabash Ave. and Jackson Blvd.
New York: 642 Fifth Avenue

Licensed under U. S. Patents 1,666,032 and S. N. 266,223. Other patents applied for.

The above illustration shows the organ with pedals folded underneath the keyboard.

*

A music rest is attached to the music desk (not shown on cut).

*

Tilting tablets are used instead of the usual stop knobs.

*

To obtain maximum volume, raise top lid and rest same on top of music desk.

*

We do not supply, free, the extension cord or plug for connecting organ to lighting circuit or floor plug. Secure from your local electrician.

THE ESTEY TWO MANUAL PRACTICE ORGAN

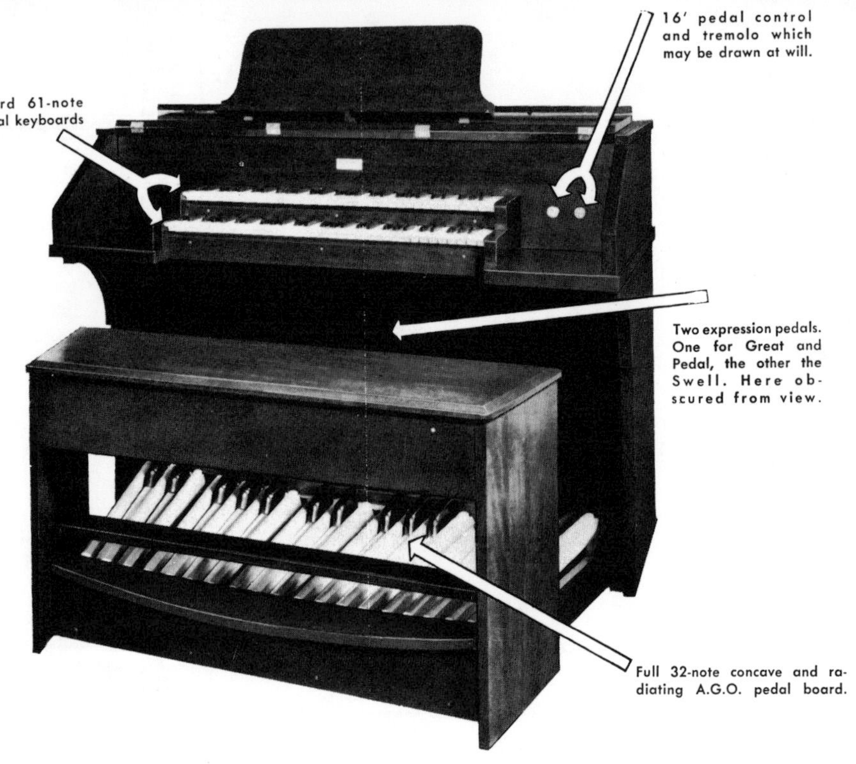

TWO MANUALS and pedal board give full compass. All measurements throughout meet standards set by American Guild of Organists.

CASE AND PEDALS require less than four feet square space. Case and bench design is simple and attractive. Wood is yellow birch with walnut finish. Weight is less than 500 pounds.

FOUR SETS OF REEDS, one hundred and eighty-six reeds in all, arranged one 8′ set each manual with 8′ and 16′ sets in the pedal.

STOPS are provided so that the 16′ Bourdon and the Tremolo may be drawn at will.

TWO SWELL BOXES are controlled by their respective expression pedals, one for Great and Pedal, the other for the Swell.

DYNAMIC RANGE of swells is so wide that either manual may be used as solo or accompaniment.

PERFECT REPETITION and staccato response.

3¼-Oz. MANUAL TOUCH reproduces the "feel" of a modern pipe organ so important to technique.

ELECTRIC MOTOR BLOWER UNIT, exceptionally quiet in operation, is built into the case as an integral part. Current consumed costs less than ½ cent per hour.

TWO MANUAL PRACTICE ORGAN

For a surprisingly small investment, you can have all the convenience of practicing on an organ built to A.G.O. specifications . . . the ideal solution to mastering technical problems from pre-Bach to post-Karg-Elert . . . and right in your own home.

Practice when you wish, as long as you wish, limiting church work to registration details. Here is an instrument that meets all essential requirements for the study and exercise so necessary to polished performance.

The Estey Practice Organ, illustrated and described in detail on the spread of this folder, is built by a company which has been intimately associated with the development of musical arts in the United States for over one hundred years.

The same unrivaled workmanship, trouble-free action and peerless tone quality on which Estey's reputation has been founded is yours in this model, as well. Practice has indeed been made perfect for the professional organist and for his pupils.

DIMENSIONS

Length	57″
Height	42¾″
Depth	27″
Depth with pedals and bench	41½″

WEIGHT AND CUBAGE

Weight of organ boxed	485 lbs.
Weight of pedals boxed	135 lbs.
Cubic feet, organ	58
Cubic feet, pedals	15

THE Estey Practice Organ is noted for its portability and ease of installation. A flexible cord connects the organ with any convenient electric outlet and the instrument may therefore be readily moved.

Estey
ORGAN CORPORATION
Brattleboro, Vermont

Since 1846 • America's Oldest Organ Builder

Practice made perfect

THE ESTEY PRACTICE ORGAN

COMMON REEDS

TOTAL NO. = 90

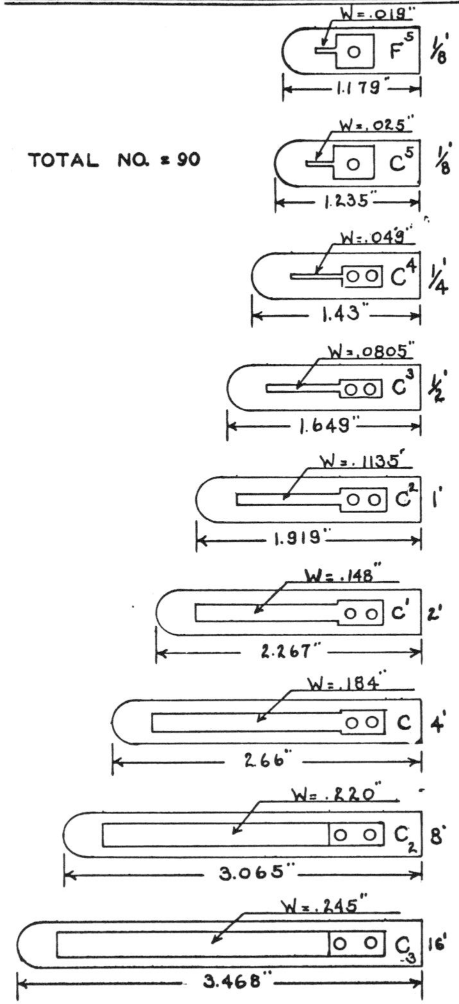

W=.018" F5 1/8' — 1.179"
W=.025" C5 1/8' — 1.235"
W=.049" C4 1/4' — 1.43"
W=.0805" C3 1/2' — 1.649"
W=.1135" C2 1' — 1.919"
W=.148" C' 2' — 2.267"
W=.184" C 4' — 2.66"
W=.220" C2 8' — 3.065"
W=.245" C3 16' — 3.468"

PHILHARMONIC REEDS

TOTAL NO. = 72

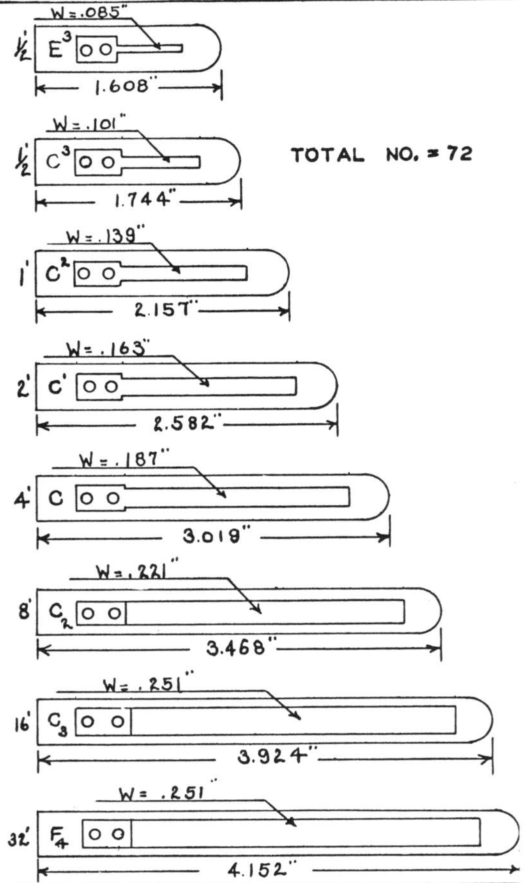

W=.085" 1/2' E3 — 1.608"
W=.101" 1/2' C3 — 1.744"
W=.139" 1' C2 — 2.157"
W=.163" 2' C' — 2.582"
W=.187" 4' C — 3.019"
W=.221" 8' C2 — 3.468"
W=.251" 16' C3 — 3.924"
W=.251" 32' F4 — 4.152"

ESTEY ORGAN CORPORATION

REED ORGAN REEDS

WIDTH ALL MANUAL REEDS = .4195"
THICKNESS ALL MANUAL REEDS = .095"
SCALE — FULL SIZE
FEBRUARY 1, 1940

SUB-BASS REEDS

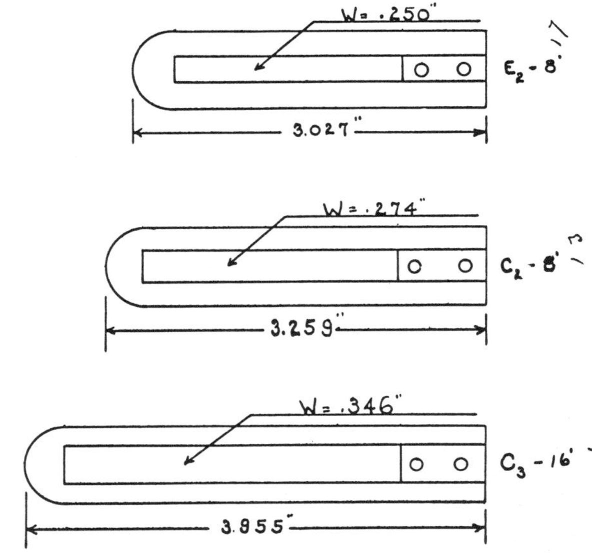

TOTAL NO. = 17

ESTEY ORGAN CORPORATION

REED ORGAN REEDS

WIDTH SUB-BASS REEDS = .695"
THICKNESS SUB-BASS REEDS = .095"
SCALE - FULL SIZE
FEBRUARY 1, 1940

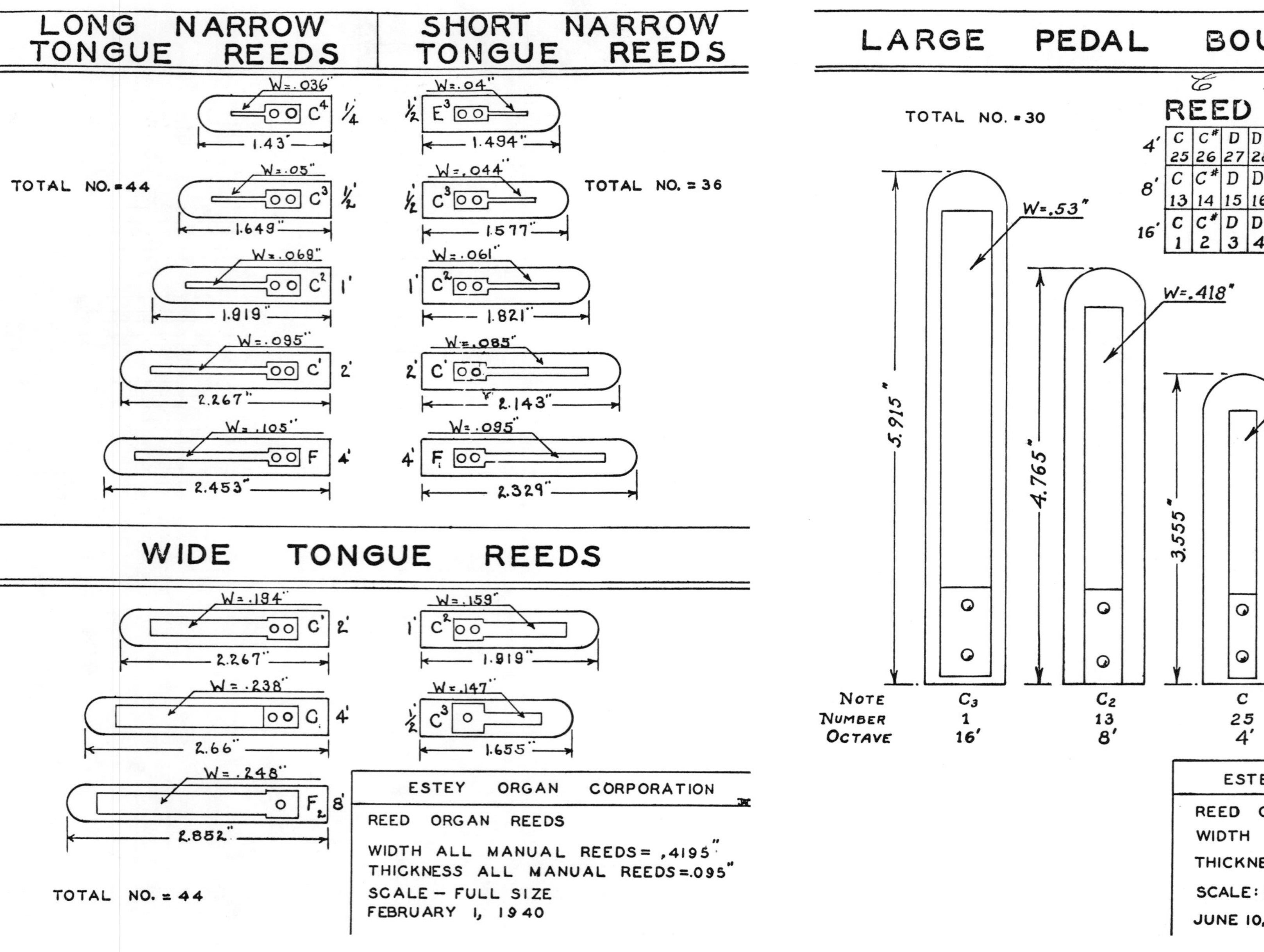

4'	C 25	C# 26	D 27	D# 28	E 29	F 30							Third Octave
8'	C 13	C# 14	D 15	D# 16	E 17	F 18	F# 19	G 20	G# 21	A 22	A# 23	B 24	Second Octave
16'	C 1	C# 2	D 3	D# 4	E 5	F 6	F# 7	G 8	G# 9	A 10	A# 11	B 12	First Octave

THICKNESS OF REEDS AT POINT OF TONGUES

JANUARY 29 1952

	F	F#	G	G#	A	A#	B	C	C#	D	D#	E
0 OCTAVE								.075	.075	.070	.070	.070
1 ST OCTAVE	.060	.060	.048	.048	.044	.044	.042	.042	.038	.038	.034	.034
2 ND OCTAVE	.030	.030	.026	.026	.025	.023	.021	.019	.017	.015	.013	.012
3 RD OCTAVE	.011	.0105	.010	.0095	.009	.0085	.008	.0075	.007	.0065	.006	.0055
4 TH OCTAVE	.005	.00475	.0045	.00425	.004	.00375	.0035	.00325	.003	.00275	.0025	.00225
5 TH OCTAVE	.00225	.00225	.00225	.002	.002	.002	.00175	.00175	.00175	.0015	.0015	.0015
6 TH OCTAVE	.00125	.00125	.00125	.00125	.00125	.00125	.001	.001	.001	.001	.001	.001
7 TH OCTAVE	.001											

SALESMEN'S

Net Price List

of

Estey Reed Organs

January 1, 1914

ESTEY ORGAN COMPANY

Factories, Brattleboro, Vt.

WAREROOMS

23 West 42nd Street, New York
17th and Walnut Streets, Philadelphia
120 Boylston Street, Boston
1116 Olive Street, St. Louis

ORGANS FOR THE HOME

5 OCTAVES

STYLE		PRICE	STYLE	PRICE
17–32	Oak or Walnut Finish	$ 70	28–38	$110
17–35		80	15–32	95
17–38		90	15–35	105
18–32		75	15–38	115
18–35		85	N 32	100
18–38		95	N 35	110
3–32		90	N 38	120
3–35		100	S 32	115
3–38		110	S 35	125
28–32		90	S 38	135
28–35		100	S 47	150

6 OCTAVES ONLY

STYLE	PRICE	STYLE	PRICE
28–72 Oak	$100	15–72 Wal.	$105

PIANO CASE

7 1-3 OCTAVES ONLY

STYLE	PRICE	STYLE	PRICE
IXL 74 Mah.	$135	IXL 75 Mah.	$150

We strongly recommend the actions containing the larger number of reeds. The small additional expense is more than offset by the variety of tonal effects the player may produce.

CHAPEL ORGANS

STYLE	PRICE	STYLE	PRICE
14–42	$60	H 38	$130
6–32	65	H 97 X	150
6–35	75	O 97	275
6–38	85	O 94 X	300
11–32	75	O 67	325
11–35	85	V 94	350
11–38	95	V 67	375
R 32	90		
R 38	110		
R 97	130		

Transposing Keyboard furnished in Models 14, 6, 11 and R, $15.00 extra.

TWO MANUAL AND PEDAL ORGANS

STYLE	PRICE	STYLE	PRICE
E 54	$325	X G 61 Pipe Top	$750
T 60	450	G 61 Low Top	725
T 61 X	500	X	

ARTISTS' ORGAN

Z 56 . . . . $275

In Walnut only

ACCLIMATIZED PORTABLE ORGANS

STYLE	PRICE	STYLE	PRICE
JJ	$35	200	$150
2	60		

PIPE TOPS

STYLE	PRICE	STYLE	PRICE
H	$40	V	$65
O	50	T X	75

All previous Lists cancelled.

Net Price List of Estey Reed Organs

October 1, 1929

ESTEY ORGAN COMPANY

FACTORIES, BRATTLEBORO, VT.

WAREROOMS
642 Fifth Avenue, New York
1702 Walnut Street, Philadelphia
Park Square Building, Boston
Wabash Ave., & Jackson Blvd., Chicago

ORGANS FOR THE HOME

5 OCTAVES

CASES	ACTIONS 32	35	38	97
17 W. F.	$110	$125	$	$
18 Oak or W. F.	120	135		
3 Oak	120	135		
3 Wal.	135	150		
S Wal.	185	200	220	260

ARTISTS' ORGAN

Z 56 Oak	$410
Z 56 Walnut	410

We strongly recommend the actions containing the larger number of reeds. The increased variety of tonal effects obtainable amply warrants the slight additional investment.

CHURCH AND CHAPEL ORGANS

CASES	ACTIONS 32	35	38	97
6 Oak or W. F.	$100	$115	$	$
11 Oak or W. F.	105	120		
R Oak	135	150	170	210
R Wal.	150	165	185	225

PHILHARMONIC SERIES

CASES	ACTIONS 38	97	98	81	83
H Oak	$190	$235	$290	$	$
H Wal.	220	265	320		
O Oak				410	480
O Wal.				430	500

Transposing Keyboard furnished in small Chapel Styles including Style R, $15.00 extra. The same feature in Style H, $25.00 extra.

ACCLIMATIZED PORTABLE ORGANS

JJ Oak	$60
C Oak	70
2 Oak	90

TWO MANUAL AND PEDAL ORGANS

E 54 Oak	$620
T 61 Oak	795
T 61 Oak Pipe Top	920
G 61, Pipe Top Oak	1065
New Studio, Oak	1150
New Studio, Mahogany	1275

Foot Blow Pedals on T, G and E, $12.00 extra.

PIPE TOPS

H Solid Oak or Walnut Finish	$75
O Solid Oak or Walnut Finish	110

Our Prices include boxing and delivery on board cars, Brattleboro. Freight and handling extra.

Customers please notice that the letter or first number designates the case, while the second number indicates the action; Example, 17-32 means case 17, with action 32.

January 1, 1936

All Prices F. O. B. Factory

Transposing keyboard for 6, 11, R $15 extra; for H and Gothic $25 extra.

All small organs have finished backs except 6.

Styles H and O when furnished with pipe tops have unfinished backs.

Special finish for 6, 11, R $15 extra; large single manual organs $20 extra; two manual organs $25 extra.

SINGLE MANUAL PEDAL OPERATED

CASES	ACTIONS 32	35	36	38	39	97	98	Special
6 Oak or W.F.	$106	$122	$130	$140	$148	$	$	$
11 Oak or W.F.	110	126						
Modernistic	125	145		165				
R Oak	134	150		168		212		
R W. F.	150	166		182		226		
H Oak				190		236	290	
H Walnut				220		266	320	
Z Oak								410
Z Walnut								430
O Oak								484
O Walnut								506

SINGLE MANUAL MOTOR OPERATED

CASES	ACTIONS 32	35	38	97	98	Special
Modernistic	$200	$220	$255	$300	$345	$
Gothic Oak			255	300	345	
Gothic Wal.			285	330	375	
Melodeon						270

PORTABLE

Children's	$ 25
JJ Oak	78
C Oak	86
2 Oak	108

TWO MANUALS

E 54 Oak	$565
T 61 Oak	710
T 61 " pipe top	835
G 61 " pipe top	915
Studio Oak	970
Studio Mahog.	1100
Student, Mahog. finish cur. 110v-60S-A.C.	700

MISCELLANEOUS

H pipe top Oak or W. F.	$ 80
O pipe top Oak or W. F.	115
Bench Oak or W. F.	5
Foot blow pedals T, G, E, extra	10

BLOWERS

ORGOBLO	Alternating current 110v 60 cycle, single	Direct Current
Regular	$105	$110
Special (quiet)	115	120
Soundproof box for blowers	20	20

Net Price List
of
Estey Reed Organs

January 1, 1941 Edition

Estey Organ Corporation
BRATTLEBORO, VT.

SALES OFFICE
5 West 52nd Street, New York

TWO MANUAL	
ELECTRO-PNEUMATIC, Blower and Generator, Walnut Finish	**$1185.00**
PRACTICE ORGAN, Blower, Walnut Finish	**425.00**

SINGLE MANUAL, MOTOR OPERATED

CASES	ACTIONS						
	32	35	38	97	98	56	Special
Modernistic Walnut Finish	$255	$273	$355	$428	$468	$519	$
Gothic Oak			319	397	437		
Gothic Walnut			391	470	510		
Z Oak						600	
Z Walnut						680	

SINGLE MANUAL, PEDAL OPERATED

CASES	ACTIONS				
	32	35	38	97	98
6 Oak	$133	$147	$	$	$
6 Walnut	144	158			
11 Oak	137	151			
11 Walnut	149	164			
Modernistic W.F.	200	218			
Gothic Oak			288	366	404
Gothic Walnut			360	439	477

BENCHES

Standard Oak or Walnut Finish .	$ 9.00
Modernistic Walnut Finish . .	16.00
Gothic Oak	14.00
Gothic Walnut	18.00

PORTABLE

Children's (Pedal) Finishes listed below	$25.00
Children's (Motor) Walnut or Maple Finish	40.00
Junior (Pedal) Walnut or Maple Finish	65.00
Junior (Motor) Walnut or Maple Finish	85.00
JJ Oak	75.00
2 Oak	125.00

Finishes for children's: Walnut, Maple, Black with Silver Trim, Black with Gold Trim, Green with Buff Trim, Buff with Green Trim, Buff with Blue Trim.

ESTEY

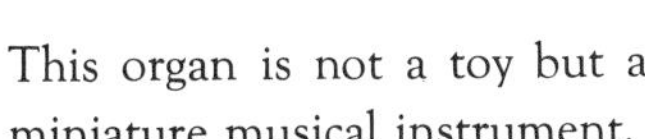

This organ is not a toy but a miniature musical instrument.

It is an invaluable aid in the early musical training of younger children and finds a definite place in the nursery, kindergarten and primary school.

In this instrument you will find the tone, action and other desirable characteristics of the reed organ concentrated within the smallest imaginable dimensions.

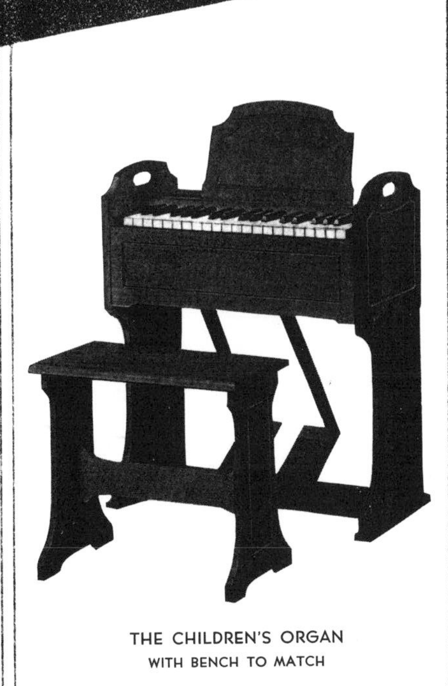

THE CHILDREN'S ORGAN
WITH BENCH TO MATCH

The organ contains one three octave set of Diapason reeds 8 foot pitch C scale. The reeds are tuned A440 pitch.

The case is either maple or birch and can be furnished in any finish or in colors.

MEASUREMENTS

Length. .2 feet
Height to top music rack 32 inches
Height to top of Keyboard . . . . 23 inches
Depth. . . . . $11\frac{13}{16}$ inches
Height bench. . . . .$15\frac{1}{2}$ inches
Weight organ. . . . . .31 pounds
Weight bench. . . . . .6 pounds

CHILDREN'S ORGAN

THE ESTEY MINIATURE ORGAN

FASCINATING

EDUCATIONAL

STURDY

PORTABLE

MADE BY
ESTEY ORGAN CORPORATION
BRATTLEBORO, VERMONT
Makers of the
WORLD'S FINEST ORGANS

THE ESTEY JUNIOR ORGAN

MODERN

TUNEFUL

ATTRACTIVE

INEXPENSIVE

ESTEY ORGAN CORPORATION
BRATTLEBORO, VERMONT

MODERN ORGANS FOR HOMES

THE ESTEY MINIATURE ORGAN

THE ESTEY JUNIOR ORGAN

Here is a practical inexpensive organ that will delight any youngster — encourage appreciation of music. The Miniature Organ is a thoroughly fine musical instrument scaled down to little folks' size with easy-to-work pedals. It has a range of three octaves with standard keys and keyboard. The Miniature Organ weighs only 31 pounds and can be carried from room to room or put away when not in use. Height: 32 inches. Length: 24 inches.

VARIETY OF FINISHES

The Estey Miniature Organ comes in a wide variety of finishes: Walnut, Maple, Green with Buff trim, Buff with Green trim, Black with Gold or Silver trim, Buff with Blue trim. The Estey Junior Organ comes in two standard finishes, Walnut and Maple, and special finishes are available at a small extra cost. Matching benches are included in the price of both instruments.

KEY RANGE

In the Miniature Organ the three octave set of reeds has a range from C to C^3, tuned to A-440 pitch.
The Junior Organ has a four octave set of reeds with the volume controlled by a knee swell. The key range is from CC to C^3, tuned to A-440 pitch.

MADE BY ESTEY

Made by Estey Organ Corporation, makers of the world's finest organs since 1846, both instruments are sturdily constructed to last years without repairs. Guaranteed as advertised in Good Housekeeping Magazine.

STANDARD KEYBOARD

Both instruments have standard size keys on a standard keyboard. The Estey Miniature Organ is designed primarily for children, but it can be played conveniently by older people. The Estey Junior Organ is larger and is definitely not a toy. It is designed for grown-ups and older children.

Now every family can enjoy the luxury of fine organ music in the home. It is extremely easy to play The Estey Junior Organ — the newest, modern musical instrument. Full, rich organ tones are produced from a set of reeds with a compass of four octaves on a standard keyboard. When not in use the music rack folds down flat to form a compact (32" x 30"), good-looking piece of furniture. The price is amazingly low.

Estey Melodeon

Then
(1860)

Now
(1934)

ESTEY ORGAN CORPORATION
BRATTLEBORO, VERMONT · U. S. A.

THE NEW

Melodeon

WITH BENCH

Length 47 inches, width 24 inches, height 36 inches.
Approximate weight boxed, 280 pounds.
22 cubic feet.

THE old-fashioned melodeon is still highly regarded by lovers of old furniture, but to musicians it is a curiosity—an object of unfavorable comparison with modern musical instruments.

We have gone seventy-five years into the past and have taken the beautiful design of the old melodeon and have added to it the mechanical and tonal improvements of today. The result is the melodeon of 1934, which we present with pleasure and much pride.

Its design and specifications are intended for the residence or studio. It is in no sense a church organ. The melodeon of 1934 is the reproduction of a lovely antique and a beautifully voiced modern musical instrument in combination.

Complete description and specifications will be found upon the back page of this folder.

Specifications and Description

THE melodeon contains five octaves, six stops, one hundred twenty-two carefully voiced reeds.

Mechanical Accessories

BASS coupler, treble coupler, tremolo, grand organ, crescendo and diminuendo pedal,* organist's bench, electric motor,† extension cord.

* The crescendo and diminuendo pedal is an entirely new device for the control of expression. By its use the volume of tone may be instantly regulated from the softest pianissimo to the loudest forte.

† This model is equipped with an electrically operated bellows which is silent in operation and eliminates the objectionable foot pumping. The motor is made to operate from any available current and the extension cord is equipped with plug to be used in any type receptacle.

THE case of the melodeon is of solid walnut beautifully finished in the natural color of the wood.

ESTEY ORGAN CORPORATION
BRATTLEBORO, VERMONT · U. S. A.

MODERNISTIC ORGAN

for
Residence
Lodge
Broadcasting Studio
Orchestra
Studio

ESTEY ORGAN CORPORATION
BRATTLEBORO, VERMONT
U. S. A.

ACTION 32

Five octaves, ten stops, two sets of reeds, one hundred twenty-two reeds. The Dulciana is derived from the Diapason, and the Flute d'Amour from the Flute. The Vox Jubilante reeds are tuned sharp, and the stop draws the Vox Jubilante and the Diapason together.

Bass		Treble	
Diapason	8 ft.	Diapason	8 ft.
Dulciana	8 ft.	*Dulciana*	8 ft.
Flute	4 ft.	Vox Jubilante	8 ft.
Flute d'Amour	4 ft.		

Bass Coupler — Tremolo — Treble Coupler

ACTION 35

Five octaves, eleven stops, two sets of reeds and the double set of Harp Aeolienne of two and one-half octaves, one hundred eighty-four reeds. The Dulciana is derived from the Diapason, and the Flute d'Amour from the Flute. The Vox Jubilante reeds are tuned sharp and the stop draws the Vox Jubilante and the Diapason together.

Bass		Treble	
Diapason	8 ft.	Diapason	8 ft.
Dulciana	8 ft.	*Dulciana*	8 ft.
Flute	4 ft.	Vox Jubilante	8 ft.
Flute d'Amour	4 ft.		
Harp Aeolienne	2 ft.		

Bass Coupler — Tremolo — Treble Coupler

ACTION 38

Five octaves, fourteen stops, three sets of reeds with one octave of sub bass reeds, one hundred ninety-six reeds. The Dulciana is derived from the Diapason, and the Flute d'Amour from the Flute. The Vox Jubilante reeds are tuned sharp and the stop draws the Vox Jubilante and the Diapason together.

Bass		Treble	
Diapason	8 ft.	Diapason	8 ft.
Dulciana	8 ft.	*Dulciana*	8 ft.
Vox Jubilante	8 ft.	Vox Jubilante	8 ft.
Flute	4 ft.	Flute	4 ft.
Flute d'Amour	4 ft.	*Flute d'Amour*	4 ft.
Sub Bass	16 ft.		

Bass Coupler — Tremolo — Treble Coupler

The above action specifications are for motor-operated organs. In the pedal-operated organs, the Flute d'Amour stops are eliminated, and all actions have Forte I and Forte II stops.

SPECIFY CURRENT CHARACTERISTICS

The Modernistic Organ

The Modernistic Organ is an up to date musical instrument, especially designed to meet the demand for organ music outside the Church. It is ideally suitable for residences, lodges, broadcasting studios, and orchestras: composers and students of music not only find this modern organ a distinctive addition to their studio furnishings, but a valuable aid in their work.

The Modernistic Organ can be furnished with pedals for foot pumping, or with a motor-operated blowing apparatus enclosed in the case. The motor-operated organ is furnished with an expression pedal and a grand organ pedal.

A choice of three actions is offered in the Modernistic case.

Cable address, ESTEY BRATTLEBORO

CODE

	Pedal Operated			Motor Operated		
Action	Black	Walnut Finish	Maple Finish	Black	Walnut Finish	Maple Finish
32	moat	mold	mope	mace	maid	mane
35	mock	monk	more	made	make	mark
38	mode	mood	moth	magi	male	mass

SPECIFY CURRENT CHARACTERISTICS

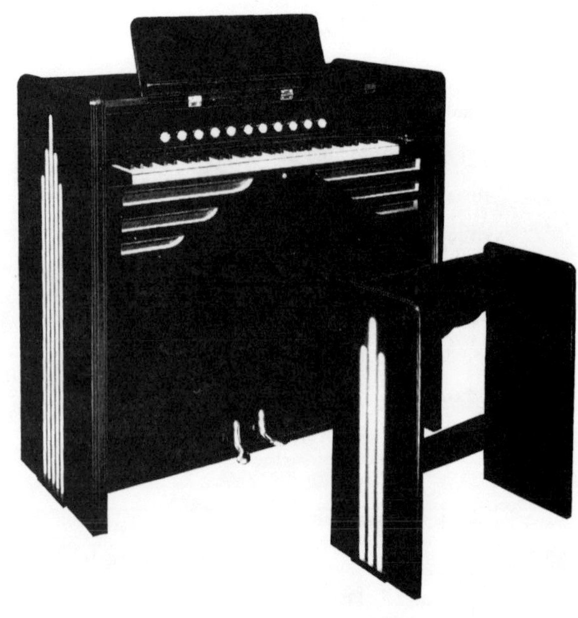

Available in Black trimmed with White, Walnut Finish and Maple Finish

Length 3 feet 8 inches, height 3 feet 6 inches, depth 1 foot 9½ inches. Boxed for shipment, approximate weight with motor 380 pounds; with pedals 350 pounds. 33 cubic feet.

Jewel-like tones . . . Flawless workmanship

THE ESTEY *Chorus*

Your Whole Family Can Enjoy Glorious Organ Music at Home

What fun you and your family will have enjoying musical discoveries with this thrilling Estey Chorus Organ!

Here is an exclusive model in a budget-price range, offering rich, jewel-like tones expected only from large pipe organs. Over 100 years of fine organ building by Estey have resulted in a flawless workmanship unmatched anywhere else in America.

The Big organ features of your Estey Chorus Organ will provide hours upon hours of varying entertainment. Choose any type of music – moving hymns, stirring marches, lively dance music, nostalgic melodies. A wonderful medium when entertaining friends!

This electrically-operated Estey Chorus is easy for the beginner yet brilliantly versatile for the experienced player. Children find its convenient size most enjoyable. Both in performance and appearance this is a superb instrument uniquely rewarding in musical experience at modest cost.

Big Organ Features • Never Needs Tuning

Electrically-Operated • Modest Cost

ESTEY . . . AMERICA'S LARGEST SELLING REED ORGANS

EXCLUSIVE STOPS

To enhance the glorious orchestral effects, the 4 ft. set of reeds is covered with a mute, operated at will by two stops. The left hand stop is the Solo Bass, operating the Bass two octaves of the 4-foot set; the right hand stop is the Solo Treble, operating the Treble two octaves.

UNIQUE EFFECTS

For exciting volume or intriguing shades of expression, use the convenient, dynamic swell pedal. As easy as accelerating a car!

Occupies Small Space

Approx. 3 ft. x 2 ft.

BIG ORGAN FEATURES

Four octave range. Two full sets of reeds; 8 ft. Diapason and 4 ft. Flute. Dynamic swell pedal. Attractive seasoned hardwood case, finished in limed oak, walnut or mahogany.

Your Estey Chorus Organ is Big organ music scaled down for home, Sunday School, small church, school room or club.

Estey, the oldest organ builder in America, is the *only* company in the world that can offer all major categories of organs—Reed, Electronic and Pipe. Behind every Estey organ stands more than a century of *experience* plus the latest concepts of tonal design and constructive achievement. Estey reed organs outnumber all other makes combined.

Since 1846, America's Oldest Organ Builders

The Estey Organ Plant

For over one hundred years generation upon generation of precision workers have here fashioned world-famous Estey Organs. One present 94-year-old employee has worked for Estey over 72 years! Four each have records of more than 50 years. Superior craftsmen have built your Estey organ.

NON-TRANSFERABLE

DOUBLE

Guarantee Certificate

CERTIFICATE NO. ______ ORDER NO. ______

ESTEY ORGAN CORPORATION (DEL.)

This is to certify that the Estey ______ *Organ*

sold to ______ *by* ______

It is *Guaranteed* to the purchaser ...

This is a DOUBLE GUARANTEE backed both by our dealer and the world-famous ESTEY ORGAN CORPORATION, makers of fine organs for more than a century.

ESTEY ORGAN CORPORATION (Del.)

ARNOLD BERNHARD, President

Authorized Dealer

Double Guarantee Certificate

ONLY ESTEY offers you an exclusive Double Guarantee Certificate—written contractual reassurance of reliable materials and performance — backed by both your dealer and the manufacturer, America's oldest organ builder.

ORGAN MEASUREMENTS		
Length 36⅜″	Width 22½″	Height 32¼″
Weight 112 lbs.		

ESTEY ORGAN CORPORATION
Brattleboro, Vermont

Makers of Fine Organs Since 1846

THE GEM OF SMALL ORGANS

ESTEY *Chorus*

A Picture Gallery

When the Estey factories in Brattleboro were closed in the 1950's, several fortunate collectors were able to get there just in time to "rescue" much valuable paper material. The pictures on this and the opposite page were found by Reed van Gorder of Flemington, New Jersey, and are of particular interest.

In the one above, note how an Artist's Organ Case Design Z from the 1920's (see p 120) was moved outside the factory to gain the advantage of sunlight for the photographer. Jacob Estey's picture was hung above the organ, and then the photographer in his studio proceeded to block out the surrounding details on his negative. The finished picture was then used in a catalog or other promotional material, with the reader oblivious to the conditions under which it was taken.

The technical details of the organ on the opposite page are missing, but surely this must have been one of the most elaborate "pipe top" reed instruments made by Estey.

Ed Jameson of Berlin, Massachusetts, a professional photographer, hit a real jack-pot when he acquired a large quantity of original glass plate negatives that supplied many of the pictures used to produce the catalogs reproduced in this book. Note the evidence of deterioration of the emulsion on several of them. Compare the pictures with the 1886 Chancel organ on page 42.

This picture was probably used to prepare the engraving of Style Z of the 1895 catalog, shown on page 69.

One has to wonder at the function of what appears to be a "Towel Bar" on the front of this early instrument. Note the pumping handle at the rear,

Note that the design on the music desk of this instrument is the same as that on the organs on pages 86, 89, 99, 108, and 143.

The "Pompadour" type back decoration seems to have lasted until around 1900. Note that this organ also features the "towel bar", the intended purpose for which one can only speculate in this day and age.

"Grab-rail" finials on the top of an organ were in great vogue with many customers. Note the mirror image of a tarpaulin, perhaps a painter's drop-cloth.

Note the similarity of this picture to many featured in the 1903 catalog, starting on page 82.

The "wardrobe trunk" design at the upper left is most unusual.

There is no evidence to indicate that Estey ever made "lap organs", but the picture above was made by a Brattleboro commercial photographer and this certainly suggests that the distinguished-looking gentleman may very well have been playing a Estey-made experimental instrument.

At left we see what is alleged to be the only three-manual organ that Estey ever made. Note that it has been moved outside the building to a carpeted platform for the best possible advantage of natural sunlight to produce a top-quality photograph.

The organs on the opposite page are from the author's private collection.

Organs from the author's private collection. Top, left: No. 22827, Nov. 1870, "Flat-Top" design. Top, right: No. 31980, ca. 1871, "Flat-Top". Center, left: Chapel Organ, Gothic case Style H, No. 359916, January 1907; see page 101. Center, right: Boudoir organ, No. 94956, late 1870's. Lower left, Style 2000 case No. 243891, February 1892. Lower right, Style A case, 6 octaves, No. 257335, January 1893. See page 65.

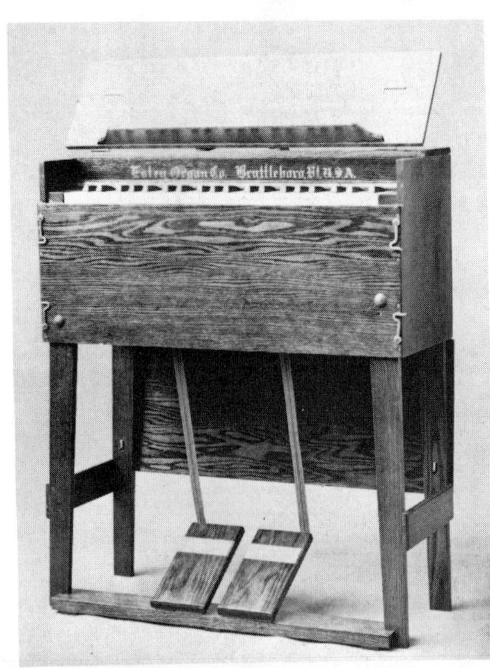

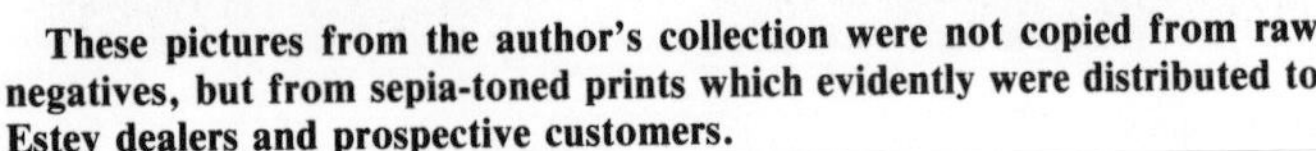

These pictures from the author's collection were not copied from raw negatives, but from sepia-toned prints which evidently were distributed to Estey dealers and prospective customers.

Estey organ number 100,000. This is owned by Bob and Diane Yates of Glenshaw, Pennsylvania, and is a style 900 with pipe top. The serial number is painted, and over the years has deteriorated and become difficult to read.

In the 1881 catalog, Estey implied that the instrument was the same as the one shown on page 39, but we see here that this is not the same case design.

SERIAL NUMBERS OF ESTEY REED ORGANS

From the beginning of business in 1846 until the end of reed organ manufacture about 1960, the Estey firm made about 510,000 reed instruments. The company maintained a list of the organ serial numbers and dates of manufacture. By sending a letter to the company, giving the serial number of an Estey organ, a person could find out the date of the organ.

At the Brattleboro factory there was a huge quantity of old Estey catalogs, advertising broadsides, photographs, trade cards, business records, and other paper memorabilia, including the serial number list. After the closing of the plant, a number of persons acquired in various ways this material. Some of it has surfaced and been offered for sale through the years, but unfortunately the existence or location of the serial number list is not known.

Some serial number dates are certain. About 8,000 melodeons or organs were made from 1846 to the fall of 1863. Organ No. 8,700 was shipped out in May, 1864; No. 100,000 was completed in 1880; No. 250,000 in 1892; No. 350,000 in 1905; and No. 500,000 in 1951.

There are complications, however. The Estey Virtuoso Organs have special serial numbers, such as V 375, instead of the regular series of numbers. Perhaps other special styles were treated similarly. Also, cases have been observed of two organs of different styles where the lower serial number had the later date. This suggests that a run of serial numbers was assigned to each style of organ currently in production, so that the organs were not necessarily made consecutively.

Until the official Estey list surfaces (if ever), the following list, based on catalogs, Estey material, and observation of organs, will date an organ within a few years.

1850	400	1884	146,000	1908	365,000
1855	2,400	1886	170,000	1910	375,000
1860	5,600	1888	194,000	1912	385,000
1865	9,500	1890	221,000	1915	400,000
1867	14,000	1892	250,000	1920	425,000
1870	24,000	1894	284,000	1925	449,000
1872	35,000	1896	298,000	1930	469,000
1874	48,000	1898	310,000	1935	483,000
1876	62,000	1900	322,000	1940	493,000
1878	79,000	1902	334,000	1945	496,000
1880	100,000	1904	345,000	1950	499,000
1882	122,000	1906	355,000	1955	506,000

INDEX

ESTEY'S COTTAGE ORGANS!

ESTEY'S HARMONIC ORGANS!

ESTEY'S BOUDOIR ORGANS!

ESTEY'S PERFECT MELODEONS!

40

Different Styles and Prices!

40

MADE AND SOLD EVERY WEEK!

PRICES FROM $100 TO $400.

The Best and the Cheapest!

12,000 NOW IN USE!!

FOR THE PARLOR! THE LODGE ROOM! THE CHURCH!

Send for a Circular to

442 Broadway, Albany, N. Y.

A. C. ROSE, Agent.